P9-CEX-878

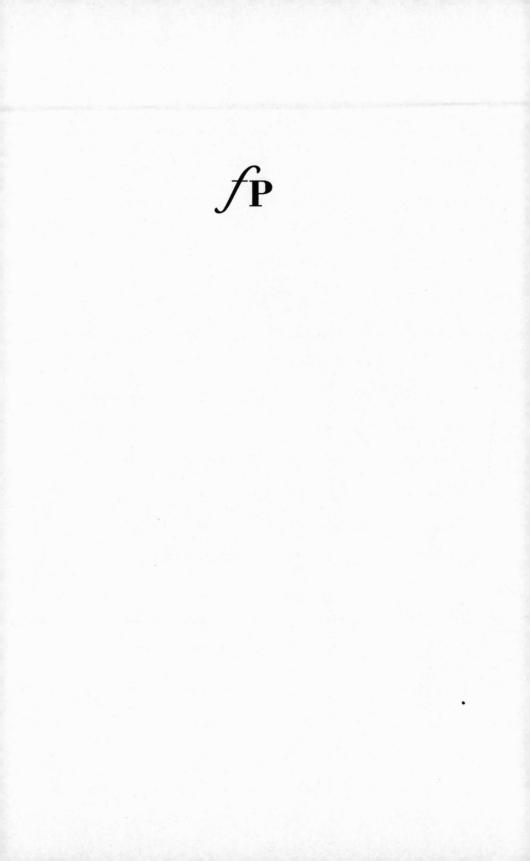

OTHER BOOKS BY DAVID W. SHAW

The Sea Shall Embrace Them

Flying Cloud

Daring the Sea

Inland Passage

AMERICA'S VICTORY

The Heroic Story of a Team of Ordinary Americans—
and How They Won the Greatest Yacht Race Ever

DAVID W. SHAW

THE FREE PRESS

NEW YORK   LONDON   TORONTO   SYDNEY   SINGAPORE

*f*P

THE FREE PRESS
A Division of Simon & Schuster, Inc.
1230 Avenue of the Americas
New York, NY 10020

Copyright © 2002 by David W. Shaw

All rights reserved, including the right of
reproduction in whole or in part in any form.

THE FREE PRESS *and colophon are*
trademarks of Simon & Schuster, Inc.

Insert photographs and art courtesy of
The Mariners' Museum, Newport News, Virginia

For information about special discounts for bulk purchases,
Please contact Simon & Schuster Special Sales:
1-800-456-6798 or business@simonandschuster.com

Manufactured in the United States of America

1   3   5   7   9   10   8   6   4   2

Library of Congress Cataloging-in-Publication Data

Shaw, David W., 1961–
America's Victory : the heroic story of a team of ordinary Americans,
and how they won the greatest yacht race ever / David W. Shaw.
p.   cm.
Includes bibliographical references and index.
1. America's Cup. 2. America (Yacht). 3. Yacht racing—History—19th century. I. Title.
GV830 1851 .S52 2003
797.1'4—dc21   *2002075702*

ISBN 0-7432-3516-9

For Elizabeth, my inspiration and strength

CONTENTS

LIST OF ILLUSTRATIONS

FOLLOWING PAGE 140

Yankee Doodle sent to town,
His goods for exhibition;
Everybody ran him down,
and laughed at his position:
They thought him all the world behind;
A gooney, muff or noodle;
Laugh on, good people—never mind—
Says quiet Yankee Doodle.

Yankee Doodle had a craft,
A rather tidy clipper,
And he challenged, while they laughed,
The Britishers to whip her.
Their whole squadron she outsped,
And that on their own water;
Of all the lot she went ahead,
And they came nowhere arter.

—from *Punch*

INTRODUCTION

On August 22, 1851, the schooner *America* beat seemingly impossible odds and bested the fastest yachts in all of Great Britain in a race against fourteen competitors around the Isle of Wight off the south coast of England. Based on a revolutionary hull design by a brilliant young naval architect, her construction represented the cutting edge of innovation. The British did not know what to think of her, and their immense surprise when she won the race was profound enough to induce English yacht designers to copy her lines. But *America*'s dazzling and unexpected success achieved far more than an adaptation of new thinking in building fast sailboats.

The victory of a lone yacht from the United States against a superior fleet of British vessels captured the imagination of the American people. The nation's merchant fleet, both sail and steam, set speed records that summer of astounding proportions, grabbing headlines on each side of the Atlantic. America enjoyed bountiful wealth from the gold pouring into the national treasury from the diggings in California, and continued to advance in the settlement of the vast new lands added to its territories from recent wars and acquisitions. Yet the country remained insecure at its young age of only seventy-five years. The nation searched for a sense of identity, a spirit, and yacht *America* seemed to embody it.

The romance of the battle against all odds smacked of other stands, the brash and brave contests at Bunker Hill, Lexington, and Concord when a few took on the many. The race of yacht *America* was far more compelling than a momentous swift passage of a clipper ship or a steamer, though the record-setting eighty-nine-day voyage of *Flying Cloud* from New York to San Francisco this same year did indeed inspire wonder at American ingenuity, drive, and daring, as did the records set by the luxury steamships of the Collins Line. *America*'s triumph, though, was the essence of what the United States was coming to stand for, the very grist for its burgeoning and shaping identity as a nation and a people.

The victory had another lasting impact as well, one that still makes itself felt today in ways both large and small. The owners of *America* won a silver cup from the British—not very valuable, nor very pretty. It was a rather bulbous thing with great Victorian curves, scrolls, and decorative curlicues. Several years later, the owners gave the cup to the New York Yacht Club as a perpetual challenge trophy, meaning the holder of the cup must defend against all comers and relinquish it if beaten. In 1870, the first challenge race for the cup was held before thousands of spectators aboard boats in New York Harbor and crowded along the shores. Races for the cup, named in yacht *America*'s honor, have been held ever since.

The victory of *America*, which started the America's Cup tradition, illuminates the soul of the United States—it is a beacon of courage, innovation, and a willingness to push on despite what appear to be impossible odds. And now, more than one hundred years later, its legacy captivates sailing fans around the world, enthralling millions of sailors and nonsailors alike as the drama of each successive challenge race plays out on the screens of televisions and on the pages of newspapers in many languages.

The story of *America* is well known among people who race sailing vessels, and it lingers like a distant cloud of recognition in the minds of the general public. But there was much more to it than winning a sailboat race and bringing home a gaudy little cup. There is beneath the end result a story never told before about the forgotten heroes that made the great moment possible—the working-class men with strong backs and dirty hands who designed, built, and sailed the yacht, and who never really got credit for their efforts. These ordinary men who achieved the extraordinary are the subject of this book. To some they may represent the millions of Americans striving for their own version of the American dream without ever realizing much chance of making history. Most possess the spirit to achieve greatness, if only given the opportunity, and they do achieve it just by going to work, raising a family, and contributing individual efforts to make a collective good possible. Today, as in 1851, these people make this country what it is.

In New York, there exists a group of men and women who guide ships into the port, ensuring that the vessels do not run aground. They are known as the Sandy Hook Pilots and their tradition traces back to 1694. It is a proud order, one that stresses courage, honor, and integrity. These individuals have remained obscure, as they were back in 1851, when one of their profession left his post long enough to sail *America* across the North Atlantic and bring her to victory in England. His name was Captain Richard Brown, a big man with a hearty laugh and a soft-spoken manner. He did not search for glory or fame. He did not strive for enormous wealth. His main concern was for his men and the boat, and to carry out his word to the owners to the best of his ability. In this he succeeded. However, he is mentioned in name only in all accounts of the race. History has overlooked him as an individual, in spite of the contributions he made.

The first mate of *America*, Nelson Comstock, also remains a mere name in the history books. An expert sailor from a long line of mariners, Nelson Comstock stood at Brown's side as an essential member of the team of men that sailed the yacht to victory. Together, Brown and Comstock brought the schooner through storms and calms, and overcame the dangers of the sea that nearly crippled the boat on the voyage across the North Atlantic. They knew every one of her nuances, quirks, and foibles. A sailing vessel is almost a living thing. No two are alike. They require a subtle and knowing hand at the helm to perform to maximum potential. There is no room for any other focus but on the boat, and Brown and Comstock possessed the ability to carry through and find that focus.

Less obscure, but no less important to the victory was the rather timid, shy genius of naval architecture, George Steers, whose innovation changed the face of yacht design in the United States and in

Europe. He designed and supervised the building of *America*, incorporating in her the very latest theories of hull form, sails, and rigging. Like Brown and Comstock, he had no formal education. Like them, he acquired his skill from the school of life. Steers accompanied Brown and Comstock on the voyage across the North Atlantic, and provided invaluable insights in terms of how to get the most speed from the schooner. Yet he, too, received little more than a footnote in the history books.

Without the contributions of these three men, the victory of *America* would not have occurred. A rare moment in history would have been lost. Their stories as they came together that extraordinary afternoon on August 22, 1851, are the stuff of American legend.

AMERICA'S
VICTORY

CHAPTER ONE

RISING STORM

An unusually light and warm southwesterly wind for mid-February stirred the stands of dune grass on New Jersey's barrier islands. Dried and speckled with salt left behind by the procession of gales during that harsh winter of 1846, the tawny blades swayed in an almost breathlike rhythm. Up beyond the berm of the dunes in nooks low and sheltered from the prevailing winds, holly and cedar grew in small woodlands. Fallen leaves and twigs covered the ground, creating a bed of deep, soft vegetation ideal for rabbit and fox, and the gulls that came to roost in the shadows beneath the ragged canopy.

The dunes, the woodlands, and the band of surf stretching away as far as the eye could see compounded the desolate, wild, and inhospitable feel of New Jersey's outer coast. Like a broken chain with ribbons of blue ocean running through the inlets into the back bays beyond, the islands extended for more than one hundred miles from the curved tip of Sandy Hook southward to the broad protrusion of Cape May. On all this land, there were only a few small villages, little more than clusters of shacks tucked in the lee of the dunes.

The inhabitants of the barrier islands led simple lives. They raked oysters from the shallows of the bays behind the islands and fished in the surf on the ocean side. They hunted duck and geese from flat-bottomed boats in the marshes fronting the vast reaches of pine forests that covered much of the state. The men ranged inland to shoot deer and rowed back to the islands with fresh meat for their wives and children. Their lives were far removed from the prosperity, culture, and vigor of New York City, although the metropolis was less than a day away by horse and steam ferry. But at times, especially during the winter, there was a form of perverse commerce between the residents of the city waiting for goods to come in on sailing ships, and those of the dunes who could not afford the most basic household items.

When the winter gales swept in from the northeast and sent towering waves to break on the shores, the children of the islands offered God a special prayer. Kneeling in front of their beds, the tiny fingers of both hands clasped together at their chins, the children whispered: "God bless Mom and Pop and all us poor miserable sinners, and send a ship ashore before mornin'."

On stormy nights or during evenings shrouded in thick fog, the fathers of some of these children crept from their shacks out to the beach. Together, a group of men piled hay up in mounds ten feet high. They hung lanterns from the sides of their horses and walked the animals around and around the haystacks. From offshore aboard the pitching deck of a sailing ship the effect resembled the loom of lighthouses, the lights blinking a welcome to safe harbor. The unwary captain, thinking he was near Sandy Hook, turned westward only to find his ship stranded on the shoals, trapped and at the mercy of the islanders, many of them notorious for the age-old practice of wrecking. They were called land pirates, these New Jerseyans, and they were very good at their opportunistic trade.

There were other residents of the barrier islands, however, who did not actively lure ships ashore with false beacons. They waited until the ocean delivered a wreck. There was no need for deception. Men, women, and children lined the beach with long poles and fished the wreckage and bodies from the surf, taking whatever they found of value. School teachers and preachers were allowed to use the longest poles to afford them a better chance at the best salvage. Passengers and crew aboard the stricken vessel often looked on and begged for help while the looting took place, until the ship broke apart and anyone aboard drowned in the breakers. The loss of life and property was just the natural way of things on the barrier islands, the redistribution of wealth by indiscriminate nature. Sometimes, though, the sea was exceptionally cruel. Cruel enough to shock the most rugged of islanders.

SHIPPING LANES AND PILOT BOAT CRUISING GROUNDS

In the early 1850s, pilot boats sailed as far as six hundred miles offshore in search of ships to guide into New York Harbor. When an inbound ship was sighted, a pilot went aboard to guide it safely across the treacherous shoals of Sandy Hook bar. The tough, dangerous work kept pilots at sea in all weather and all seasons.

Pilots referred to scouting the waters off Nantucket and Nova Scotia as "sailing the eastern chance." Cruising the waters off Cape Hatteras and Bermuda was known as "sailing the southern chance." The old saying derived from the distinct "chance" that a ship might be found in the well-established lanes channeling traffic into New York from ports all over the world.

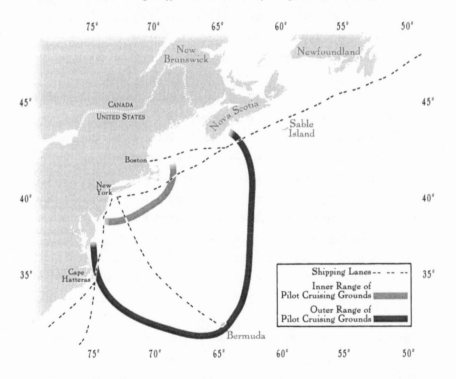

* * *

Sailing off New Jersey on that mild Saturday morning of February, 14, 1846, was the pilot schooner *Blossom*, heading slowly south with a gentle breeze off the bow. The fickle wind painted dark swaths across the smooth, shiny backs of the swells rolling in from the North Atlantic. The sea and sky blended into an expansive world of gray. The three remaining pilots aboard the schooner removed their frock coats and silk top hats.

They loosened their cravats, mopped their brows, and gazed uneasily to the northeast at the parade of heaving hills of water washing toward them from midocean. The boat pitched and jerked with each passing wave. The wooden booms and gaffs on the main and foremast slammed and creaked against their fittings. The canvas main, foresail, and jib thundered and shook as the sails emptied and filled.

The pilots cursed quietly. Bad weather was right over the horizon. The men knew the signs well. Sailing slowly, however, their schooner stood less of a chance to chase down some of the many ships bound for New York, put aboard the remaining pilots, and run for port before the storm hit. A large blue flag indicating that pilots were still available and ready to work flew from a long slender pole mounted at the truck of the main topmast more than fifty feet above the deck. It was every man's wish to see that flag down off the mast and stowed below. Home and loved ones waited. With the voyage almost done, the apprentices, pilots in training who served as the schooner's crew, were anxious to get back.

Not far from *Blossom* were at least half a dozen ships heading north toward New York Harbor. The schooners *Pioneer*, *Alabama*, and *Register*, the bark *New Jersey*, and the full-rigged sailing packets *Orleans* and *John Minturn* ghosted along with the wind fair astern. Most of these ships had already taken on a pilot, a special breed of mariner whose livelihood depended on guiding ships safely into port. But several of the ships, including *Orleans* and *John Minturn*, still required a pilot. At approximately nine o'clock, *Blossom* sighted the brig *Moses* and dispatched a pilot, leaving two aboard. Shortly thereafter, two other ships hove into view. Slowly, *Blossom* sailed up to the nearest vessel and sent pilot Thomas Freeborne to board her.

Standing on the poop deck of the packet *John Minturn*, Captain Starke watched with indifference as the nearby pilot boat lowered her yawl, a swift rowboat used to ferry the pilot to the waiting ship. (A yawl is also a two-masted sailboat.) The flags indicated the schooner was one of the New York boats. Starke had heard stories about them. Bad seamen, mere political appointees out for easy money, that was the scuttlebutt along the waterfront regarding the New York boys. He much preferred boats from the Sandy Hook Pilots, an organization that came into being in 1837 to boost the quality of piloting services for the harbor. That one of his lifelong friends, Captain Richard Brown, was a Sandy Hook Pilot no doubt strengthened his bias.

"Some of the New York boys are every inch a sailor," Brown had said on one of those many occasions when Starke and Brown drank together, while both of them were in New York at the same time, he at the close of a voyage up from New Orleans, Brown between stints offshore aboard the pilot boat *William G. Hagstaff*. But on this day Brown's opinion did not move Starke. He did not trust the man in the yawl below who stood ready to help.

"Keep her sails full and drawing," Starke said to his first officer. "Perhaps the man will see he's not wanted here."

In such faint winds, the oarsmen in the yawl had no trouble catching up to the ship. As the yawl pulled close to the vessel, Thomas Freeborne noted that there was no ladder hung over the ship's side to allow him to climb aboard. He sighed. Craning his neck, he peered up at the officers on deck. "This is Thomas Free-borne of the pilot boat *Blossom*. I'll come aboard, Captain!"

Starke strode to the rail and gazed down at Freeborne. "Off with ye, now!" he yelled. "I'll not take a man from a New York boat."

"As you wish, Captain. Put her about, lads," he said to the ap-prentices at the oars of the yawl. The boys glumly struck out for the row back to the schooner. Off on the horizon, the ship *Orleans* ghosted on a northerly heading. *Blossom* slowly sailed to her, offered a pilot, and received the same rejection. Piloting had come to a sorry state in 1846, one year after the laws regulating the service were re-pealed and the unity and honor of the business seemed to have vanished. Some of the older salts clung to the hope that the situation might change for the better, and they had reason to hope. The business might attract a disreputable few, but by and large the best of the pilots, whether from New York or New Jersey companies, were among the most skilled sailors in the world.

The pilots of Sandy Hook received years of training to learn their trade. They served for nine years as apprentices studying the ways of the sea and the location of every channel, sandbar, reef, and navigation aid in the harbor, until they could draw a harbor chart from memory. After the apprenticeship, the pilots started work on the smallest of vessels. Gradually, they progressed to the largest of the sail and steam packets and became known as Full Branch Pilots.

Though the job demanded sacrifice and was often dangerous, the Full Branch Pilots enjoyed far more freedom and a better chance to put roots down ashore than a sailor serving before the mast or even as a ship's master. The pilots did not have to play host to wealthy passengers and listen to their prattle at the captain's table, as was the case with the commanders of the packets sailing between New York and Liverpool. They did not have to bend to a shipowner's wishes and run the risk of landing permanently on the beach if a shipowner became displeased. These were independent seamen head and shoulders above the majority of those then serving in the United States merchant marine, and as traffic coming into New York increased, their jobs played a crucial role in keeping the commerce of the city going.

New York City was the busiest port in the United States. Ships from all over the world came and went without pause, hundreds of them every month, even in the midst of winter when the risk of disaster increased. The inbound ship coming from the southern ports of the United States, the West Indies, or South America first had to pass New Jersey, which offered no safe harbors. The inbound ship coming from Europe had to pass the equally inhospitable and dangerous south shore of Long Island, which, like New Jersey's, was over one hundred miles in length. Together, these landmasses formed a funnel, with the approaches to New York at the tip. Across the narrow opening to the safety of the upper harbor lurked additional obstacles. These took the form of sandbars that grew and shifted with each passing storm and the daily cycle of the tide.

The dangers off Sandy Hook had been well known since the earliest times Europeans ventured across the Atlantic Ocean to the present-day northeastern United States. Sailing for the Dutch in 1609 in search of the elusive Northwest Passage aboard *Half Moon*, Henry Hudson was aware of the shoals. He took great care as he probed his way up the lower bay and through the Verrazano Narrows into the river that eventually bore his name. One of the ship's company, Robert Juet, described the harbor: "The Land is very pleasant and high, and bold to fall withall . . . we stood along the Northernmost [portion of the harbor near the Narrows] thinking to have gone into it, but we found it to have a very shoald barre before it, for we had but ten foot water." Other captains followed Hudson. Adriaen Block, Hendrick Christiaensen, and Cornelius May explored the lower and upper harbors for the Dutch entrepreneurs that eventually established New Amsterdam in 1626. They, too, noted sandbars and the best channels weaving across them to the final approach in the upper harbor off Manhattan.

Ships of the day were not deep-keeled. They could operate in relatively shallow water. As a consequence, the shoals, which came to be known as the Sandy Hook bar, were not a serious hindrance to the development of the port. But by the end of the 1600s, with Great Britain then in possession of the island settlement of New Amsterdam, and all of what was formerly New Netherland (renamed Manhattan and New York respectively) since 1664, the Sandy Hook bar caused enough problems for shipping that the government took action.

On March 9, 1694, the Assembly of New York passed "AN Act for Settlying Pylotage for All Vessells That Shall Come Within Sandy Hook." Part of the text reveals the nature of the hazards mariners encountered.

> Whereas the late Easterly storm there were severall banks thrown off at the south of the Harbour at sandy Hook whereby the entry is rendred very difficult and dangerous to all vessells

bound for this Port and required an attendance of men at the hook to be in readiness to pilot them in to safety, be it Enacted and Ordained by the Gouveneur and Councill and Representatives Convened in Generall Assembly and it is hereby Enacted and Ordained by the authority of the same that there shall be four men appointed and commissioned by his Excellancy the Gouveneur who shall constantly attend at some convenient place near the Hook with a boat to give all aid and assistance to all vessels bound for this Port which they are obliged to pilot up as far as the narrows.

So much had changed from those early days of piloting. Yet, much of the job remained the same. The shoals still claimed ships. The New Jersey and Long Island coasts still posed a real danger. The basic need for the pilot was if anything more acute than ever before.

Throughout the day *Blossom* cruised up and down the coast looking for inbound ships, and throughout the day the weather deteriorated. The southwesterly wind increased, suddenly shifted to the northeast, and came in strong. Waves formed atop the swells and gradually began to break. The temperature plummeted to below freezing and it began to snow. At around five o'clock, *Blossom* again caught sight of *John Minturn* and this time she signaled for a pilot.

Thomas Freeborne gripped the rails of the yawl as the apprentices worked hard at the oars, their muscles bulging unseen under their oilskins with every stroke. The bow of the little rowboat plunged deep into the breaking crests. Spray and snow soaked Freeborne's face, his southwester pulled low over his head, partially obscuring his weathered cheeks. His silk top hat he had left behind aboard the schooner. However, he still wore his heavy frock coat and a knit wool sweater underneath it to keep warm. *John Minturn*'s hull towered above him. His boatmen drew close alongside. Timing the rise and fall of the yawl with the rhythm of the sea, he stood up in the boat as it rose to the top of a large wave, and grabbed the rope ladder hung over the side of the ship. In less than a minute, Freeborne was aboard.

Captain Starke clasped Freeborne's hand and apologized for waving him off earlier that day.

"I understand. There are many of us who wish things were different," Freeborne replied, turning his back against the wind to peer westward through the whirling snow. He estimated the dangers of the beach lay just four miles away. "We've got to get her offshore!" Freeborne shouted.

Ashore in the gathering gloom of night, the islanders looked out the doors of their shacks. The wind billowed the canvas that covered the cracks between boards nailed over the openings of the glassless windows. It whistled through the eaves. The roar of the surf carried to them in the lulls between gusts. Although some of the islanders welcomed the storm for the salvage it might bring, others donned their oilskins and checked the gear at the wreckmaster's station. They made certain the surf boats were equipped with rope and life buoys. They checked the mortars used to fire lines out to ships caught in the breakers, lifelines the people aboard might need to get from the wreck to the beach. When these tasks were completed, the men faced the fury of the rising storm, tasted the salt in the air, felt the sting of sleet against their cheeks. The cold wind cut through their warm clothes and chilled them to the bone. Straining to see into the night, the men searched for the telltale lights of a ship too close to shore, minutes away from breaking her back on the sandbars below the roiling waves. But they saw nothing, nothing at all.

CHAPTER TWO

TRAGIC LOSS

The ocean merged with the night made all the blacker from the blizzard as *John Minturn* plunged and labored in the heavy head seas. Solid water roared over the bow, crashed against the deckhouses, and almost washed away the crewmen clinging to the lifelines run fore and aft along the ship. Thomas Freeborne, with Captain Starke at his side, stood on the poop deck, his mind racing. As the pilot, Freeborne had the command and the responsibility for the ship, her fifty-one passengers and crew, and her cargo worth approximately eighty thousand dollars. He calculated the amount of drift to the west he knew occurred every minute the ship tried to claw her way off the coast. He checked his watch and turned to the northeast to gauge the increasing velocity of the wind, estimating that the ship was just two miles from the beach. Freeborne leaned close to Captain Starke and shouted, "We're losing ground, Captain. She'll not go to weather in this sea."

A dark look crossed Starke's face. The situation was perilous, a commander's worst nightmare. He had allowed his ship to get too close to the coast. When the wind shifted to come in from the northeast he had little sea room between him and the shoals. It was a bad mistake, one he should not have made with all his experience at sea. But he was not alone in the error. At that very moment, dozens of ships faced the same fate as *John Minturn*. Others farther offshore lay hove-to in a fight for survival against the worst storm to strike the coast in memory, even among the boatmen of the upper harbor of New York, who had seen the hazards the sea had to offer in their time.

A few moments later, the main topsail split and blew to tatters with a resounding boom. It was a new sail, strong and tightly woven of the best canvas. But the wind was too powerful for it to stand up against the pressure. The first officer stationed forward sent the best of the sailors up the mainmast to furl the remains of the sail. The men inched out onto the yard and struggled with the stiff, frozen canvas, their hands bloodied and bruised as they worked. A fierce gust laid the ship on her side and waves thundered over the windward rail. Down below in the black, cold, and wet interior of the ship the men, women, and children among the passengers cried and screamed. The violent motion of the vessel hurled them against the bulkheads and the sides of the hull.

"We've no choice but to wear ship, Captain, and run her bow in to the shore," Freeborne yelled. "We'll be in the breakers in minutes no matter what we do, sir!"

Starke considered his options and found he had none. If his packet went ashore with her side exposed to the fury of the breakers, she might roll over and sink in minutes. If she went in bow on, her stern would take the brunt of the pounding. She might last long enough to launch the boats and get the passengers off. "Aye, Mr. Freeborne. I see. I see," he said. "We will wear while we still can."

Freeborne gritted his teeth against the cold. He could no longer feel the tips of his fingers or his toes. The men forward were even worse off. Soaked to the skin, the water froze on their pea jackets, boots, and mittens. Ice coated the rigging, masts, and yards. He shouted to the helmsmen to turn toward the beach. Her bow paid off, and the ship, flying just her staysails and jibs, slowly headed west toward the roar of breakers audible over the noise of the storm. In another minute, *John Minturn* rose on the back of a crest and dropped down on a sandbar one hundred yards beyond the breakers. Another wave hit the ship, slewed her stern around, and turned her broadside to the wind and seas, sending the masts and yards falling to the deck. She was a stout ship. She did not sink right away.

As dawn broke on Sunday morning, people began to die of exposure. The day dragged on, and rescue attempts from people ashore all failed. *John Minturn* broke apart that night, leaving only thirteen survivors. Ten ships drove ashore on the New Jersey coast during the storm, including *Register, Pioneer, Alabama, Orleans,* and *New Jersey,* which had taken on another pilot from *Blossom.* Bodies littered the beach. After riding out the gale, *Blossom* limped into port on Tuesday, February 17. Word had already reached New York about the unprecedented number of wrecks and the heavy loss of life.

The New York Herald's bold front-page headline told the story: "The Terrible Storm." The text in part read:

> Many years have elapsed since we were called upon to describe a greater calamity to life and property than that of the night of the 14th last and the morning of the 15th. About sixty lives have been lost in one wreckmaster's district [Squan Beach, where *John Minturn* sank, along with *Alabama* a short distance away]. . . . By this most melancholy dispensation of an all-seeing Providence many a heart that a few days since throbbed high with hope has forever ceased to beat.

The New York pilots sent *Blossom* and other schooners to search for Thomas Freeborne and the other pilot put aboard *New Jersey,* hoping both men had survived. Several days later, Freeborne's body was discovered on the beach miles from the wreck site. He was covered in ice as he lay sprawled amid wreckage strewn above the high water mark. He wore no coat or sweater. Survivors from *John Minturn* said they had seen him give his coat to Captain Starke's wife, and his sweater to Starke's child. He had frozen to death because of his kindness on Sunday afternoon long before the ship broke apart. Testimony from survivors of the shipwreck about Freeborne's actions appeared in *The New York Herald* and made him a hero. Talk of the gale, which later became known as the John Minturn Storm, and the many fatalities lasted for days in New York.

Upon hearing the news of the death of his good friend, and the deaths of Starke's family, Captain Richard Brown fell into a period of mourning. Along with three other young men from Mystic, Brown and Starke had run away from their homes to pursue lives in the merchant marine. The sea had killed them all now, all except for him. The sad turn of events made a deep impression on Brown, one that remained rooted in the back of his mind for the rest of his life.

Brown was a tall, stocky man in his mid-thirties, soft-spoken despite his size, with a squarish face fronted with a spade beard in the style of deacons of the day, and bright blue eyes accented with laugh lines. He was relatively new to the piloting service, having received his license from the Sandy Hook Pilots in 1841, just five years earlier. He regarded the plans to honor Freeborne as just and fair. The rival pilot had shown kindness to his friend in a time of need, and lost his life in the disaster. Brown had always felt disinclined to generalize about the New York pilots, or for that matter any group or organization. There were good and bad men in every profession. It was unfair to make sweeping judgments. Knee-jerk responses reflected ignorance of the highest order.

Brown had learned early in his life that the world was not cast in distinct borders of black and white. No situation was exactly as it appeared. There was always room for another interpretation. Born in 1810, Brown was a young child during the dark years of the War of 1812. His earliest memories were of his father, a ship's carpenter in Mystic, one of the many shipbuilding ports in New England that provided plenty of work for men handy with a saw or an adz. Like many men, his father railed against the British, painting them as devils.

Yet, when the war ended in 1815, Americans scrambled to buy cheap British goods that the merchants across the Atlantic were only too willing to sell. Was it possible that a person, or a people, could rank as a devil on one day, and a business partner on another? Evidently, life was not a clear-cut matter. Brown saw more to build his sense of people, and the unpredictable way of things in any complex web of relationships, when he went to sea at the age of sixteen. Trade between Great Britain and the United States flourished in the

1820s. To a young Connecticut Yankee, the sea promised a bright future for the rugged man who also possessed a keen mind. The sea proved a good teacher for Brown. Its serenity and cruelty, beauty and ugliness, and its indifference to the often petty-minded nature of men, be they sailors before the mast, officers aft, or the wealthy merchants and shipowners ashore, instilled a sense of how in the end the works of mankind paled in comparison to nature. That realization put matters into perspective. It fostered in Brown a code of personal ethics, a belief in self-reliance, a deep respect for one's place in the world and one's unique ability to fashion it to best advantage.

So when people spoke out against the New York pilots and called them "slugs" and "lubbers" to a man, Brown knew enough to doubt. He also knew that it was the way of things to have good and bad in a strange sort of coexistence, a balance that swung one way or another. The same human foibles and frailties that afflicted the New York pilots might well have surfaced among the men of Sandy Hook had there been more of them. It was easier to keep order, demand a high level of skill from apprentices as well as pilots, and a sense of honor and ethics when the number of individuals in the group was small. As it was, there were only a handful of men and just a few schooners associated with the Sandy Hook Pilots in 1846.

Brown attended the funeral of Captain Starke, his wife, and his child. Brown's wife and children tried to comfort him as he laid to rest his friend whom the sea had taken at the prime of life. Then he, along with other pilots from Sandy Hook, joined their competitors from New York on the day of Freeborne's funeral in a form of salute fitting to their calling. Riding a southerly wind across Raritan Bay toward the shores of Brooklyn, fifteen pilot boats, nearly the entire fleet of all those serving New York, sailed in a line to the north up the bay at the eastern edge of the lower harbor. With the breeze tousling his short brown hair and caressing his tanned and slightly creased cheeks, Brown held his silk top hat over his chest and gazed up at the United States flag as it snapped and fluttered against the mainsail of his pilot boat, *William G. Hagstaff*. The flag was only hauled halfway up the length of the halyard, a sailor's form of half-staff. The fleet sailed as near as possible to the hills of Greenwood overlooking the bay, and smartly tacked back and forth, each boat executing the maneuver in perfect formation.

After several passes, the pilots turned their schooners back toward the sea. The busy harbor of New York never slept. There was always more work to do, more ships to meet. The formation broke as the boats scattered and set full sail to outpace their rivals. Some steered toward New Jersey to search for ships bound from the southern ports carrying valuable cargoes of wheat, corn, hides, and most precious of all, bales of cotton. Massive quantities of cotton were exported to Great Britain, where factory workers sweated at mechanized looms to convert it into ready-made clothing popular among the burgeoning middle-class residents of New York City. Others steered eastward toward Nantucket Shoals to search for vessels from Europe loaded with manufactured commodities, ranging from textiles to lengths of iron track needed to build the railroads connecting the city to its rural outposts.

Ashore, the crowds gathered at Freeborne's grave in Greenwood Cemetery and listened to the sonorous voices of preachers and dignitaries eulogizing a public hero. Then they, too, turned toward the broad blue ocean, seemingly alight with the sparkles and diamonds of the sunshine on its undulating surface, and watched the white sails of the pilot boats grow small in the distance.

CHAPTER THREE

THE PILOT'S TRADE

Dick Brown stood at the helm of his new sixty-six-foot schooner, *Mary Taylor*, sailing on what pilots called the eastern chance, where swift freighters and liners from Le Havre, Bremen, Hamburg, Southampton, Portsmouth, and Liverpool gradually merged into tight lanes to mingle with the schooners out of Gloucester on the east side of Georges Bank. Closer still to New York lay Nantucket Shoals, a series of sandbars fanning southeast from the island more than twenty-five miles. It was there that the ship captains turned from a more southwesterly course to nearly due west on their final approach to New York Harbor, and it was there that Captain Brown sailed *Mary Taylor* on those brisk autumn days and nights of 1849.

As he steered *Mary Taylor*, his hand on the tiller and his legs braced against the motion of the boat, he felt her powerful, clean advance through the gently breaking waves. One after another the crests broke, rumbling white and flashing deep green. Just as suddenly, the ocean reverted back to the nearly uniform gray in the weak light penetrating through the dark layers of an overcast sky 120 miles off the coast of Massachusetts.

Brown checked the trim of *Mary Taylor*'s mainsail. It was the typical gaff-rigged main of a pilot boat, with a long boom at the lower edge that extended well beyond the stern. A smaller spar, called a gaff, was rigged aloft along the top of the sail, giving it an almost rectangular shape. Several feet below the gaff the bold black number five painted on the canvas identified the boat as one belonging to the Sandy Hook Pilots. Satisfied that the mainsail drew fair, Brown turned his attention to the other sails. The foresail set on the foremast also had a boom at the lower edge and a gaff at the top. The triangular sail flown at the bow strained at the lines holding it in place on the schooner's bowsprit. This sail was known as a jib. Both the foresail and the jib were also in excellent trim.

Another gust ripped across the waves and the schooner tilted her lee rail under, washing the decks with solid water. The hemp rigging hummed and vibrated. Spray pattered on the foredeck. A fine, straight wake rolled and whirled. It disappeared a boat length or two behind the schooner amid the flash of whitecaps and layers of foam.

Brown gazed up at the apprentice perched at the top of the mainmast. The young man held a spyglass in his right hand and clutched the shrouds with the other. His heavy wool work coat flapped in the wind and exposed the pale blue of his denim pants. He wore a wide-brimmed hat pulled low to keep the chill off his ears. Every few minutes he scanned the horizon and brought the glass to rest on the sails of a competing pilot boat several miles to leeward and slightly ahead of *Mary Taylor,* also heading east at a high rate of speed.

"Keep a weather eye on our friend there," Brown shouted up to the apprentice. "Let me know if she changes course."

"Aye, sir," the boy replied. "She's holding steady, bearing south-southeast by a half east. All clear otherwise."

It was an old game, watching a competitor's heading. If the competing boat suddenly changed course, it might well point to a ship just outside the scope of the lookout's vision. From his post roughly fifty feet above the deck, the lookout's maximum visual range extended to a radius of eight miles around *Mary Taylor* to objects at or near sea level. The topgallants of a sailing packet or the deckhouses of a steamer showed up at a much greater distance. The same eight-mile scope of vision held true for the lookout on the other boat. Separated as they were by several miles, both observers together commanded a visual horizon nearly double that of a single man armed with a spyglass and a good set of sharp eyes. The cunning captain used every skill, every trick to come out the winner in these informal races against each other. A fast boat was only part of what was needed for victory and the decent wages every man aboard counted on to feed his family ashore.

Dick Brown had ordered his new schooner with financial considerations in mind. If he and his fellow pilots concentrated on the steamers and the larger sailing packets, it meant a jump in their standard of living because the bigger, deeper ships paid more for piloting service than the smaller, shallower coastal vessels. The pilots earned well above the usual income for a common sailor. The Jacktar serving before the mast was paid an average of twelve dollars a month. A lucky pilot aboard a swift pilot boat took home $1,500 to $2,000 or more per year, enough to buy a modest house and the comforts of a middle-class lifestyle. The pilot's life, though, was much less certain than that of an office worker or even that of a ship master paid a salary of $3,000 to $5,000 per year, if he performed at the top of his profession. The pilot's wages depended on meeting and guiding ships into port. His financial standing depended on the speed of the pilot boat, his captain's ability to find and sail down inbound ships, and the performance of his compatriots once they were put aboard for the eventual trip across Sandy Hook bar, when the ship arrived off New York Harbor.

The typical pilot schooner carried six to eight pilots out to sea. The wages of all the men, which were paid to them by the owners of the ships they guided into port, were pooled and divided among the pilots, their apprentices, and the owners of the boat. Fees were based on the draft of the vessels they guided into port. Ships drawing fourteen feet or less paid a dollar and fifty cents per foot. Those whose keels extended eighteen or more feet below the water paid two dollars and twenty-five cents per foot. A steamship drawing twenty-one feet was a real prize, bringing in a total of forty-seven dollars and twenty-five cents to the pilot boat. There was additional profit in winter when surcharges were added to the usual rate, and a further charge for any ship taking on a pilot more than fifteen miles from Sandy Hook.

Brown knew he needed a very special boat to ensure the best chance of securing a good livelihood for him and his men. At one of the East River shipyards was a young man well known to men of the waterfront for his ability as a designer of fast-sailing vessels. He had designed yachts for members of the New York Yacht Club, a bastion of the most elite and wealthy families of the city who raced boats for personal status and glory. He had built commercial craft as well as several pilot boats, including *William G. Hagstaff* for the Sandy Hook Pilots, one of the fastest in the fleet. The name of George Steers was associated with speed and quality and innovation in design. Brown sought him out to design and build his new schooner.

Steers warmed to the idea immediately. While he was busy at the time designing the hulls for the new American steamships that were built for Edward Knight Collins, a New York shipping magnate intent upon winning the fine freight, passenger, and mail trade from Samuel Cunard's steamships, Steers designed the hull of the schooner that was to become *Mary Taylor*. She was different in form from almost every other boat, something quite new at her launching in early 1849. During the building of the boat, there was considerable anxiety about whether Steers's instincts were right, at least on Brown and his partner's part. Steers swore he knew what he was doing and voiced no concerns, perhaps wisely so, if he in fact harbored any.

Traditional sailing ships and boats of the day were built with wide bows thought necessary to keep the vessel from driving the front end under in a gale. The widest section of the hull was forward of the midpoint and the stern section was tapered into much narrower proportions than the bow. The resulting profile as seen from above looked something like a fish, and, indeed, the design of traditional vessels was called "cod's head and mackerel tail" to denote the fishlike shape. Ships and boats with this conventional design pushed the waves aside, creating considerable resistance and drag. Steers, and other designers working on the clipper ships, tried a new approach that reversed the form. Instead of having a wide, bluff bow and a thin stern, these designers made the bow thin and the stern wide. Steers tried his theory out on *Mary Taylor*, and she was, as Brown and the pilots competing against him discovered, faster than any boat of her size in the harbor.

Mary Taylor's bow was sharp, almost knifelike. Her draft was shallowest at the bow and gradually increased toward the stern. Her widest section was in the middle, or midships, portion of the schooner, not closer to the bow, as it was with traditional craft. As a result, she achieved greater speeds with the same spread of sails of boats of similar weight. She was more stable and better able to stand up to the heavy seas Brown often encountered offshore, and her motion at sea was smooth, less violent, which meant the crew tired less easily.

When it came time to name his new boat, Brown chose not to christen her after a famous shipowner or one of the founding fathers, as most of the other pilots did. True to his sense of irreverence and general lack of conservative convention he named her after a sexy, scandalous actress of the day. Back in 1844, at the popular Niblo's Gardens, the actress Mary Taylor raised eyebrows among conservatives when she introduced the polka to New York audiences. The dance caught on, despite its new and boisterous character, or perhaps because of it, and its disapproval among the more staid citizens of the city, who thought it uncivilized. A member of a prominent New York family, George Templeton Strong, described the polka upon first witnessing it as a "kind of insane Tartar jig." Mary Taylor remained very popular for her role in the hit play *A Glance at New York*, which had opened the previous year to rave reviews. Considering her radical new design, it struck Brown as fitting that his boat should honor a beautiful lady who was the talk of the town.

"She's changing course, sir!" the apprentice shouted from the masthead.

Brown raised his spyglass and peered at the bouncing image of the other schooner magnified in the orb of the lens. So she is, he thought, and heading downwind at a good clip to the southwest.

Brown watched as the schooner's mainsail spread out on one side of the boat, the foresail on the other, sailing wing and wing, as sailors called it. The other man's actions told him the westbound ship, still invisible below *Mary Taylor*'s horizon, was probably still east of the other schooner. To compensate for the ship's speed the pilot had to steer ahead of the vessel if he hoped to intercept it, much like a hunter fires ahead of a duck in flight to bring it down. Brown was pleased. His fellow master had made a tactical error. It was a natural mistake, following basic human nature to sail right to a specified point in a straight line. Yet, with the wind dead aft a sailboat lost the aerodynamic lift created when wind channeled through the slots created by the sails. Sailing downwind was slow. Brown had the chance he needed to get the better of the other man and his crew.

Brown ordered the men to the sheets, lines used to control the sails, and smoothly pushed the tiller to turn the bow away from the wind. Quickly, the schooner paid off. The wind moved from just forward of the left side of the bow back toward the stern. Brown issued commands, and the men worked the sheets to bring all the sails over at once as the wind came across the stern in a maneuver modern sailors call a jibe. *Mary Taylor* did not slow a bit as she came round and gathered speed with the wind now blowing over the right side of the stern, a perfect slant for sailing fast.

Instead of sailing directly after the schooner, Brown intended to sail west to get ahead of his competitor on the faster point of sail. At the same time, if he was lucky, he expected *Mary Taylor* to stay ahead of the inbound ship while the slower schooner dropped behind. Brown might sail a longer distance, but sailing at a greater speed he also might well win the contest.

Mary Taylor cut through the water without kicking up much foam at the bow. The little water that was disturbed hissed and sizzled as it flowed along on either side of the hull. The waves slapped against the stern and rolled under her, pushing her along with short bursts of speed from their imparted momentum. Brown concentrated on his work at the helm, feeling the pull of the tiller, and the balance of the sails as they propelled the hull. The cool touch of the wind against the skin on the back of his neck helped him guide the boat. He constantly looked aloft to check the trim of the sails and he ordered his men to make fine adjustments on the sheets whenever he felt it was necessary. Periodically, he jibed, making a zigzag course downwind. He gained steadily on the other boat until the men aboard her became clearly visible on deck.

"I see the ship, Captain Brown!" the apprentice on watch duty called. "She's a steamer bearing southeast by a quarter east, about seven miles."

Seeing at last what Brown was up to, the captain racing against him changed course to counter his moves. Both boats now sailed the faster zigzag course downwind. The crew on Brown's boat crouched low on the windward side of the deck aft of the mainmast to reduce the resistance of the wind against their bodies and to use their combined weight to keep the schooner in the best sailing trim. When it came to getting the most speed out of a sailboat, the small details counted.

Brown maneuvered *Mary Taylor* to keep her upwind of the other schooner, as the distance between both boats grew shorter with each passing minute. No one aboard spoke. Every man tended to his duty and concentrated on Brown's stream of quietly issued orders. He seemed to will his schooner to move faster, as if his very spirit was in close harmony with the wind and the sea, the vessel an extension of his body and mind. When his competitor jibed, Brown followed. *Mary Taylor* sailed close enough for her crew to see the faces of the other pilots. Their expressions ranged from annoyance to admiration.

The bow of *Mary Taylor* drew even with the other boat's stern. Brown took her close, very close, as if he might run his bowsprit into her transom. The sound of the vessels racing through the waves mingled with the wind, the flutter of canvas, the creak of blocks. In desperation, the other captain turned to cut across *Mary Taylor*'s bow to force him to bear away, creating an opening of clear air. Brown was ready and countered the maneuver. His well-trained crew acted fast and as one. *Mary Taylor* held the advantage.

Slowly, the disturbed air extending downwind from *Mary Taylor*'s sails robbed the competitor of wind. It was as if she had sailed behind a landmass that suddenly blocked the full force of the breeze from hitting the sails. The rival schooner slowed and *Mary Taylor* surged ahead. Brown's crew cheered. They stood up and waved good-naturedly to the men on the other boat's deck as her bow dropped astern.

"Well done, boys!" Brown said as the tension ebbed from his face. He smiled broadly, then with false severity, he said: "Now mind yourselves. The race is not won till our man's aboard that steamer."

The race indeed was not over. Although *Mary Taylor* was faster than the other schooner, they sailed in close company as the steamer drew near. There was always the possibility the competing pilots might still beat them to the prize. A tactical blunder, or a failure of gear or rigging, might change the odds. The only sure element at sea was its complete unpredictability.

Brown recognized the steamer as *Hibernia*. She was one of the mail ships from Cunard's line of Great Britain, which had ruled the sea since its founder, the Nova Scotian-born Samuel Cunard, won government subsidies from the British Admiralty to establish regular steam service between Liverpool, Halifax, and Boston. He began operation in 1840 with four nearly identical steamships capable of cruising at an average speed of eight knots. *Hibernia* was the first of the company's ships to begin eastbound service from New York to Liverpool on New Year's Day, 1848. That was a day all the pilots remembered well. It marked the first time reliable, regular steamship service had come to New York City with any frequency worth noting. Prior to that, Boston had held the distinction of being the only United States port where a traveler could catch a Cunard liner and cross the sea in under two weeks, even against the westerly winds that so taxed the masters of the sailing packets from New York as they sailed home from Europe.

Later in 1848, Cunard fielded four new liners, *America, Niagara, Canada,* and the famous *Europa*. With steaming speeds of ten knots, these were the fastest steamers afloat in the world. As a consequence, they drew the best in the passenger and freight trade, including the lucrative privilege of carrying the United States mail to and from Europe. Passengers paid as much as $125 per trip. A round-trip fare on a Cunard liner cost the equivalent of one third of a man's annual salary working in the city's shipyards, along the docks, or as clerks or copyists in the stores and countinghouses of the business district in lower Manhattan. The rise of the steamers at the port of New York was yet another example of the push for speed in the merchant marine, a symptom of the times when the pace of life seemed increasingly frenetic.

The desire for speed did not solely reside with the shipmasters and shipowners engaged in the transatlantic trade. It rippled through every aspect of maritime commerce emanating from New York City. Coastal packets bringing cotton to New York from New Orleans, Mobile, Savannah, and Charleston sought the best routes for the swiftest passages, and designs for newer, faster ships were coming into operation. The packets in the East India and China trade pushed for speed as well. On March 25, 1849, the clipper ship *Sea Witch* astonished New York with her record passage of seventy-four days, fourteen hours from Canton to New York, a record never broken on that route in the days of sail.

Gold had been discovered late the previous year in the California territory newly ceded to the United States from Mexico after the close of the Mexican-American War in 1848. Bands of men throughout New England formed mining companies and set off aboard all manner of vessels, many of them ill-equipped, on voyages around Cape Horn at the tip of South America bound for the goldfields. Merchants in New York were beginning to realize enormous profits from the sale of merchandise at the port of San Francisco. A new market had suddenly emerged and men at shipyards that were already hard at work designing and building the new type of freight-carrying vessels known as clipper ships for the China trade increased their activity to put still more of these ships on the California run. Overall, the economy of the United States boomed, and so, too, did the port of New York. Imports had doubled in tonnage in just four years. The pilots were never busier, nor as prosperous.

As Brown sailed *Mary Taylor* to meet *Hibernia*, leaving the competing boat far enough astern for him to relax a little, it was once again very clear that Steers had done his job well. Brown brought the schooner close to the ship, almost within easy hailing distance.

Well-dressed first-class passengers lined the decks and waved. They looked small at the rails of the big 1,422-ton steamship. Her paddle wheels churned the water. A prodigious bow wave curled and hissed. All her sails were set to add power to her engines chugging and heaving down below, each with the strength of 500 horses. The boilers converted water into steam and the fires in the furnaces sent a black plume of smoke up the stack that the wind carried off over the sea.

Brown sailed *Mary Taylor* even closer, taking care to stay out of the lee of the ship, to ensure that the massive hull did not block his wind while bringing the schooner in behind the potentially lethal paddle wheel. Standing on top of the half-moon-shaped paddle wheel box covering the wheel, the captain of the steamship gazed across the waves at the grand sight of the schooner slicing through the water, a wedge of white foam at her bow. He shouted to an officer on deck to signal the engineers below to slow the engines down, allowing the steamer to ride forward on her momentum alone. He could spare a little time with the pilot boat close and sailing fast, just enough to take a pilot aboard in preparation for the ship's arrival off Sandy Hook.

Brown nodded to the apprentices at the yawl, and the pilot who was to go aboard. "Off with you now, boys. We haven't much time," he said, as he calmly and quietly issued orders to the apprentices on deck at their sail stations. Brown hove *Mary Taylor* to. Her jib backed with a pleasing snap. She slowed nearly to a stop. The apprentices launched the yawl. The pilot clambered over the side into the boat, trying not to get his fine clothes wet. The crew pushed off. In seconds, their oars dug deep and propelled the yawl swiftly toward the rope ladder dangling against the side of the ship aft of the paddle wheel. The rowboat quickly dropped behind the paddle wheel and the waves it created sent spray flying over the bow. With the practice and skill of hundreds of boardings, the apprentices brought the boat alongside. The pilot grabbed the ladder and climbed twenty feet up the clifflike side of the steamer. The yawl dropped astern and bounced in the ship's wake.

When the yawl cleared the steamer, Brown picked up his men.

He told them they had done well, his voice cheerful and jolly. The boys beamed back at him, their eyes sparkling, their shirts soaked with sweat from their hard work, despite the autumn chill in the air. *Mary Taylor*'s sails filled as the apprentices hoisted the yawl aboard and secured it. The schooner heeled to the breeze and once again cut through the waves, heading back east in pursuit of the other pilot boat already well away on a new search. Brown was ready for yet another race, yet another difficult task of putting a man aboard a moving ship. After years of practice, Brown was also ready for a different sort of competition, a contest in a far-off land where the honor of his country would shine or fade based on his abilities as a Yankee schoonerman.

CHAPTER FOUR

THE COMMODORE'S PRIDE

The well-liveried coachman wiped away beads of dew that sparkled on the woodwork and brass fittings of the four-in-hand carriage in the early spring morning air. In places, where the light was just right, the wood glistened enough for him to see a distorted reflection of his face in the finish. All around him the sounds of New York City wide awake and busy with the day penetrated his concentration. The clatter of wheels and the clop of hooves on the cobblestone streets, the brusque shouts of omnibus drivers, and the cry of newsboys hawking their editions of *The New York Herald* or the *New York Tribune* merged into a singular hum of vitality. Detailing the carriage, tending the horses, and harnessing the four magnificent creatures in preparation for the master or lady's departure was part of his daily routine.

When all was ready the coachman waited. Soon the man of the house, John Cox Stevens, emerged from his palatial Greek Revival home, tucked on a corner of the Columbia College campus in lower Manhattan near Washington Square, where he had been a student years earlier. His late father, John, a colonel for the Continental Army during the Revolutionary War, had also gone to school there and studied law, though he never practiced it. But that was way back in time, back when the venerable institution bore a different name, King's College, and the Stevens family was one of the wealthiest and most influential in Great Britain's American colonies.

"Good morning, Mr. Stevens," the coachman said, opening the door for his employer. The athletic-looking man of medium height, showing signs of his sixty-five years in the form of wrinkles and his long, wavy gray hair, paused before climbing into the richly appointed interior of the carriage. John Cox acknowledged the salutation with a nod, removed his top hat, and stepped inside. The coachman closed the door and took his seat. With a slap of the reins and a shout to the horses, the coachman drove off toward the docks of the Stevens family's Hoboken Ferry Company situated on the New York and New Jersey shores of the Hudson River. Stevens may have intended to catch the ferry to Hoboken on an errand to the New York Yacht Club, or perhaps to conduct some business at the family estate at Castle Point. The nature of Stevens's excursion was none of the coachman's concern, however. His sole purpose in life at that moment was to convey his master to the pier on time and without incident in the chaotic traffic.

The neighborhood around Columbia College, once rural in character and rarefied in the nature of its wealthy residents, had changed considerably since Stevens had built his city home there in 1846. It was the same story elsewhere in the city as well. The economic boom times had spurred growth, hiked real estate values, and led to a reshuffling of the wealthy enclaves from their former haunts in lower Manhattan up Broadway to Fifth Avenue and beyond. Just the same, John Cox and his wife, Maria Livingston, herself from one of the wealthiest families in New York, were happy living in the city. It kept them close to the heart of the high society they belonged to and enjoyed, his interests in the financial and insurance businesses, and the luxury of running water, indoor plumbing, central heating, and other amenities that were available in New York. When John Cox required a diversion he sailed his yachts in the company of friends or he raced against other members of the New York Yacht Club. He and Maria also retired to their country estate in Hyde Park or visited friends who owned summer "cottages" at Saratoga Springs and at Newport, Rhode Island.

While John Cox and others of his ilk maintained the rhythm of their aristocratic lifestyles, the city continued to change with an increasing rapidity. These changes threatened to strip away whatever insulation money provided for those who did not wish to acknowledge the growing divide between the classes. The wealthy watched with uneasiness as a tide of humanity from the "lower order" swept over the city and quickly reshaped it into a cosmopolitan mix of rich and poor mingled together in residential neighborhoods and on the busy thoroughfares.

Low- and middle-class people funneled into the city from the hinterlands of New Jersey, upstate New York, and Connecticut. They were drawn by the promise of work and better wages than they could earn in the countryside. Irish, German, and English immigrants flooded the town at an average of 157,000 new arrivals every year, and many of them stayed. The total population of New York had grown in just one decade from 312,000 to more than 515,000 in 1850. As the coachman drove west across town to the ferry landing, he passed brownstone mansions surrounded by brick boardinghouses, shops, and groggeries. Wooden tenement buildings crammed to capacity grew more numerous closer to the river. The city presented the observer with a stark juxtaposition of prosperity and poverty, but such contrasts mattered little to men like John Cox. He barely noticed them, except when they became apparent in his own neighborhood near his beloved alma mater.

Stevens pulled his simple black frock coat close against the chilly breeze blowing off the waterfront as he boarded the ferry. He gazed out at the river filled with all manner of vessels. Hudson River sloops, low and wide and cumbersome, sailed upriver on the incoming tide that flowed up the estuary as far as Albany, 150 miles to the north. Tugs with large sailing vessels in tow headed down the upper bay toward the Verrazano Narrows and the open sea beyond, weaving among the fleet at anchor off Governors Island near the Battery. Steam ferries on the seven-hour run to Albany hooted and hissed. The water churned white as the paddle wheels turned. Across the river in Jersey City, Cunard's transatlantic steamships lay moored at the new docks. Buildings dotted the wooded shoreline of the river north of Hoboken, itself still in a quasi-pristine state, though more suburban than rural.

The dockmen cast off the lines of the ferry, and her captain skillfully steered her away from the rickety wharves, decaying from lack of maintenance. Although maritime commerce accounted for the bulk of economic activity in New York, the city planners chose not to fund the expensive repairs needed on nearly every pier on the East and Hudson Rivers. Rather, they thought, and perhaps wisely, that it was best to keep the dockage rates low to encourage packet shipowners to call at the port instead of at Boston, Philadelphia, or Baltimore, where rates were three or four times as high. Across the river in Hoboken, however, the docks on the Stevenses' land were kept in good order. Cunard's new docks in Jersey City were likewise examples of money well spent, a manifestation of the principle that to make a profit one must spend some of it to further a business enterprise.

John Cox was known about town more for his love of sports than for his powers as a businessman. Of all his passions, yachting ranked as his most cherished pursuit. In 1809, at the age of twenty-four, he built his first yacht, a twenty-foot sloop he called *Diver*. At the age of thirty-one, in 1816, he frequently instigated informal races against the harbor workboats aboard his fifty-six-foot yacht *Trouble*. He often bested the old salts on the waterfront. Winning at all costs became a driving force behind his personality as it evolved and grew with the passing decades. The competitive nature was not isolated to him alone. His father and brothers, particularly Robert Livingston and Edwin, all were imbued with it. However, they competed in business while John Cox stuck largely to sports.

Over the years, John Cox had a series of at least four yachts built for him. He raced friends and cruised to New England for pleasure. In Boston, the members of high society also owned and sailed yachts, even going so far as to form a loose sort of yacht club, though it did not last. The Bostonians and the New Yorkers often met at popular anchorages in the balmy summer months, where they dined like kings and queens in the well-appointed main saloons below decks or ashore in the dining rooms of the numerous estates built as retreats for the wealthy anxious to escape the heat of the big cities. They were acting out a style of yachting that dated back to the Dutch in the seventeenth century, when sailing first began as a recreational sport, a sport of the nobility. The favored rig was the schooner, and these fleet little craft were known as *jaght schips,* meaning swift boats, or yachts, in English.

The year of 1844 proved quite eventful for John Cox. He launched the latest of his boats, the fifty-one-foot schooner *Gimcrack,* and on July 30, he and eight other yachting enthusiasts formed the New York Yacht Club. The informal ceremony was held aboard *Gimcrack* in New York Harbor, and John Cox was appointed commodore. The nine men planned the first formal club cruise to the burgeoning resort of the rich: Newport, Rhode Island. The annual summer cruise became a tradition, one much enjoyed among the members of the club.

During that summer full of boats and sailing, parties and banquets, John Cox was smitten even further with his love of yachts, which were essentially very expensive toys for him to play with. Having just launched *Gimcrack,* John Cox commissioned his favored builder, William Capes, who owned a boatyard in Hoboken and had built *Gimcrack,* to build him a sloop expressly for racing. Designed by Robert Livingston and named after John Cox's wife, Maria, she was launched in 1845. She was the pride of the New York Yacht Club's fleet, measuring ninety-two feet on deck, with a beam of more than twenty-six feet, and a draft of just five feet, two inches without her centerboard lowered. A centerboard is a movable extension of the keel, which can be raised or lowered as conditions merit. *Maria's* centerboard extended her draft to twenty feet.

Maria's single mast was ninety-two feet long and the boom for the mainsail was ninety-five feet long, which meant it protruded well over the stern. Her mainsail and jib totaled 7,890 square feet. The huge spread of canvas set on such a tall rig, together with her shallow draft, made *Maria* a challenge and sometimes dangerous to sail in a stiff breeze. She saw her first action in a regatta held on October 6, and, to the immense pleasure of John Cox, she soundly beat the rest of the fleet over a forty-mile course in New York Harbor. *Maria* was the purpose of John Cox's excursion to Hoboken on that early spring day in 1850.

As the ferry approached the dock, John Cox went over in his mind the improvements William Capes was to have made on *Maria*. The work was nearly done, or at least John Cox expected it to be completed. He counted on Capes to have her ready in time for the first regattas of the summer, and he felt making an appearance at the boatyard might help guarantee the men carried out their promises. A notice in *The New York Herald* added other worries to his concerns about *Maria*'s readiness for the sailing season. The short yachting news item read: "It is said that considerable difficulty is being encountered in obtaining crews for yachts. It is probable that the yacht sailors who go into deep water during the Winter have not yet returned, but during the next two weeks they will be ready to report for the coming season." Good reliable labor, both in the boatyard and for captains and crews, was a chief worry to yachtsmen. As yachting was seasonal in nature, the men needed to sail the big racers sought work offshore on the fishing smacks. The best of them applied for positions aboard the yachts during the summer. The pay was better, conditions more comfortable, and the work less demanding.

As soon as the dockmen secured the ferry, John Cox disembarked and headed over to William Capes's boatyard. Workers darted about the premises with mauls, saws, and adzes. Other men drove teams of horses that dragged timbers, already squared but in need of more shaping, to the yachts and workboats under construction on the stocks. The sounds of the boatyard filled the air, the whack of mauls, the jangle of chains, the rhythmic whine of the two-man pit saws. The smell of freshly cut wood, woodsmoke, and horse manure mixed with the tang of the salt brought in on the breeze off the river.

John Cox was comfortable in the chaos of the boatyard. He knew its workers well, though he seldom spoke to them, except the foreman or William Capes. He thought highly of their craftsmanship, their ability to fashion swift yachts out of an odd assortment of oak, pine, and rock maple. He made his way across the boatyard and craned his neck to look at the hull of yacht *Maria*, pleased that the work he ordered done to lengthen her bow a full eighteen feet seemed well near finished. Men swarmed over her decks. They stood on plankways on either side of the bow to complete planking and caulking the hull.

"Good morning, Mr. Stevens," some of the men called down to him.

John Cox touched his fingers to the rim of his top hat and nodded. He walked around the yacht, admiring her new lines, which were based on Richard Brown's pilot boat *Mary Taylor*. Brown had risen from obscurity to command the respect of the pilots, merchants, and shipowners of the city. He had worked for the United States Coast Survey aboard the brigs *Washington* and *Somers* in charting the shoals and channels of the Sandy Hook bar, and he had tended the navigation aids, the various buoys, lights, and day beacons placed at points along the coast from Sandy Hook to Delaware Bay. Captain Brown knew the harbor better than most men. But it was his abilities as a schoonerman that had caught John Cox's attention, that and the sailing qualities of his new boat. Good sailors and fast boats did not go unnoticed in John Cox's wide circle of yachting friends.

As he surveyed *Maria*, John Cox recalled previous sailing seasons with the yearning typical of any yacht owner anxious to see his boat afloat once again soon after the spring thaw. He delighted in *Maria*'s swift sailing abilities and savored the excitement of reaching speeds of well over ten knots. Spreading nearly 8,000 square feet of canvas, she sailed faster than traditionally built merchant ships twice her size. His crew of fifty men manned the huge mainsail and jib, and jumped to the orders of the captain, and his, when he chose to step in. He stood at her helm, with a harbor pilot at his side to provide navigation advice when it was needed, the wind whipping his hair under his broad-rimmed hat, which he wore when out on the water. To his guests he served simple meals of fish chowder, and strong spirits to the men. With the modifications to *Maria*'s bow, John Cox looked forward to sailing faster than ever before.

Robert Livingston had designed *Maria* in the traditional form, with a rounded, bluff bow and a fair clean run aft to the stern, and she had performed well enough. She indeed possessed some striking innovations, including hollow spars to reduce weight aloft, a small aft centerboard for sailing off the wind, and rubber compressors fitted to her main sheet traveler to lessen the strain on the rig. *Maria* was the first yacht to use rubber compressors, which essentially acted like shock absorbers as the main boom swung over for a new tack. The previous year, when George Steers's new design for *Mary Taylor* proved so successful, John Cox decided to try the concept on *Maria*. The expense was of no consequence. Over the time he owned *Maria* John Cox spent more than $100,000 on her, the equivalent of $1.8 million in today's currency.

Steers first came to John Cox's attention fourteen years earlier, in 1836 during one of the sailboat races he sponsored. It was a competition open to all comers. Steers, then only sixteen years old, built a sixteen-foot racing boat, *Martin Van Buren,* and bested all challengers. Gradually, as the young boy became a young man, Steers's accomplishments made him well known as a skillful yacht designer. Though he was only thirty years old, Steers's abilities won him respect in the yachting community ordinarily granted to older, more established naval architects. He designed John Cox's *Gimcrack,* and the yachts *Una, Cygnet,* and *Cornelia,* among others. *Mary Taylor*'s radically new lines intrigued John Cox, whetted his curiosity to see them applied to the largest sloop in the yachting fleet, his yacht *Maria.*

Thus, under his orders, William Capes's men removed the rounded, bluff bow and rebuilt it to the sharp, nearly concave lines of *Mary Taylor.* Expanded to 110 feet on deck, *Maria*'s new lines struck John Cox as unorthodox, but beautiful. They also excited in him a desire to sail his boat as soon as it was possible to get her back into the water. He patted the side of the sloop and dreamed of the coming season, the races and the victories, the thrill of competition that made him feel more alive than in most any other aspect of his life.

CHAPTER FIVE

GREAT
EXHIBITION

As the spring of 1850 gave way to summer and the fair southerly winds blew the fresh scent of the sea across the teeming island of Manhattan, the city continued on with its rapid expansion. The packets and steamships came and went, reaching the height of traffic for the year. Tea clippers brought in valuable cargoes from the Chinese ports of Amoy, Foochow, Ninghsien, and Shanghai. The California clippers set sail loaded with merchandise for the port of San Francisco, the population of which had grown from under one thousand residents in 1848 to well over 20,000. The gold rush dominated the talk along the East River piers, fashionable Broadway to the slums of Five Points, in countinghouses, taverns, fancy restaurants, and at private soirees held in the homes of high society.

The promise of the times reached far from Manhattan to cities on the Great Lakes such as Rochester and Chicago. The 9,000 miles of railroads linked major cities to the small towns, and gradually replaced the much slower and less efficient transportation on the canals, when they were navigable. During the cold winters in the Northeast and Midwest, canals remained frozen an average of three months out of the year. Opportunities to earn a living and the basics of a comfortable life extended farther west for thousands of teachers, doctors, shopkeepers, shoemakers, millers, blacksmiths, and farmers. Telegraphs sped the dissemination of news and information vital to commerce.

On the frontier, west of the Mississippi River and east of the Rocky Mountains, the westward migration extended the reach of American interests beyond the national borders into the plains and foothills of the Great American Desert, as this area of North America was called. There seemed to be an endless amount of land for the country's nearly 24 million citizens, and the flood of immigrants coming from Europe. In 1850 alone, more than 400,000 Irish, Germans, and English emigrated to the United States, and while many stayed in the Northeast, others pushed west. An anonymous writer, who went by the name of "Big Block," wrote of his travels in the western lands in 1849:

> The only places on the Plains, in the wide stretch of two thousand miles, where the crude elements of Civilization could be seen, were at Forts Kearny, Laramie and Bridger, with Salt Lake City on one route and Fort Hall on the more Northern road, and at none of these places could food or the comforts of life be obtained to supply our wants.

Headlines in the New York newspapers highlighted the political unrest boiling in the United States at the time. The North–South sectional split over the issue of slavery in the new territories flared up in Congress, as it had intermittently since the war with Mexico began in 1846. The temperance and women's rights movements also commanded headlines.

Tucked in among all of the hot domestic issues of the times was news from Europe. New York merchants paid close attention to the improving economy of Great Britain, which directly benefited them, and to the temporary easing of political tensions in Central Europe that had threatened to throw the continent into a widespread state of war in 1848. Troubles had erupted in Germany, Poland, Switzerland, France, Austria, and Italy. Much of the unrest stemmed from a rebellion of the working classes against the iron rule of despotic governments. The merchants also noted the stories that began to spread concerning The Great Exhibition of the Works of Industry of All Nations.

Great Britain's Prince Albert, consort of Queen Victoria, had hatched an idea to hold the first international world's fair in London the following year. New York merchants read with amusement the London newspapers that came over on the packets. Story after story showed just how resistant the British Parliament was to Prince Albert's plan. The politicians were not alone. The British press lampooned the prince with its typical acerbic barbs and cruel cartoons. The pettiness of the opposition to a fair meant to promote an exchange of ideas, greater intercourse between nations, and peace in Europe was not lost on discerning readers in the United States.

The controversy in June of 1850 centered on the location of the exhibition site and on what kind of edifice to build to house all the displays. The newspapers also crowed about the likelihood that the exhibition was certain to turn London into a mecca of the lower order, that prostitutes and thieves might corrupt the good-hearted citizens of the city, and that the millions of attendees expected to view the more than ten thousand displays from more than thirty countries was a sure invitation for plagues. Prince Albert was at the point of despair. He wrote during the preparations for the exhibition:

> Now our Exhibition is to be driven from London; the patrons who are afraid, the Radicals who wish to show their power over the Crown Property [Albert was referring to Hyde Park], *The Times,* whose solicitor bought a house near Hyde Park [and presumably did not want all the rabble in his neighborhood], are abusing and insulting.

And at another time, in response to stories about "aliens" conspiring to use the exhibition for the purpose of terrorism, the prince wrote:

> The opponents of the Exhibition work with might and main to throw all the old women here into a panic and to drive myself crazy. The strangers, they give out, are certain to commence a

thorough revolution here, to murder Victoria and myself, and
to proclaim the Red Republic in England.

Albert was of German descent, prince of Saxe-Coburg, a small
duchy in the German confederation, prior to his marriage to Queen
Victoria in 1840, when he became a British subject. He spoke with a
thick German accent. His progressive thinking on foreign and domestic policy, particularly with regard to the importance of bettering
the lives of working-class people in Great Britain, did not endear
him to politicians. He was viewed as an unwelcome foreigner whose
ideas seemed outlandish and completely against the traditions of
the kingdom. Nevertheless, he put aside the unpleasantness and
worked behind the scenes with Victoria, writing letters to the pow-
ers-that-be at home and abroad, held meetings and implemented
plans to further British interests, and overall helped to run the country as an unrecognized and often unappreciated king.

A once handsome man, the prince was showing signs of over-
work. He put on weight. His hairline receded and he was subject to
bouts of depression. Nevertheless, he believed so strongly in his
Great Exhibition, and what it might mean for the world, that he endured the ridicule and infighting that even went so far as to concern
itself over felling not a single elm tree in Hyde Park on the twenty
acres that were eventually set aside for the exhibition site.

Just two years earlier, the notion that Great Britain might hold an
international exhibition as a showcase for her superior technological advances, and invite others to do the same, would have been
considered ludicrous. The famine in Ireland and the high price of
grain that caused misery for the poor and discomfort for the rich
led to unrest in Britain in 1847 and 1848. During this period as
much as one seventh of the entire population of Great Britain was
receiving full or partial government assistance to obtain food. In
England and Wales alone, the population jumped from nine million in 1801 to double that amount by 1851, setting up a large disenfranchised horde of unemployed, hungry, and angry citizens.

There were riots in Ireland and in England from Trafalgar Square to Glasgow Green.

Although the Industrial Revolution had spawned new jobs for the growing population in factories and coal mines, the largest segment of Great Britain's working class scraped their livings out of the nation's agricultural enterprises operated on land owned by the nobility and gentry. Nearly two million workers labored on the estate farms. The second-largest source of employment was for domestic servants, comprising more than one million individuals.

The forties were known as the "hungry years" in Great Britain because of the potato famine, which began sweeping through Ireland in 1845. The famine brought to the fore what was already a deep groundswell of smoldering support among certain segments of the British population for an advancement of free trade and the repeal of protective import laws. The most famous of these were the Corn Laws that prevented the importation of grain products into Great Britain, despite the fact that millions of her citizens were starving, and not just in Ireland. Famine struck in industrial cities such as Manchester as well as out in the countryside, largely due to the high cost of grain kept artificially inflated by the restrictive laws.

The question of whether to repeal the Corn Laws was a divisive issue in Parliament, and there was uncertainty as to which side might come out on top, those who wanted free trade, or those who did not. New York merchants anxious to sell grain to Great Britain were crying out for the latest news, news that meant the potential for quick money for those who were first to open up a new market. This led to the dispatch of a pilot boat by a group of Wall Street newspaper publishers to England to gather the latest news in the late spring of 1846.

On May 31, 1846, rival publisher James Gordon Bennett of *The New York Herald* was lucky enough to scoop the Wall Street "gang," when his own newsboat, a swift schooner based on the pilot boat design, met *Yorkshire* inbound from England off the east end of Long Island. She carried the latest news of the debate, which was taken off the packet and brought to New York via foot, horse, train, and ferry—for publication the next day in the *Herald*.

The Corn Laws were repealed in the summer of 1846, and, as expected, the action led to a huge increase in trade between Great Britain and New York City in the form of exported flour. Shiploads of flour and other grain products poured into New York via the Erie Canal, on railroads, and on Hudson River sloops. New steam-grain elevators proliferated. The new market in Great Britain added to the export of tobacco and cotton, which remained the lion's share of United States exports through New York until the American Civil War put a temporary end to the business in 1861. According to a Congressional report on exports in 1852, "more than 800,000 tons of the navigation of the United States engaged in the foreign trade are employed in carrying American cotton to Europe and elsewhere, and upwards of 40,000 American seamen are given employment in such vessels." Total exports of United States goods in 1851 amounted to $188 million. Cotton comprised sixty percent of that total dollar value and most of it and the money it generated flowed through New York.

In addition to the Corn Laws, Great Britain repealed its highly restrictive Navigation Laws in 1847, which further opened up the country for imports from the United States and Europe. The Navigation Laws, in place since 1651 and modified over the centuries, were intended to favor British shipping while putting ruinous economic burdens on other countries wishing to trade with Great Britain.

The United States responded to these positive developments in Great Britain with a lifting of many of its own protective trade policies. The actions of both nations spurred the economies of each. Still, the conditions for the average British citizen remained grim in the late 1840s, though the improvements to come in the early 1850s were starting to become more apparent. James Alexander Hamilton, the third son of Alexander Hamilton, who was aide to General George Washington and later secretary of the United States Treasury, wrote to a friend in New York during a visit to Europe in 1848:

> When I turn my thoughts back from this Old World in her
> state of decrepitude and decay, to our happy land, so new in its

institutions, but so much further advanced towards true civilization, where the mental and physical properties of man are so much more vigorously developed than in any part of Europe, England with all her pride not excepted, the undoubted result of our free institutions, I thank God *I am an American* [Hamilton's emphasis].

The grand idea first announced in our Declaration of Independence and practically illustrated in the Constitution of the United States that the only true foundation of government is the will of the people, and its only true aim, the greatest good of the greatest number, has never on this side of the Atlantic been the object of the faith, or the rule of action of its statesmen or politicians when engaged in forming or administering their Governments. On the contrary, it is deemed by them a dangerous heresy, subversive not only of thrones, but of the power and influence of the classes who consider themselves born with boots and spurs on, to ride at will the submissive people. . . .

You may have heard of "Merry England." If ever she was so, she is so no more. Her joys are all turned to sorrows. You have heard of "the roast beef of old England," there is certainly much of that there, but the masses not only do not eat it, but they do not know its taste.

The repeal of restrictive laws on imports and exports, combined with better harvests in Great Britain in 1849, marked a decrease in the tensions at work in the country. The booming trade between the continent and Great Britain, and with the United States ushered in prosperity for many of the disenfranchised of the British working class. Hope and optimism spread across the island nation in 1850. Although there were millions left out of the good times, there was a middle class whose lives were far more comfortable than they had been just several years earlier. The prince's idea for the Great Exhibition was a manifestation of this sense of well-being. As time went on, the population of the country warmed to it, embraced the concept, and became proud of the prince for pushing for its implementation.

The thorniest obstacle to the successful execution of the Great Exhibition was removed in mid-July 1850, by an associate of the Duke of Devonshire, an engineer named Joseph Paxton. Paxton devised a plan for a radical new type of building to house the displays for the exhibition. Essentially, it was a giant version of the Victoria regia greenhouse at Chatsworth, which he called the "palace of glass" and *The Illustrated London News* dubbed the "Crystal Palace." He convinced members of the Executive Committee who were reviewing and rejecting thousands of designs, all based on bricks and mortar, to consider his "palace." After much debate, Paxton's plans were approved on July 15.

No building of its kind had ever been constructed. It seemed fitting for an exhibition dedicated to the "new wonders" of the world. The provisions of the agreement to use the Hyde Park site stipulated that the elms of the park had to remain in place, and that the structure had to be removed at the close of the exhibition, if that action was deemed desirable to revert the park back to its unblemished beauty, a haven for strollers, picnickers, and grazing cows. Constructed with iron, wood, and glass, Paxton's Crystal Palace enabled him to enclose the tall elms and make them part of the building's unique appeal. The design also allowed for easy deconstruction, whereas bricks and mortar did not.

Work commenced on July 26. The iron foundries near Birmingham began turning out the thirty-nine miles of iron pipe, columns, and girders needed for the skeleton of the 1,000-foot-long, three-tiered structure. One third of Britain's annual production of glass was needed to construct the walls, roofs, and the one hundred-foot-tall transept, under which were some of the majestic old elms, fountains, and statues. While work went on at the factories and the components were shipped via rail to London, more than 2,000 men gathered in Hyde Park to put the giant puzzle together. Iron pipes, girders, and trusses were shipped and assembled sometimes within eighteen hours of their exit from the foundries. Glass panes were secured. The effort involved in constructing the Crystal Palace was one of the major engineering wonders of the nineteenth century.

Teams of horses and dozens of laborers raised the first columns of the Crystal Palace in September. Large crowds of Londoners came to watch the work as it rapidly progressed day by day. Vendors set up concession stands to feed the workmen and the spectators. Other entrepreneurs opened groceries and restaurants. The city itself underwent a face-lift with the construction of new housing and roads. Almost 14,000 exhibitors with more than 100,000 displays were expected. Plans indicated eleven miles of tables were needed to show off the technological and often whimsical contributions from most of the world's major countries.

The excitement over the Great Exhibition thrived like tea roses in an English garden. While the talk in America dwelled on gold and profits, in England, all classes of the population talked of Prince Albert and the exhibition. One English merchant found himself as swept up with enthusiasm for the exhibition as his peers, and in his fervor he wrote a letter to a powerful American merchant in Manhattan with whom he conducted frequent business. He noted that the United States was going to be a large contributor to the Great Exhibition and suggested that New Yorkers might consider sending over one of their swift pilot boats to demonstrate the advances in American shipbuilding that were producing some of the fastest sailing vessels in the world. It was, of course, not to be an official part of the exhibition, but a nice addition to the contributions the United States intended to send in an official capacity.

The reputation of the American pilot boats had indeed reached the shores of Great Britain. That these boats were fast was not new information. Early American pilot boats, based on the sharp lines and deep V hulls of the Baltimore clippers, had outsailed slower British vessels during the War of 1812. These privateers, in essence legalized pirates, captured English ships off the coast of the United States, and they roamed to the West Indies to harass shipping there.

After regular packet service began between New York and Liverpool in 1818 with the start of the Black Ball Line, the newsboats, also of pilot boat design, were well known among the captains. When steamships began replacing the packets as mail carriers the newsboats turned to Cunard's liners as sources for the latest reports from Europe, also making an impression on English captains. Every ship clearing in and out of New York Harbor encountered the pilots, and witnessed their races against each other. Of them all, the pilot boat *Mary Taylor* and her skipper, Dick Brown, were talked about on the Liverpool waterfront. Word of a radical new boat that outsailed even the best of her competitors was of keen interest to both British and American businessmen involved in maritime commerce.

The British merchant's suggestion was made in an honest appreciation of the American schooners and the men who sailed them. A love of the sea and grand ships was fundamental to Great Britain's national character. That America might want to share the best of its small craft as an unofficial part of its contribution to the Great Exhibition seemed a foregone conclusion, and it was a correct assumption. But the merchant's letter set in motion a chain of events no one could have foreseen.

CHAPTER SIX

DECISION

The pungent aroma of Cuban cigars filled the expansive drawing room of John Cox Stevens's New York City home. The six men gathered together sipped brandy or port from crystal glasses while they smoked. A fire burned in the fireplace and dissipated the autumn chill. The globes of the gas lamps and the candles needed to augment the light illuminated the room in a warm, yellow glow that set off the luster of the dark mahogany easy chairs, amply cushioned and made more comfortable with throw pillows. A velvet upholstered sofa, a pedestal table, a sideboard, and a grand piano accounted for some of the other furnishings. Heavy velvet curtains hung across the windows helped keep out drafts. Family portraits and paintings of landscapes adorned the walls covered with the finest European wallpaper.

Like many of New York's elite, the Stevens family had emerged from the Revolutionary War with its wealth intact. John Cox's father, John, freely spent his money on establishing transportation businesses that helped build the new nation and in the process had vastly expanded his fortune. A visionary, Colonel John, as he was known, believed in the superiority of railroads versus canals. He believed in steam-powered vessels as opposed to the use of sail for water transportation on the coast, its bays, rivers, and sounds. As early as 1804 he was experimenting with steamboats when he launched *Little Juliana,* a steamboat driven by twin screw propellers.

As Colonel John's sons grew older, two emerged as the key players in building the family fortune, Robert Livingston and Edwin. Both young men worked on inventions related to steam locomotion on land and water. Both also worked closely with their father to establish and operate the Union Line, with Edwin as its president, and Robert Livingston and John Cox as the other owners. The Union Line ran freight and passengers via steamboat from New York to the harbor of Perth Amboy on Raritan Bay, and from there via stagecoach to Trenton, where riders and freight were transferred to the Stevenses' Delaware ferry company for through service to Philadelphia. The trip took only twelve hours instead of days. The family established steamboat service on Long Island Sound, and between Hoboken and Manhattan in the 1820s.

Few people in the early years of the nineteenth century believed in Colonel John's insights. Canals were built, not railroads. Turnpikes and toll roads were hacked out of the forest. Some of these actually featured a system of crude wooden rails to facilitate travel over the rough ground. Horses pulled the freight wagons. It was slow and laborious work getting from one place to another, even using a turnpike. Rightfully clinging to his belief in the superiority of steam locomotives over horses, Colonel John became the first man in the United States to receive a charter to build a railroad, when he convinced the New Jersey Assembly in 1815 to "erect a rail road from the river Delaware near Trenton to the river Raritan at or near New Brunswick." As good as his idea was, Colonel John's "vision" was met with laughter and none of his wealthy friends stepped forward to back his scheme.

Undaunted, Colonel John, together with Robert Livingston, designed and built the first American-made steam locomotive in 1825. The design was lifted from specimens of locomotives then coming into use in Great Britain. The Stevenses were at that time developing their estate in Hoboken into an early form of amusement park and resort. They built a hotel and a pavilion they called the Colonnade, a promenade along the river front, and planted English gardens around the estate. In addition, they built Ferris-like wheels and other amusements.

The most impressive attraction was their half-mile circular track on which paying passengers rode in cars pulled behind the Stevenses' steam locomotive. It was an outlandish looking contraption, with a vertical tubular boiler resembling a wine bottle. But the little engine hit speeds of twelve miles per hour and thrilled the riders. In the 1830s, city dwellers rode the Stevenses' ferries to Hoboken, stayed in their hotel, paid for amusement rides, food, and refreshments, and played baseball and cricket at the family's Elysian Fields. As many as twenty thousand people came to the Villa Stevens, as it was called, on holiday weekends during this era.

In 1830, when Colonel John was in his early eighties, Robert Livingston and Edwin won a charter to build a railroad between Perth Amboy and Camden, realizing a long-held dream of their father. The Union Line was folded into the Camden and Amboy Railroad and Transportation Company. The railroad was completed in 1834. The tracks were a special invention of Robert Livingston. Known as a T-rail, these tracks allowed for mounting directly to the crossties, something other forms of tracks could not accomplish. The old-fashioned rails tended to lift and form what were called snakeheads, as the iron ribbons twisted and often pierced through the wooden floors of the train cars—to the alarm of passengers. Robert Livingston's T-rail did not form any snakeheads; it is still in use today. He also invented a special claw spike to use in mounting the track.

The Camden and Amboy Railroad was not the first railway in use in the country. But it was one of the earliest to get started and provide effective service and consistent profits to the owners and stockholders. Also under construction were the Baltimore and Ohio, the Albany and Schenectady, the Lexington & Ohio, and several others. These early railroads were uncomfortable for passengers, but they also represented a much faster way to get from one place to another. People put up with all sorts of inconveniences and the danger that the engine's boiler might explode. Even in the early 1850s, after significant improvements to steam engines had occurred, the danger of explosions was still great enough for the lawmakers in New York

City to prohibit steam locomotives south of thirtieth street.

Author Charles Dickens described a ride on an early American line, New England's Boston & Lowell Railroad, in his humorous book, *American Notes,* about a trip to the United States in 1842.

> The train calls at stations in the woods, where the wild impossibility of anybody having the smallest reason to get out, is only to be equalled by the apparently desperate hopelessness of there being anybody to get in. It rushes across the turnpike road, where there is no gate, no policeman, no signal: nothing but a rough wooden arch, on which is painted, "WHEN THE BELL RINGS, LOOK OUT FOR THE LOCOMOTIVE."

Like many of the early American rail lines, the first steam locomotive used on the Camden and Amboy was imported from Great Britain, the country to which Americans looked not only for technological developments in steam but also for the British nation's superior ability to manufacture the massive amount of iron track needed to construct the railroads. Robert Livingston's T-rails were made in Wales and brought over on sailing vessels. However, the Stevenses soon improved on the British locomotives and began building their own at their machine shops in Hoboken, staffed with technicians "fresh out from England." They bought coalfields in Schuylkill County, Pennsylvania, to obtain fuel for the trains at the lowest prices. Through-service from New York to Philadelphia took just nine hours, three hours shorter than was possible on the old Union Line. By 1840, the company owned seventeen locomotives, 136 passenger and freight cars, and eight steamboats. The Stevenses' holdings in stock, companies, real estate, and other assets and investments made them one of the wealthiest families in the nation.

All of the men present in the room occupied positions in society every bit as lustrous as those of John Cox Stevens and his brother, Edwin, who was there as well. They hailed from the ranks of the old rich whose families had settled the country when it was under Dutch or British rule, and had gone on to expand the fortunes they inherited. They looked down on those whom they called the new rich, men who had built their wealth through their own sweat and talent. Men like Cornelius Vanderbilt, a Dutchman to be sure, though not of the old Knickerbocker group, were considered socially unacceptable. When Vanderbilt applied to become a member of the New York Yacht Club, he was snubbed based on the fact that he was something of a scoundrel, a womanizer, and a drunk—which was true. (The club finally did admit Vanderbilt later in the 1850s.)

Seated on John Cox's right was Hamilton Wilkes, a charter member and vice-commodore of the club, who had driven into the city for the meeting from his home at Hyde Park. The son of a wealthy banker, Wilkes was a large, colorful gentleman known about town as an excellent shot with a pistol and for showing off his skills as a horseman. He demonstrated his abilities with his team of four black horses harnessed in white leather by placing an egg in the middle of Hyde Park's main road and driving around it in figure eights at top speed, the horses plunging and kicking up dust as the four-in-hand carriage slid on the tight turns. He was fascinated with yachts from a technical standpoint, how they were built, how a new design might offer more speed. And he liked to go fast, whether he was driving horses or steering a yacht.

Edwin Stevens occupied the seat to John Cox's left. Edwin was regarded as the "flywheel" of the family, a whiz kid with a sense of business administration none of his brothers matched. As treasurer and manager of the Camden and Amboy Railroad, Edwin had exceeded the financial expectations of everyone involved in the venture. It all started with the sale of one million dollars of stock in one day needed to help finance the building of the railroad, and the success continued in the form of annual returns to stockholders ranging from six to thirty percent. The Camden and Amboy never missed paying a dividend even when the United States economy slumped into widespread depression in 1837 and many railroad and canal companies went bankrupt.

Edwin held several patents for inventions that helped build the nation. He and Robert Livingston invented a special plow used in construction, and they designed a closed fire-room system of forced draft for steam applications. Edwin also invented the rather prosaic two-horse dump wagon used for hauling garbage in New York City. It was a wagon with removable sides, facilitating the quick discharge of refuse at city dumps.

Edwin loved all kinds of vessels, from the steamboats he worked on with Robert Livingston to John Cox's yacht *Maria*. He and Robert Livingston were currently engrossed in the development of a new type of warship, an ironclad, for the United States Navy. Called *Stevens Battery*, the ironclad was designed to withstand shells while pounding the wooden ships of an enemy navy to pieces. The two brothers were having difficulties, however, because the development of increasingly efficient naval shells and guns forced them to keep changing the design. Some of Edwin's ideas were ahead of his time, much the same as many of his father's.

Seated side by side were George L. Schuyler and his father-in-law, Colonel James Alexander Hamilton, with whom he was very close. Schuyler was heir to a great fortune and a member of one of the oldest families in New York. His family line traced back six generations to Philip Pieterse of Amsterdam, who married Margarita Van Slichtenhorst in Albany in 1650 and established the Schuylers in the New World. From the start the family was well-to-do and continued so as control of New York passed from Dutch, to British, and finally to American hands.

Schuyler's grandfather, Philip, served in the Continental Army as a general. After the war, he was a member of the New York State Senate. Philip took an active role in furthering the career of his son-in-law, Alexander Hamilton, cementing a long alliance between the Schuyler and Hamilton families. Relatives of both families frequently intermarried, as was the custom of the wealthy. The Schuyler fortune came from real estate and stock in the Bank of the United States, which Alexander Hamilton helped found as secretary of the treasury. The Schuyler money also stemmed from stocks in the Bank of Albany and from holdings in the Northern and Western Inland Lock Navigation companies, among other interests.

As a result of his grandfather's role in the founding of the United States, George L. Schuyler, a studious, bespectacled man of thirty-nine, spent much time researching and recording the history of the Revolutionary War. He ran a shipping company and harbored a deep love of yachting.

A veteran of the War of 1812, Colonel James Alexander Hamilton was a strongly nationalistic man with a deep-seated mistrust of Great Britain as a world naval power. His feelings were understandable. Both he and his father, Alexander Hamilton, fought against the British, and they both viewed the "American experiment" as the very essence of an enlightened system of government, which further polished their patriotic sentiments. Yet, while they looked down on the British way of life, seeing the nobility as oppressors of the "submissive people," they also entertained considerable lack of confidence in the ability of the working classes in America to decide matters of national importance for themselves. Alexander Hamilton referred to the American people as "the great beast." James Alexander Hamilton referred to them as the "lower order."

James Alexander Hamilton earned his living as an attorney, and he was a tough, canny businessman. He briefly held the posts of secretary of state of the United States and United States district attorney for the Southern District of New York. A vehement advocate of slavery up until the American Civil War, Hamilton was known as a smooth talker full of charm and wit, which he combined with his keen mind for business and politics. This won him favor with Presidents Andrew Jackson and Martin Van Buren, and many other important and powerful men.

Hamilton frequently conveyed his numerous opinions regarding domestic and foreign United States policies to influential people at every turn. He felt it was his patriotic duty to inform those whom he felt were misinformed or ignorant of the full implications of the issues of the day. He got this trait from his cantankerous father.

The fifth visitor in John Cox's drawing room was the only gentleman there who did not profess an open love of yachting. His name was John K. Beekman Finlay. Well known in the highest circles of New York society, Finlay was independently wealthy, a man of leisure who dabbled in whatever struck his fancy at any given time, then moved on to other interests. Finlay responded to John Cox's invitation to join the five members of the New York Yacht

Club on this evening, because he considered their proposition an opportunity to put some of his money behind a patriotic cause.

On the table was the letter from the English merchant suggesting the Americans send a pilot boat to England the following summer, with the view toward racing against the best yachts in all of Britain to test the merits of the New World in opposition to those of the Old. The men talked about the idea, saw its potential, and then went one step further. Why not, the group decided, build the fastest yacht in the nation, design her expressly for racing, and send her over with a top-notch crew?

"Of course," John Cox said, "we won't be there to show her. We'll be over there to race!"

The men nodded in agreement.

"And we can't lose," Hamilton said. "It would be a national disgrace."

More nods of agreement.

"There will be much expense involved in the construction of such a yacht, and much risk to us if she proves herself a poor sailer," Schuyler said.

The men talked about the best way to proceed. Any of them could have spent lavishly on building a yacht capable of sailing across the Atlantic Ocean that might still stand a chance of besting the cream of the British racing fleet. Such a boat, though, had never been seen. *Maria* was the fastest racing boat in the United States, but because of her tall rig and shallow draft she could not brave the seas of the North Atlantic. The objective was patriotic and one that might bring glory, or dishonor, to the men behind the venture. None of them wanted to go it alone, nor were any of them interested in tangling with the British unless there was good evidence their boat stood a better than even chance of winning.

The hour grew late as the men discussed the matter. Finally, they decided to put up $30,000 to build the yacht, an unprecedented sum equal to $540,000 today. But there was a catch. The man who built her had to shoulder some of the risk. His yacht had to prove in trials of speed against any vessel the men fielded as her rival that she was indeed the fastest boat in the United States, faster than even *Maria*.

If the builder failed to provide a winner, he would not be paid.

"Who would take such a wager?" Edwin asked, laughing at the complete lack of business sense it would take for a man to agree to a deal like that. "I don't know a man on the East River that courageous, or potentially stupid."

"There is George Steers," John Cox said. "If any man can build a yacht to best all others, it is he. He's working with William Brown at his yard. Brown's wealthy enough to take the loss, if Steers's yacht turns out to be a bad sailer."

The men turned to George L. Schuyler, who was young, almost a contemporary of George Steers, and a man who knew the law and how to get the most from a contract. Schuyler agreed to explore the idea with William Brown and George Steers. As they said their good-byes that night, the men realized they had formed a group to back the world's first international yacht race, a novel and exciting concept in itself. Their plan might come to nothing. But they were determined to follow it through to the next phase, and the next. First they needed the right yacht, then a seasoned sailor to skipper her. Having hatched their plan, it now depended on a racing team to ensure success—men like the shipyard owner William H. Brown, George Steers, the designer, and the as yet undetermined man skillful enough to take the yacht safely across the Atlantic Ocean and sail her to victory.

CHAPTER SEVEN

DEMANDING TERMS

A cold wind gusted off the East River, lifting flakes of dirty snow into the air to collect in layers against the windward side of the pilings along the waterfront. Chunks of ice gathered in the still water out of the swift current of the river beneath the docks and surrounded the vessels at rest in their berths. The weak light of the sun shone through breaks of the clouds that seemed low enough to almost sit atop the squat brick buildings fronting the shore, and faded when the clouds came together again, lengthening the shadows of the late afternoon. All was quiet, save for the sounds of nature—the whistle of the wind and the occasional mournful cry of a gull on the wing. The clatter of horse-drawn drays on the cobblestones, the shouts of the stevedores and longshoremen working on the piers, and the incessant hammer bangs and sawing in the shipyards yielded to a silent desertion when Sunday came round and the city slipped into a day of rest after the exertions of the work week.

In the shipyard of William H. Brown, a lone figure stood in front of a schooner on the stocks. The skeletal protrusions of her frames—strong, durable ribs fashioned from hackmatack, cedar, chestnut, locust, and white oak—rose like bones above the planks of the hull. He lingered, his hands jammed deep in his pockets, his breath billowing in front of him until the wind dissipated the vapor.

He was just over six feet tall and built large, giving him a commanding stature. However, there was a gentle quality to him that the ladies found pleasing. He had piercing eyes, and a close-cut swath of a beard covered his lower jaw, leaving the rest of his face set off in the brown oval of his sideburns and the dark shag of his hair. The man turned around at the sound of boots squeaking in the snow. A smile crossed his lips and his eyes brightened. For a moment, the worry and fatigue washed away, and in its place arose an almost cheerful look.

"Good to see you, Captain," the man said.

"And you," Captain Brown replied, as he shook George Steers's hand. "There is no rest for the weary, eh, George?"

George Steers nodded. He turned back to look at the schooner and sighed. "We may not have her finished by April," he said. "I'd have the men here on a Sunday, but that's unthinkable, you know."

Brown nodded. "Every man needs a rest, including you."

The men walked around the schooner and stooped to examine the workmanship for imperfections. They ran their fingers along the three-inch-thick white oak planks of the hull where the treenails had been driven and faired to ensure the outer surface was as smooth as a beach stone. They sighted fore and aft, surveying the schooner's underbody from her knifelike bow to the arc of her midpoint, aft to the well-balanced stern. The yacht stretched eighty feet along the keel with the deepest draft aft at eleven feet. Amidships her beam extended to twenty-three feet, making her quite narrow for her overall length on deck. Accounting for the overhangs at the stern and bow, when completed she would measure ninety-five feet on deck and displace one hundred seventy tons. (Other sources indicate she was 101 feet from stem to stern.)

For George Steers her designer, she was a work of art, a physical manifestation of the many hours he spent carving the wooden scale model used to lay off the lines of the vessel following the consummation of his and his partner's agreement with George Schuyler in November. He had sat up late at night, his nephew holding a sperm whale oil lamp for him, so that he suffered as little eye strain as possible while working. When he finished the first model he found it imperfect and threw it away. He went through the carving process again and again to refine his thinking. The vision he had of the yacht's underbody remained elusive and difficult to transform from thought to reality. During those long nights of work after finishing his routine assignments at the shipyard, it lived only in his mind and demanded much trial and error before it translated into tangible form.

"She's shaping up nicely," Brown said. He was greatly interested in the schooner. She was based on *Mary Taylor*'s lines, but Steers went well beyond her with this new yacht. He respected Steers for many reasons, not the least of which was his genius as a designer and his courage to go against conventional wisdom. He admired Steers for his willingness to bet on his own abilities and come out a winner. That he may have fallen victim to his ambition and a desire for profit might prove true in the end, if he missed his deadline for completion and the men that inspired Steers to create his latest masterpiece voided the agreement between them. Yet, despite the danger of hubris, Brown liked the young man's gumption. It appealed to Brown's Yankee pride and sense of self-reliance.

"You think so? I wonder," George said quietly. "I wonder how fast she really will be."

Brown laughed and shook his head. "Just look at her, George! I don't think you have much to worry about."

Brown's words provided little comfort for his friend. As George gazed at the yacht, he thought about the delays due to the unusually harsh winter weather and the usual troubles associated with building a vessel. He thought about the many modifications he had insisted on making from the start, which put him even further behind schedule. Schuyler and the others demanded the impossible, and he was foolish enough to think he was the man to give it to them. It had all seemed so exciting in November, the chance and challenge to build the fastest yacht in the nation, in the world, in fact, and the prospect that if he accomplished it, the profit from the venture would surely mark a leap forward for his career.

Boatbuilding was very much a part of Steers's life. It was not just work, but rather it provided him with a sense of who he was, his own personal identity as well as a place of recognition in the larger world. In this Steers was no different from his late father, a man whose influence continued to drive him forward to seek new innovations in a trade that had long been in the family and had saved them all from poverty. The Steers family originally hailed from Dartmouth, England, where his grandfather owned considerable property until bad times reduced his fortune in the late 1700s. Instead of enjoying the lifestyle of a member of Britain's moneyed class, his father, Henry, went to work as an apprentice at the shipyard of Newman of New Quay. Henry proved a talented builder. He went on to find work at the Royal Dockyard in Plymouth, and later, after emigrating to the United States with his wife and four children in 1819, at the Washington Navy Yard. Henry's fifth child, George, was born on August 19 that same year.

Henry Steers remained in the United States and pursued his version of the American dream. He also made his own modest contributions to improving the nation. While not as grand as the Stevens family's Camden & Amboy Railroad and other business pursuits, Henry Steers came up with innovations in the design of marine railways used for hauling ships from the water more efficiently. He conceived, designed, and installed a system of semaphore towers for the approaches of New York Harbor to speed word of incoming ships to owners and agents in the city. With the proceeds earned from salvaging treasure from a wreck off the Mexican coast, he opened a shipyard on the East River on Tenth Street, just two blocks away from the booming yard of William H. Brown, who later became his good friend and a friend of his son George as well.

Henry Steers and his wife had thirteen children, and of them all it was George who showed promise in carrying on the family business. Steers built his first boat in his early teens. It was not an auspicious start to his career, however. The boat leaked, sailed poorly, and in the view of his older brothers, James R. and Henry T., it was unsafe. Worried that their little brother might drown in the very likely event the boat sank, they broke it apart. Steers considered his brothers' actions as a challenge. He accelerated his studies of boat design and construction at his father's yard. He never finished grade school. He focused solely on boats. He went on to build *Martin Van Buren,* which won a race sponsored by John Cox Stevens and earned him the attention of the powerful, wealthy yachting enthusiast. A couple of years later, Steers designed and built a thirty-foot rowing shell, which he named after John Cox Stevens. As his father's shipyard prospered, Steers continued building boats and experimenting with improvements in their hull designs. At the death of his father in 1841, the yard was sold. Steers went to work for the shipyard of Smith & Dimond, along with his brother James, who also shared an interest in the shipbuilding trade, though not as a designer.

In 1845, George Steers, together with a partner, opened the Hathorne & Steers shipyard on the Brooklyn side of the East River in Williamsburg. Over the next four years he built schooners for the Great Lakes trade, pilot boats, and yachts for the city's elite. His reputation as a designer began to shine, most particularly with the launch of *Mary Taylor.* Eighteen forty-nine was a good year for Steers. He had found a new friend in Captain Brown, and Brown's outstanding performance with his new pilot boat added to the increasing luster of the Steers name along the waterfront. It was also a strange year, because at the seeming cusp of prosperity with his own shipyard, his partnership with Hathorne ended (the record does not indicate why), and he found himself looking for work.

His father's friend, William H. Brown, offered him a position. He was not Brown's employee in the usual sense. Steers was more a working partner who offered his well-known talents as a designer to the already successful operation. With Steers associated with the yard, its owner knew it was good for business, and he was right. When Edward Knight Collins secured subsidies from the United States Congress to establish a new line of steamships to compete with those of Samuel Cunard, Collins turned to George Steers to design the hulls, and to William H. Brown's yard to build two of the four vessels of the Collins Line, *Atlantic* and *Arctic.* The contract was worth nearly $1.5 million, the equivalent of over $25 million today. It made William H. Brown one of the richest men in New York City.

The workload was intense throughout 1849 and 1850, as the two enormous sidewheel steamers took shape on the stocks and were launched before crowds of more than 20,000 spectators. In addition, Steers built another pilot boat based on *Mary Taylor*'s lines, named after Moses H. Grinnell, head of the New York office of Liverpool's Swallowtail Line.

Steers was riding high in November 1850. The Collins steamships were setting speed records, in part the result of his design work on their hulls. *Mary Taylor* continued to outsail the rest of the pilot boat fleet and his design was copied by no less a personage than John Cox Stevens for modifications to his yacht *Maria*. Anything seemed possible the previous fall. But as George shared a few quiet moments with Captain Brown, both men peering at the yacht wondering about her seakeeping and racing characteristics, there was a degree of panic in the young designer. His agreement with Schuyler amounted to the biggest gamble, both financial and from the standpoint of reputation, that Steers ever imagined he might take.

On November 15, Schuyler put their agreement in the form of a letter from William H. Brown, which expressed the proposal as if it came from Brown, not the men in what modern sailors call a syndicate. Schuyler also wrote a letter accepting the proposal. Why he chose to do this we cannot be sure, but the letters are both plainly in his own hand. Below is the letter Schuyler addressed to himself and which he wrote pretending he was William H. Brown:

New York, November 15, 1850

George L. Schuyler, Esq.

Dear Sir,

I propose to build for you [George Schuyler] a yacht of not less than 140 tons custom house measurement on the following terms—

The yacht to be built in the best manner, coppered, rigged, equipped with joiner's work, cabin and kitchen furniture, table furniture, water closets, etc., etc., ready for sea—you are to designate the plan of the interior of the vessel and select the furniture.

The model, plan and rig of the vessel to be entirely at my discretion, it being understood however that she is to be a strong seagoing vessel, and rigged for ocean sailing.

For the vessel complete and ready for sea you are to pay me $30,000 upon the following conditions—

When the vessel is ready, she is to be placed at the disposal of Hamilton Wilkes Esq. as umpire, who after making such trials as are satisfactory to him for the space of twenty days, shall decide whether or not she is faster than any vessel in the United States brought to compete with her.

The expenses of these trials to be borne by you.

If it is decided by the umpire that she is not faster than every vessel brought against her, it shall not be binding upon you to accept her and pay for her at all.

In addition to this, if the umpire decides that she is faster than any vessel in the United States, you are to have the right, instead of accepting her at that time, to send her to England, match her against anything of her size built there, and if beaten still to reject her altogether.

The expense of the voyage out and home to be borne by you.

The test of speed in England to be decided by any mode acceptable to you and consented to by you in writing.

Respectfully yours,
W. H. Brown

Below is Schuyler's response to his own proposal:

W. H. Brown, Esq
Dear Sir,
Your proposal to build for me a yacht of not less than 140 tons custom house measurement for $30,000, payable on certain conditions detailed in your letter of the 15ths inst., has been submitted by me to some of my friends interested in the subject.

The price is high, but in consideration of the liberal and

sportsmanlike character of the whole offer, test of speed, etc., we have concluded that such a proposal must not be declined.

I therefore accept the proposal, and you will please go ahead without loss of time. I only stipulate as a condition on my part that the yacht must be ready for trial on the first day of April next.

Very truly yours,

George L. Schuyler

New York, Nov. 15, 1850

Based on the terms outlined in Schuyler's letters, George Steers and William H. Brown shouldered the bulk of the risk in the venture. The agreement with the syndicate showed little promise of turning out well. Indeed, it was a Faustian pact. Yet, both men felt compelled to take the wager based on Steers's talents. For William H. Brown the financial loss did not pose a ruinous burden in the event that Steers failed. For George Steers, however, who was to put up as much as $10,000 of his own money during the building and testing of the yacht, failure meant a crushing economic blow from which he might well have difficulty in recovering. Doubts ran through his mind constantly as the work on the yacht dragged on and the months passed from December into early February. On that quiet Sunday in the shipyard, the enterprise had lost something of its romance and adventure.

Steers turned to face Captain Brown, his words of encouragement still ringing in his ears. Threads of ice ran through the big man's beard. His blue eyes sparkled and danced, a bit mischievous and boyish.

"George, you don't have much to worry about, even if you think you do." Dick Brown clapped Steers on the back. "A man willing to pay thirty thousand dollars for a yacht . . . a lovely thought!"

George smiled. "It does tend to warm the heart on a day like this, as long as Schuyler and the rest end up paying and not me."

A gust of wind whipped across the yard, sending curtains of snow over the yacht, veiling her for a moment in a ghostlike whirl. The sun emerged from a break in the clouds to the west, low over the tops of the buildings. Shadows reached across the yard and made the cold more penetrating. Brown rubbed his hands together, flexed his fingers to keep them from freezing. Out at sea, under the charge of his partner, *Mary Taylor* sailed on the eastern chance, the pilots and everyone but the apprentices on watch huddled below around the stove. Although the shipping traffic from Europe decreased in winter, it never stopped completely. Sometimes, though, especially on days like this one, Brown wished it might halt long enough to give the men an opportunity to rest. There were times no man should be at sea, times when simple human comfort and security meant more than all the money in New York.

"We shall see what happens, George. It's too late to have doubts now."

After a pause, the designer replied, "She *is* a fine boat."

Despite the difficulties and worry associated with the yacht, she represented a culmination of his work as a naval architect. Both beautiful and revolutionary even in her incomplete form, the vessel promised greatness—for him, and the nation, if he only succeeded in meeting the terms of his agreement with the syndicate and could show all the world just how fast this unique schooner sailed. It was more than a simple leap of faith on the part of the designer. Based on his many years of experience, despite his young age and the self-doubt that came with it, Steers sensed the yacht's marvelous potential.

Dick Brown visited the shipyard of William H. Brown throughout the winter of 1851 to see how the work progressed and to give his friend encouragement as he struggled to complete the yacht on time. It appeared that the weather conspired with the syndicate to further stack the odds against Steers. Strong northeasterly storms blew in from the Atlantic and blanketed New York with a thick, heavy fall of snow. The yacht lay half-buried beneath the drifts, and the yard workers had to dig her out before they proceeded with the job of building her between the frequent spells of inclement weather.

Oddly, Steers did not have a shed built to keep her out of the elements, nor does it appear that shed-building in commercial shipyards was common elsewhere on the waterfront. Bad weather was just something else to work around. It did not merit the cost and bother of building temporary shelters for half-finished vessels.

As the delays continued, Steers began to look increasingly haggard and worn out from the stress. Brown grew uneasy for him, sensing his mounting desperation. By the spring thaw, it was clear that Steers had lost his race against time and the relentless elements. The yacht remained unfinished and the April 1 deadline passed. Steers sent word to George L. Schuyler asking for more time and waited anxiously for a response.

Among the mail delivered to the shipyard of William H. Brown on April 2 was a letter from George L. Schuyler. Steers paced in William Brown's office while his partner read the letter. He shook his head and passed it to Steers.

W. H. Brown

Dear Sir,

I have this morning laid before the gentlemen associated with me your proposal to renew the contract between us for building a yacht, the time for delivery to be fixed on the 1st of May next.

The delay has been one of more consequence to the convenience of some of these gentlemen than I had supposed. One of them is obliged to sail for Europe on the first of May, and consequently will lose all the trials, and another who is ready to sail at that time is obliged to change all his plans.

I propose to continue the contract between us, which expired April 1st, to May 1st, 1851, as the time for the delivery of the vessel, all other conditions to remain as before, providing you consent to the following alterations in your letter of Nov. 15th, 1850:

On the first page, after the words, "The expense of these trials to be borne by you," you [Brown] agree to insert the words, "The vessel to be at my risk as regards loss, or damage from any source." The last clause of your letter to read as follows: "In addition to this, if the umpire decides that she is faster than any vessel in the United States, you are to have the right, instead of accepting her at that time, to send her to England, match her against anything built there, which in your judgment gives her a fair chance in a trial of speed, and, if beaten, reject her altogether; the expense of the voyage out and home to be borne by you [Schulyer], and the vessel to be at your risk. The test of speed in England above referred to shall be decided by the result of any one or more trials acceptable to you, and to which you, or some person authorized by you, shall have consented in writing."

Please answer immediately whether you accept these changes, and if you do, go ahead without loss of time.

Yours truly,

George L. Schuyler

New York, April 2nd, 1851

George L. Schuyler's additional terms protected the syndicate from possible lawsuits that William H. Brown and George Steers might pursue to recover money to pay for any damage to the yacht that resulted during the trials or during the voyage across the Atlantic Ocean. It was a wise move. A court of law may well have ruled in favor of the builder if the yacht sustained damage while engaged in the risky business of racing against the top competitors in two nations, as well as the always dangerous endeavor of crossing a vast ocean just to satisfy the obligations insisted upon by the prospective buyers. In essence, the syndicate split the risk. William H. Brown and George Steers agreed to cover expenses for any damage or loss during the trials, and the syndicate agreed to cover expenses for any damage or loss on the transatlantic voyage and during the races in Great Britain, while still reserving the right to reject the yacht if she failed to win.

The change regarding the trials in Great Britain was disturbing. Schuyler's letter written for William H. Brown on November 15, 1850, stated that the yacht was to race against competitors of a similar size. The amendments in his most recent letter voided that clause and opened up the possibility that the yacht might have to race against a vessel of a far greater size, stacking the deck against her. The speed of a vessel is linked to its length at the waterline. The longer the waterline, the faster a boat can sail. Based on the new agreement, the British could field any yacht in the country to sail against the American boat. This was good for the syndicate because it widened the potential pool of English yachts that might compete against Steers's boat. It was bad for Steers, however, because it meant the boat he had designed must perform perfectly even against rivals with a higher theoretical ability to sail faster due to their longer waterlines.

Although he was faced with the seemingly impossible odds of the venture coming out in his favor, Steers had no choice but to continue his work on the yacht and hope for the best. The dimensions of the gamble he took had grown. Much of his personal wealth was tied up in the boat. She simply had to prove herself the fastest schooner ever built. There was no room for failure. Yet, the reality of his situation was bleak and Steers knew it. His desire for money and fame and the chance to prove that he was the most talented designer in the nation got the best of him. Steers was many things. A savvy businessman he was not. This was to become abundantly clear during the speed trials in May.

CHAPTER EIGHT

TILTED ODDS

Along the shores of southern Barnegat Bay behind the barrier islands, dozens of men in small rowing skiffs gathered the day's harvest of oysters. The mid-May morning dawned calm and humid, the
air heavy to the lungs and fragrant with the scent of pine. A dull
haze painted the sky almost white. But it did not diminish the heat
of the rising sun that brought out a sweat as the men leaned over
the sides of the boats and plunged their rakes deep into the sand beneath the shallow water. They heaved into the culling boards clumps
of ooze seeded with broken shells, crabs, and kelp. There were some
oysters as well, all destined for the plates of diners in New York
restaurants from the posh Delmonico's to the lowliest of waterfront
taverns.

Farther up the coast just south of Sandy Hook the fishing fleets
of Nauvoo and Galilee put out from the beach to Shrewsbury Rocks
in pursuit of the ground fish attracted to the shoals. When the
striped bass, blues, and giant tuna ran, the fishermen turned their
attention to them and returned to shore with their boats riding low
in the water. The day's work did not end until the fishermen stacked
the fish in cone-shaped icehouses dug deep in the sand, stocked
with ice cut the last winter from the Navesink and Shrewsbury
Rivers. The next morning, while they were out fishing again, the

previous day's catch was shipped to New York via steamboat. It was a never-ending cycle, and it created a link of interdependence between the city dwellers and the country folk.

As the sun reached its zenith on May 13, the oystermen in the bays and the fishermen at sea glanced nervously at the darkening sky to the west. Clouds rose high over the mainland in vast columns of white and gray. As the hours passed, the tops flattened and trailed off toward the north, swirling and climbing ever higher. The wind barely rippled the gray-green surface of the water. It came in fits and puffs laden with moisture. Beyond Sandy Hook, far out in the approaches to New York Harbor, the captains of the sailing packets kept a weather eye on the horizon, ready to shorten sail at a moment's notice.

A mile south of the Verrazano Narrows three yachts under full sail came abeam of the lower Quarantine off Staten Island, a popular overnight anchorage for yachtsmen, though they never went ashore. From the buildings on Dix and Hoffman Islands patients suffering from cholera and yellow fever, but who were healthy enough to sit up, looked out on the beauty of the bay and the grand sight of the yachts sailing past. The yachts represented more than a scene pleasing to the eye; they symbolized the promise of America. The passengers of immigrant ships at temporary anchor at the station nearby watched the yachts and wondered at a land where such craft existed solely for the pleasure of their owners. They waited anxiously for the Quarantine officers to board and clear the vessels, to proceed up the harbor to the receiving station at Castle Garden near the Battery in lower Manhattan.

The pilot in command of one of the yachts, the seventy-four-foot *Cornelia*, scanned the thunderheads building over the Highlands of Navesink and Raritan Bay. He reconsidered sailing on to the anchorage on the west side of Sandy Hook, where the three yachts were to meet in readiness for the races the next morning. Squalls were common in late spring and sometimes packed hurricane force winds. He spoke a few words to the yacht's owner, who agreed to bring her to at the Quarantine. *Cornelia* came about and headed for the anchorage in the relative shelter of Staten Island. The other two yachts, the

sloop *Maria* and the schooner George Steers had built for the syndicate, which they named *America,* continued sailing toward Sandy
Hook.

Aboard *America* was George L. Schuyler, whom the syndicate
designated as umpire for the trials in place of Hamilton Wilkes,
who was too ill to carry out the duty. George Steers was also
aboard, and anxious about the prospects the next few days might
hold for his future and financial well-being. As he sat aft with the
others in the boat's circular cockpit, which had a circumference of
thirty feet, the foul weather visible off the starboard bow added to
his worries.

The schooner was launched on May 3 and rushed to completion,
much too fast for Steers's liking. But he had no other option. As a
consequence of the haste, the vessel's rigging had not yet stretched
and settled into shipshape fashion fit for racing. The shrouds that
supported the sides of the two masts kept slacking off and had to be
tightened repeatedly. The wooden hull had not yet swollen tight,
making her leaky in the bilge. The crew, such as his dwindling resources could afford, worked with a will, but though the men were a
good-hearted lot, they were not the best. The well-paid and well-
trained regular crew aboard *Maria,* under John Cox's watchful eye, far
outclassed the men aboard *America.* Likewise, the crew aboard *Cornelia,* which Steers had also designed, were superior sailors. Nevertheless, given the circumstances, Steers was determined to do his
best to show the real potential for speed he knew existed in his
schooner. He thought about Captain Brown, wishing he was available
for this important moment. But again, as fate would have it against
him, his friend was at sea aboard *Mary Taylor.*

In the quiet moments in that first week of May, after the men in
the shipyard had gone home for the day, Steers stood on the docks
and stared at his creation with a mixture of pride and doubt. *America*
was indeed a splendid sight, despite the fact that her topsides were
painted a leaden gray, the primary coat only. It was not her paint job,
but her lines and spars that caught the eyes of the many people who
came to look at her as construction progressed and finally came to

SAIL & SPAR PLAN OF *AMERICA*

1 Jibboom   A *Flying Jib*
2 Bowsprit   B *Jib*
3 Foremast   C *Foresail*
4 Fore gaff   D *Main Gaff Topsail*
5 Mainmast   E *Mainsail*
6 Main Topmast
7 Main Gaff
8 Main Boom

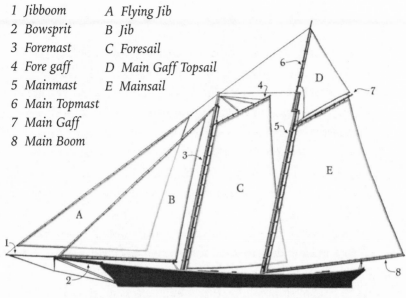

The above illustration shows America *as she was rigged during her famous race around the Isle of Wight on August 22, 1851. She carried a flying jib set on a boom fixed to the bowsprit. Her original sail plan did not include a flying jib, nor did it include a boom for the jib. These modifications were made prior to the race.*

an end. Among some of the visitors with a keen interest in the yacht was the British ambassador to the United States, Sir Henry Bulwer, who had come to the shipyard of William H. Brown in early February. He had heard members of the New York Yacht Club intended to sail the schooner to Great Britain the following summer. While back in England on business he mentioned this to the commodore of the Royal Yacht Squadron, which sailed out of West Cowes on the Isle of Wight and in so doing, along with the British merchant who had inspired the syndicate members to forge the deal with Steers, further propelled the chain of events toward their ultimate outcome.

Later in February, after speaking with Sir Bulwer, the commodore of the Royal Yacht Squadron, the Earl of Wilton, wrote the following letter to John Cox Stevens:

7 Grosvenor Square, London
22nd February, 1851
Sir:

Understanding from Sir H. Bulwer that a few members of the New York Yacht Club are building a schooner which it is their intention to bring over to England this summer, I have taken the liberty of writing to you, in your capacity of Commodore, to request you to convey to them and to any friends that may accompany them on board the yacht, an invitation on the part of myself and the members of the Royal Yacht Squadron to become visitors of the Club-House at Cowes during their stay in England.

For myself, I may be permitted to say that I shall have great pleasure in extending to your countrymen any civility that lies in my power, and shall be very glad to avail myself at any improvements in shipbuilding that the industry and skill of your nation have enabled you to elaborate. I remain, Sir,

Your servant,
Wilton,
Commodore, R.Y.S.

Lord Wilton waited for a reply from John Cox, but did not receive one until early April, about one month before the grand opening of the Great Exhibition. All of London was then in a frenzy of excitement. The displays were set up, landscaping done, concession stands erected, and already people from dozens of countries were disembarking from ships in Liverpool in preparation for the first international world's fair. While going about his business, Lord Wilton, and many others, noted an article that appeared on the front page of *The Illustrated London News* on March 15.

The headline read: "New American Yacht." Accompanying the brief story was a woodcut showing the schooner under construction. In the text, the writer reported that the boat was "to compete with . . . English yachts next summer at Cowes," and went on to say he believed the Americans would lose in such a competition. The story must have struck Lord Wilton as somewhat odd. He never mentioned a race to John Cox Stevens, only that he was interested in learning about American innovations in shipbuilding that might be applied to yachts. At the time, the American clipper ships were setting speed records, as American sailing packets had done repeatedly since the Black Ball Line went into service more than three decades earlier. It was natural he should be curious to see what the Yanks were up to. Now, it seemed, the wide readership of *The Illustrated London News* was being primed for a race between British and American yachts. Lord Wilton received the following letter from John Cox Stevens, which mentioned nothing about a race, either, though it was clear between the lines that the man wanted one.

New York, March 26, 1851

My Lord:

I regret that an accident prevented the reception of your letter until after the packet of the 12th sailed. I take the earliest opportunity offered to convey to the gentlemen of the Royal Yacht Squadron, and to yourself, the expression of our warmest thanks for your invitation to visit the Club House at Cowes. Some four or five friends and myself have a yacht on the stocks which we hope to launch in the course of two or three weeks.

Should she answer the sanguine expectations of her builder, and fulfill the stipulations he has made, we propose to avail ourselves of your friendly bidding and take with good grace the sound thrashing we are likely to get by venturing our longshore craft on your rough waters.

I fear the energy and experience of your persevering yachtsmen will prove an overmatch for the industry and skill of their aspiring competitors. Should the schooner fail to meet the expectations of her builder, not the least of our regrets will be to have lost the opportunity of personally thanking the gentlemen of the Royal Yacht Squadron and yourself for your considerate kindness.

With the hope that we may have the pleasure of recipro-
cating a favor so frankly bestowed, I remain your lordship's
most obedient servant,

John Cox Stevens
Commodore New York Yacht Club

By the time she was launched, the schooner *America* was the talk
of New York. There were great expectations regarding how well she
might perform against the best yachts the New York Yacht Club
brought out to race her. Rigged as a pilot boat for ocean sailing, her
Norwegian pine masts were raked with a dramatic tilt aft. This allowed Steers to place the seventy-nine-and-a-half-foot foremast and
the eighty-one-foot mainmast farther forward for better balance
than if the masts protruded straight up into the air like those of
most vessels. *America*'s mainmast was lengthened to even loftier
heights by her thirty-two-foot main topmast. Her working sails consisted of a gaff-rigged mainsail, a gaff foresail with no boom at the
foot, and a loose-footed jib set on a bowsprit that extended seventeen feet outward from the clipperlike bow and reached another fifteen feet aft. In all, she carried 5,263 square feet of sail, a sizable
spread of canvas for a yacht of her size, though more than 2,500
square feet less than *Maria*.

On deck, *America* was sleek and clear of structures that might
cause resistance to the wind or present weaknesses to breaking seas
in the North Atlantic Ocean. Like most pilot boats, Steers designed
her with a break in the deck forward of the mainmast, a sort of step
down to a deck set at a lower level than the quarterdeck aft. Behind
the bowsprit was a windlass, a winch that worked on a horizontal
axis used for raising and lowering the anchor. *America* was also
equipped with a capstan, a winch that worked on a vertical axis. It
was set just forward of the mainmast and was used to tug the
schooner into and out of her berth at dockside, with heavy lines secured ashore and to the capstan. A circular skylight provided light
and ventilation for the crew's quarters forward, which contained fifteen berths. A beautifully finished skylight eight feet in length was
situated above the aft cabin, where the owners and guests lived

when aboard. The only other major deck structure was a companionway house sloped forward to reduce drag from the wind and resist breaking seas, with its highest point aft at the entrance, where two double doors led from the cockpit down below to the main cabin.

The accommodations below were elegant, with furnishings upholstered in green velvet to set off the white bulkheads and ceilings. The main aft cabin measured twenty-one by eighteen feet and contained six large and comfortable berths, lockers, and china cabinets. Off the main cabin were two staterooms forward and two larger ones aft.

Other features included a washroom, a pantry, two wardrobes, two water closets, and most important, a large kitchen, known to sailors as a galley. The galley consisted of a stove, a sink supplied with fresh water from two cylindrical iron water tanks, and numerous storage lockers for provisions and cooking utensils. There was also a cavernous icebox. Wedged between heavy blocks of ice with sawdust for insulation, fresh meats could remain in a nearly frozen state for several weeks.

Under the cockpit was a simple bathroom with a tub for bathing. Even some of the better homes of the day did not have a room set aside specifically for taking baths. People preferred to set up portable bathtubs in their bedrooms. Bathing was labor-intensive, because the water had to be heated over the stove, brought upstairs, and poured into the tub. When finished, the tub had to be emptied by hand. Only the rich bathed regularly since they were able to pay servants to take care of the work for them, and the operation was therefore less of an ordeal. To have a bathroom on *America* was quite a feature well worthy of note, one that Steers installed at the behest of Schuyler and the other members of the syndicate, who, based on the agreement, were to have the choice of laying out the interior and selecting the furnishings.

Now, after all the work on the yacht was done to get her ready for her trials of speed, the proof of Steers's abilities was about to unfold. The self-doubt Steers felt was made all the worse by the look of the weather. Slowly, the clouds thickened and darkened. The first sign of the imminent approach of the squall came in the foreboding stillness that settled over the water. *America* rolled to the swells, her sails slatting and banging. The temperature suddenly decreased. Steers looked to the west and saw the bay churned into small breaking crests. The wind came in all at once and *America* tilted way over on her side as the gust filled the sails. She kept leaning farther and farther, until the lee rail was buried under solid water. The pilot quickly pointed the bow into the wind as the sailors shouted and ran about on deck. The sails thundered and shook. The masts whipped back and forth from the strain. At any moment, Steers was certain the rigging might part and send the rig crashing down on deck.

"Strike that foresail, boys!" the pilot screamed. "Get her down fast. Here it comes!"

Looking off toward Perth Amboy, Steers clenched his teeth and held his breath. The sky boiled with black and purple clouds. A greenish hue appeared above and beyond them. The light of the sun faded away, until it seemed as if evening had come early.

"Get that sail in!" the pilot shouted, repeating an order the sailors already knew they must carry out as quickly as possible.

With a roar, the line of thunderstorms tore across the bay, just as the men got the foresail down and prepared to lash it tight to the gaff. As the wind pushed the schooner's bow to leeward, the jib and mainsail filled with an explosive bang, and she immediately laid well over on her side. Steers realized that she was top-heavy and in danger of capsizing, because she was not sufficiently weighted down at the keel. Inside *America* were more than forty tons of iron weights, known to sailors as ballast. The ballast was supposed to help keep the schooner upright when the force of the wind against the sails tried to push her over. He had no way of knowing if he had laid in enough ballast until the vessel experienced her first blow. Such shortcomings were for the sea to point out, and this dangerous miscalculation on his part began to become painfully clear. However, he thought it might be best to see how she did in a strong, steady breeze before making a final assessment about the issue. Slowly, *America* found her footing and sped away toward Sandy Hook. Rain lashed and blew, thunder clapped, and lightning forked the sky.

Off to leeward, *Maria* faded in and out of the tempest. She was not built for such a blow, and yet she carried full sail. In the gusts, it seemed she might capsize. As Steers watched, the sloop's enormous jib split horizontally down the middle. The fifty-man crew aboard the yacht acted fast, lowering the sail to the deck before it blew to tatters. The best of them balanced at the tip of the sloop's bowsprit, wrestling with the canvas as they bunched it up against the spar and rigging to make it secure.

"Well done!" Schuyler said to himself, as he, too, watched the struggle aboard *Maria*.

Sailing in company, both yachts fought their way down the bay amid the shoals and ships, and came to anchor off Sandy Hook. Thunderstorms rumbled and blew throughout that Tuesday night. Feeling seasick and needing air, Steers stood at the open doors of the companionway out of the weather and watched the blurred yellow of *Maria*'s anchor light bounce and pitch in the darkness. Off to the south, atop the 200-foot hills of Navesink, the twin lights of the beacon there that marked the final approaches to New York Harbor lit the sky. It was a lonely, desolate sight, seeing the pinpricks of light as the wind moaned through *America*'s rigging and the waves broke against her bow. Steers retired to his berth and listened long to the sounds of the sea before sleep rid him of the thoughts weighing heavily on his mind.

The next morning scarcely a puff of wind from the northwest disturbed the water of the bay. The sky cleared of all but the residual clouds left in the wake of the storm. The air felt much cooler, quite pleasant in fact. The smell of hot coffee wafted up through the companionway to the cockpit, where Steers sat apart from the others, Schuyler and the friends he had brought aboard with him to see the trials. He looked out at the green hills of the Highlands of Navesink and cast his gaze north to take in the long white spit of Sandy Hook. Sandy Hook Lighthouse rose above a low stand of cedar and holly. Farther north, bay steamers, oceangoing liners, and sailing packets cruised close to the North Beacon at the tip of the sand spit, and proceeded up and down the Main Ship Channel leading to the Verrazano Narrows. The harbor's works proved endlessly fascinating to a man who loved all manner of vessels. The sights evoked a sense of pleasure in Steers, and instilled in him a rising hope for the outcome of the day's race.

The men aboard the yachts waited for the wind to build until it reached a velocity sufficient to call a fresh sailing breeze. The northwesterly wind blew off the land out to sea and kicked up short, steep whitecaps on the bay as the afternoon progressed. The day's trial aimed to test *America*'s ability to sail to windward, meaning a point of sail that held the bow as close to the true direction of the wind as possible. When a sailboat sails to windward her own momentum creates a breeze, one that combines with the velocity of the true wind and allows a boat to sail faster and in some cases closer to the true wind direction. Excellent performance to windward was a very important characteristic for a racing boat.

Joined by *Cornelia,* just down from her anchorage at Quarantine, the yachts sailed into a rough position to start the trial. It was not done with any great precision, however, not like a modern race in the age of fiberglass. The trial began at an appointed time without much effort to line the boats up together. *Cornelia* sailed about a half mile ahead of *America* and *Maria,* with the latter two yachts much closer. *America* sailed about two hundred yards ahead and to leeward of *Maria,* as the boats leaned to the wind, the spray flying over the bows, the crews working the sails to best advantage while the vessels headed west. Steers watched with pleasure as *America* gained on *Cornelia* and held her own with John Cox's sloop. But gradually *Maria* gained on *America.*

"She's losing ground, I'm afraid," Schuyler said. He checked his watch and looked astern at the sloop coming on fast.

Steers glanced aloft at the set of the sails and wondered whether he had enough ballast in his schooner. Something deep inside, on an intuitive level, told him the boat was not sailing in harmony with the elements. She felt out of balance, as if she fought the sea instead of falling into its smooth rhythm. She seemed too tender, as sailors say when a vessel leans over too much and too easily in a strong wind. Such leaning is called heel, and *America* heeled enough to bury the lee rail. After sailing about three miles, *Maria* drew alongside of *America.*

Suddenly, *America* surged ahead. Steers was elated, until he looked astern and saw the commotion aboard the rival boat. Crewmen darted about like frightened swallows in flight as the vessel turned broadside to the wind and heeled over at a precarious angle, her centerboard lodged deep in the muck at the bottom of the bay.

"She's hard aground!" the pilot at *America*'s helm said, his voice low and a little sad. That kind of mistake might cost a pilot his reputation among his peers. It certainly did not bode well for his future sailing for the wealthy owners of the city's yachts. He guided *America* on her course through the shoals back to the anchorage at the Quarantine. His colleague did the same once the sloop got free.

Steers was thoroughly disturbed as *America* rode quietly at anchor that night. He realized he had made some errors not so much with regard to the schooner's hull or rig. The basic facets of her design he still believed were superior to any other boat. But he began to think her spars were too slender, not strong enough to bear up under the stresses of a North Atlantic gale. And she heeled too easily. He met with Schuyler, John Cox, and others in the group and made arrangements to put aboard eight additional tons of ballast the next day. The expense for the extra iron, the loading and shipping it on a harbor workboat, and the proper installation of it aboard the yacht came out of his pocket.

On Thursday evening, the yachts again sailed down to Sandy Hook. A light southerly wind blew, forcing the boats to sail to windward in a series of maneuvers called tacking. Tacking requires a boat to turn her bow through the wind to bring it on the opposite side of the vessel. The maneuver is repeated to make forward progress in a zigzag course as close to the true wind direction as possible. With her new load of ballast, *America* sailed much better. Both yachts tacked back and forth together, the crews working the lines with a will. *America* gained on *Maria*, passed her to leeward, and shot ahead of the sloop. Steers smiled broadly. It seemed he had put the yacht right at last.

The wind increased as the sun sank low over the horizon to the west, illuminating the sky in pale shades of red, pink, and orange. To the east, the broad Atlantic faded into blackness. The sound of the water rushing past the hull, the hum of the rigging, the sweet smell of the land carried to him on the wind. For a moment all seemed right with the world as Steers let himself relax. Slowly, however, the pleasure gave way to mystification, and deep disappointment. *Maria* again gained on the schooner, after her crew adjusted the centerboard to a deeper draft. *America*'s pilot tacked. *Maria* followed, her well-trained crew quick with each maneuver, their shouts, the clatter of blocks, and the boom of the sails audible to Steers aboard his own vessel. She passed *America* and came to anchor off Sandy Hook seven minutes ahead.

On Friday, the third day of the trials, Steers's disappointment grew more acute. The yachts met off Sandy Hook bar for a race out to sea with a fair wind from the south. Again *America* gave *Maria* a good showing, sailing in close quarters and seeming to draw ahead for a time. Steers's mind was on his boat, how he might make her faster, when a loud crack and snap startled him. He looked aloft as the pilot shouted orders and headed the boat up into the wind. The seven-foot length of *America*'s fore masthead had badly sprung under the high loads imposed by the wind, making the rig unstable. The shrouds supporting the mast might part at any moment.

"We will have to withdraw," Steers said to Schuyler, who nodded in agreement, his face grim.

Steers turned to the pilot, his voice choked with emotion: "Take her in," he said, and turned back to look at *Maria*. Heeled to the wind making close to fifteen knots, she was a beautiful sight. The spray flying off her bow, her massive mainsail full, it was almost too much for Steers to bear. The pilot barked orders at the crew, preparing them to jibe over and run with the wind astern back toward the approaches of Gedney Channel, which led to the Narrows and the safety of Brown's yard on the East River.

As the pilot began his turn and *America* bore off toward the buoys at the mouth of the channel, the wind caught the crew off guard. It came in from behind the sails and with great force swung the fifty-eight-foot main boom and the twenty-eight-foot main gaff over to the other side of the boat in what sailors call an accidental jibe, very dangerous in a good breeze. The yacht rolled violently, skittered out of control, and turned broadside to the wind. The main gaff parted from the mast with an explosion of snapping lines and thundering canvas, and hung down like a broken limb. It tore and whipped at the sail. The stunned crew remained motionless for a second, staring at the damaged foremast, the wildly shaking sails, and the broken gaff.

"Look lively to that mainsail, boys!" the pilot yelled, stirring them to action as he tried to head the yacht back up into the wind, using the foresail, despite the risk to the foremast, and the jib to power her through the water. When he brought her bow to face the wind the men quickly struck the sail, though still with some difficulty. *America* limped home under reduced canvas, damaged and defeated, her builder in despair. Steers tried to hide his emotions from Schuyler, whose alarm the previous few moments had turned to a look of displeasure, as if he suddenly had caught the odor of rotten fish.

The press took up the story and published conflicting accounts regarding the performance of *America* during the trials. Some newspapers claimed *America* soundly beat *Maria,* and others claimed the opposite. Both George L. Schuyler and John Cox Stevens went on record as saying the schooner was a close match for *Maria,* but that the sloop was faster. The old salts along the waterfront read the stories about the trials with interest and amusement. It was no surprise to them that *Maria* outperformed *America* on the racecourse. A sloop or cutter, with its large mainsail set on a single mast, sailed better to windward and off the wind than a boat spreading the same amount of sail on two masts. A sloop and a schooner were both distinct classes of vessels, and to expect a schooner to beat a sloop of similar size was considered unrealistic. But then, of course, the whole scheme of building the yacht on speculation struck many of the boatmen as foolish, and a bit vain of George Steers. There was also the very real difference in the sailing capabilities of a centerboard sloop like *Maria* versus a full-keel, heavy displacement schooner built to ride out North Atlantic gales. But these issues never came up.

New trials were promised, as per the agreement stating Steers

had twenty days in which to prove his schooner was the fastest boat
in the United States. But the trials were not held. Instead, knowing
full well that they could not send *Maria* to England to race, that she
would never stand up to a midocean storm, the syndicate seized the
advantage over Steers and his partner, William H. Brown. On May
24, Schuyler made an offer neither man could refuse, a flat fee of
$20,000 cash for the yacht.

"He's got us against the wall, George," Brown said, handing
Steers Schuyler's letter. "We'll not find another buyer to take her."

Steers read and reread the letter. He sighed, knowing Brown was
right. "She is the faster boat. I know she is."

"Maybe. Maybe not," Brown said. "She did do poorly in the trials."

"We'll have been working almost for free if we take the offer."

Brown, a canny businessman, nodded. "But a little profit is better than a big loss. You do see that."

"Of course."

"Then I recommend we accept the new deal and be done with it."

Steers thought the matter through. He put his emotions aside
and counted the venture as a lesson learned. It dawned on him that
he might still benefit from his part in it as well, if *America* proved
successful in Great Britain. Such a happy turn of events might make
a lasting mark for his future as a yacht designer, and conversely, if
the schooner lost it might have the opposite effect. Steers resigned
himself to the fact that he could not turn back now, that he had far
more than dollars invested in *America*. He resolved to do all he could
to ensure she came out the winner. He accepted Schuyler's offer and
took the cash. He agreed to sail aboard the yacht across the Atlantic
Ocean, to take further stock of her merits and make any modifications necessary to her in Le Havre, France, where the syndicate
wanted her taken for fitting out before the races. Although the
British had still not made a firm commitment to any kind of race, it
was assumed they would oblige the Americans with a skirmish. Perhaps the most important step Steers took to ensure *America*'s success, however, came when he spoke to Schuyler about the matter of
who might act as the yacht's master.

"There is no better man for the job than Captain Brown," Steers said.

Seeing the good sense in Steers's suggestion, Schuyler discussed it with the rest of the syndicate. Like Steers, they wanted every advantage for their yacht. They sent word to Brown's wife at his home in Brooklyn asking, when he returned next from sea, if he might consider taking a bit of time off from his duties aboard *Mary Taylor*. It was for a good cause, they said, a cause in the national interest. Brown was just what *America* needed.

CHAPTER NINE

QUIET DEPARTURE

Captain Ezra Nye stood atop the wheelhouse of the steamship *Pacific* and squinted through the lens of his brass spyglass against the glare coming off the smooth surface of the water, undisturbed from any influence of wind. Only the ship moving south down the upper harbor of New York, bound for Liverpool, carried the black smoke rising from the stack aft and away from the crowds of passengers gathered on deck, out in the fresh air to take a last look at land before it vanished below the horizon. He stared for a long moment at *America*, also bound for England, as his ship overtook her in the channel. Even under tow with a steam tug pulling her along, her gaffs lowered and her sails tightly furled, she struck him as beautiful.

A veteran of the Liverpool sailing packets from Grinnell, Minturn & Company's Swallowtail Line, Nye loved all kinds of sailing vessels, the special harmony they achieved with their element, as if becoming one with the sea. The glory of driving a packet hard through the waves of the North Atlantic was not easy to give up. In the end, though, the $6,000 annual salary he earned as captain of one of the four Collins steamers won out over his more romantic side. Times were changing fast in America. A smart man kept up with the new technology steam power represented.

In early spring, Nye himself had set an example of what steam could mean for ships. On April 19, he completed a voyage home from Liverpool to New York in an astonishing nine days and twenty hours. It was the first time any vessel had crossed the Atlantic Ocean in less than ten days. The record-setting passage made him the toast of the town and earned him headlines in the United States and Great Britain.

Nye lowered his spyglass. "We'll give Brown and his men two guns and a cheer!" he shouted down to his first officer.

"Aye, aye, sir!" the first mate answered. He issued orders to the sailors on deck and they jumped to his commands with a will, feeling the excitement of the moment. They rammed black powder down the muzzle of the signal gun, tamped it snug, and ran the little cannon out through the gunport cut from the bulwark. The passengers together with off-duty stokers, firemen, mechanics, stewards, and deckhands gathered on the port side of the ship to get a better look at the schooner. She was making news on this day, June 21, 1851, as she set off to a foreign land to become the first American boat to cross the Atlantic to compete in an international yacht race. The people waved and shouted with delight when the ship drew abeam of *America*, dwarfing her in size at 2,686 tons and 282 feet to the yacht's 170 tons and 95 feet. The signal gun roared and recoiled against its tackle. The report echoed off the land. The sailors reloaded the gun and fired. More shouts erupted from the crowd.

"Cheers for *America*!" Captain Nye yelled.

The passengers at once answered his call. Their voices as one, they gave the men aboard the yacht nine lusty cheers. Captain Nye took his cap off and held it over his chest. "Godspeed, Dick," he murmured, wishing the pilot he knew well a safe passage over the 3,000 miles of open ocean. Upon Brown's shoulders rested a grand enterprise, not one for profit, but one more noble, a competition of speed matching the Old World against the New, a contest of technology, skill, and even character unblemished by the petty squabbles of the countinghouse.

The cheers of the passengers reached the men aboard *America*. George Steers beamed with pride at the sight of the steamer he had helped design, and the appreciation that the passengers showed for his latest creation. At George's side was his older brother, James, a heavyset man in his early forties with a craggy face, bushy brows, and a large curtain of a gray beard. Of the thirteen brothers and sisters in the Steers family, growing up, George was closest to James, and this extended into his adult life as well. James worked with him during his stint at Smith & Dimond, before James was appointed Inspector of Customs for the port of New York, a position he held until 1849. They later worked together for William H. Brown, continuing to build on their close personal relationship. James's seventeen-year-old son, whom everyone called "Little George," was with him as well. The Steers family waved back at the people aboard *Pacific* as the steamer drew away, the massive thirty-five-foot paddle wheels churning the ocean into boils of foam. In a few minutes, the ship was well down the channel on her way to England.

Captain Brown and his men settled down to rest after *Pacific* passed, anxious to grab the last bit of free time for themselves before the watches were set and the work of the voyage began in earnest. They sat on the deck and leaned against the masts, the skylights, and the cockpit coamings, smoking and talking together in subdued voices. These were good, strong sailors. Brown had chosen them himself. There was his first mate, Nelson Comstock, a smart, experienced schoonerman of twenty-nine. The seven crewmen and a boy, who served as the cook's assistant, all boasted plenty of time on the pitching deck of a schooner at sea. They welcomed the better pay of several dollars a week, the good food, and the relative luxury of their quarters compared to that of the common sailor. The work in summer aboard the yachts gave the best of the men along the waterfronts from Maine to New Jersey a respite from the toil and danger of their days spent fishing off the Grand Banks in wintertime.

What lay ahead on the voyage was anybody's guess. The North Atlantic seldom showed kindness to those who sailed upon it. The fast moving low-pressure systems that blew eastward across the broad ocean diminished in frequency during the summer months. But the gales still came. The hurricane season had begun, adding to the possibility that an early tropical storm might blow up from the south and catch the yacht in midocean.

British shipping merchant W. S. Lindsay considered the passage across the Atlantic between the United States and Europe dangerous in all seasons, and not just because of the weather. He wrote about the conditions Brown had to contend with.

> A voyage across the Atlantic must ever be attended with greater peril than almost any other ocean service of similar length and duration; arising, as this does, from the boisterous character and uncertainty of the weather, from the icebergs which float in huge masses during spring along the northern line of passage, from the dense fogs frequently prevailing, and from the many vessels of every kind to be met with, either as employed in the Newfoundland fisheries, or in the vast and daily increasing intercourse between Europe and America. In such a navigation the utmost care and caution requires to be constantly exercised. . . .

Dick Brown was well aware of the dangers. He had braved storms of the Atlantic and Pacific, the Southern Ocean off Cape Horn and the Cape of Good Hope, the Indian Ocean, and the China Sea during the days of his youth in the merchant marine. He knew what it was like to balance on the footropes suspended below a yard of a square-rigged ship while trying to furl a sail in a blow. He had seen the sea boil into a whirl of white spray and foam at the height of a gale, with the waves towering high above the deck. The experiences of his boyhood instilled in him a deep respect for the sea, and inspired him to leave the merchant marine in favor of a less risky life working closer to home.

Brown often told the story of coming back from sea to Mystic after a hiatus of many years. It was a moment he never forgot, in part because it reinforced in his mind how much pain he knew his running away had caused his parents. He had returned home one Thanksgiving Day in the early 1830s, a full-grown man, lean and strong, tanned and weathered, his face covered in a long, shaggy beard. At the front door of the family's modest little house, no one but his mother recognized him. She flung herself into his arms, crying, "I knew my Richard would come back. I knew you would." Brown found a place already set for him at the table. It seemed his mother had set dishes out for his meals since the day he had headed for the thriving wonderland that was to him, a simple country boy, a world of adventure, the city of New York.

After returning home, Brown went to sea aboard fishing smacks. The hard, difficult life proved as dangerous as his former occupation as a merchant seaman. His early twenties were a time of indecision, a period of his life when he urgently wanted to find his niche, but could not. He married, and soon children followed. Always interested in the mechanics behind both machinery and nature, Brown took a position aboard a coastal survey vessel engaged in updating the charts of New York Harbor. It was safer, better work, which gave his wife more peace of mind than she had when he fished off the banks. The work was also dull. It involved measuring water depth, taking hundreds of observations with the sextant and bearings with the compass, and hours of paperwork. The one major benefit of his time aboard the brigs *Washington* and *Somers* was the intimate knowledge he acquired of the harbor, its every shoal, sandbar, rock, and channel. It paved the way for him to become a Sandy Hook Pilot.

Brown needed more to keep his interest than the tedious task of making charts. The pilots he had seen while at his work off the coast caught his imagination with their swift schooners. Their fraternal order's emphasis on honor, ethics, and bravery lured him back to risky business, and in it he thrived, finding his niche at last, a sense of balance between home and excitement. His work was dangerous once again. Yet, his growing family did have more security than most others in the low and middle class, certainly more than the government worker or the doryman of a fishing smack. The pilots pooled their resources to give small stipends to retired pilots and the families of any man killed in the line of duty, thus providing a safety net of sorts, a small one, but welcome just the same.

Although the pilots were not out on the water to serve as rescuers, they helped mariners in distress whenever it was possible. It was considered part of their duty. They felt honor-bound to uphold it, and they had plenty of practice. Steamships sometimes collided with fishing schooners on the Grand Banks of Newfoundland, killing the unlucky and sending the others to drift for days in their dories until death took them as well, or a vessel chanced by to pluck them from the sea. A still more common encounter for pilots was finding a dory with her two-man crew adrift in the fog, long separated from the mother ship and at the mercy of the elements. Immigrant ships ran afoul of the shoals of Sable Island in winter gales, when ice coated the rigging of the pilot boats an inch thick, and the water was so cold the touch of spray caused a man to wince in pain as it pelted his face. Those who could be rescued were assisted at great peril to the pilots. They, of all mariners, saw more than their share of what the sea could do to ships and the people sailing in them.

No captain put to sea without a certain amount of anxiety. It was the fool who believed he was invincible, that his vessel and skill might save him even in the worst of conditions. Such a belief was to tempt the sea to break down the arrogance into abject humility and despair. Brown harbored no illusions of what he faced as the steam tug towed them down the Main Ship Channel, around the buoy of the southwest Spit just off Sandy Hook, and across the last of the bar.

When the tug reached a safe distance off the shoals her captain signaled a crewman at *America*'s bow to cast off the hawser. The sailor tossed the heavy line into the sea with a splash, and the men aboard the tug heaved it over the stern. The tug turned back toward the harbor. As she passed the schooner, the men aboard the tug waved and shouted good-bye and good luck, leaving the yacht alone to pitch and roll in the low undulating swells of the Atlantic. She drifted within sight of the Sandy Hook Lightship for hours while her captain and crew waited for wind to take them clear of the land. All the sailing traffic remained stationary, sails limp on the spars. It was as if the sailers were caught in a woodcut depicting a harbor scene for one of the city's newspapers. The bay steamers and oceangoing liners, however, went about the day's business with no loss of time and money due to the calm.

Brown smoothed his beard and glanced off to the south-south-east toward the patches of darker water that began to form on the backs of the swells. The cat's-paws increased in frequency and heralded a wind about to come up. The air felt clammy. Beads of moisture collected on the varnished cap of the bulwarks, on the slope of the companionway hatch, on the glass of the skylight. Brown knew the signs well. A fog was on the way with the coming of the wind. New York Harbor was the foggiest port south of Maine with reduced visibility occurring on an average of thirty-six days every year. Even Boston was less foggy, though not much less. Fog was most common in spring and early summer along the mid-Atlantic coast. Warm, moist air blown from the waters of the Gulf Stream roughly one hundred miles offshore passed over the cold water near the coast, cooling it below its dew point and thus creating a thick blanket of mist at the sea surface. As the inshore waters warmed with the passage of summer, the frequency of the fogs off New York Harbor decreased.

To confirm his suspicions about the imminent arrival of fog, Brown inhaled deeply and exhaled slowly, revealing a puff of vapor. It vanished in seconds, quite unlike one's breath on a cold winter's morning. But it was visible just the same. Seeing one's breath when the temperature hovered well above freezing meant thick weather was about to close in. Checking to see if one's breath was visible was an old seaman's trick and represented just one of the many in Brown's inventory.

"Fog, Nels," Brown said to Nelson Comstock.

Comstock followed Brown's gaze to the south-southeast and nodded. He pointed over the stern to the west. Already the purple hills of the Highlands of Navesink loomed amid a gathering mist. Down the coast the land disappeared in a curtain of white and gray.

"We won't have to wait long, Captain," Comstock replied.

Comstock's full name was Henry Nelson, but he preferred to be called Nels. Henry was just too formal to fit well with his plain talking, unpretentious nature. A tall, strapping man with sandy hair and features akin to those of a Scandinavian, Comstock was every inch a sailor, like so many of the men who hailed from the lowlands of the

Connecticut coast and earned their livings from the sea. He came from a family of mariners. His father was a sea captain, and four of his brothers were sailors of fishing smacks in the winter and yachts in the summer. His older brother, Peter, was commander of the yacht *Cygnet*, one of the fastest boats in the harbor. His brother, Andrew Jackson, served as mate. The Comstock boys were well known to Captain Brown. Nels considered him both a friend and a sailor whom he respected, and he was glad to serve as his first mate.

In Nelson Comstock's family pedigree ran the blood of German nobility, of the Komstohk line, though neither he nor his brothers put on any pretense of royalty. Those days were long gone, as far back as the 1500s when the patriarch of the family, Baron Charles Von Komstohk, fled to England after falling into the disfavor of the rulers in Germany at the time. But the Comstock boys were told of their heritage, and one point in particular they considered worth keeping in the forefront of their minds as they pursued the business of their daily lives. The coat-of-arms of Baron Charles Von Komstohk symbolized what was most important to Nels. It was adorned with bears, denoting courage, elephants signifying strength and personal character, and a golden sword piercing a red crescent that indicated the family had fought in battle against the Turks. Although the Komstohks were wealthy, their family motto was "not wealth but contentment," boldly stating a belief in happiness over the mad dash for money that reflected the values Nels and his brothers embraced.

The Comstocks had come to the New World in 1639 and settled in present-day Connecticut, where they have lived ever since. The family was among many English immigrants to put down roots in a small village at the mouth of a river on the mainland side of Long Island Sound. The British settlers found the location ideal, with ready access to the fishing grounds offshore and the forests that dominated the coastal lowlands. They envisioned a magnificent city that might someday occupy the land they had chosen as their own. They called their village New London and named the river the Thames. The Comstocks played a part in the settlement of New London, which officially occurred in 1646, and went on to establish themselves as whalers, coastal fishermen, and merchants. Yet, despite their long tenure in the New World, they never achieved the enormous wealth of families like the Stevenses, though they were not poor. They were not cut from silk, but rather from the canvas of the workingman, and they were proud of it. They were New Englanders.

The harsh winters and rocky soil of New England did much to discourage the inclination to farm. Many of the men turned to the sea, and as a consequence, the crews and officers of the New York packets often came from up the coast. The stoic and taciturn nature the hard living bred in the New Englander made these Yankees well suited to the rigors of life at sea. But it also bred into them a highly effective work ethic that translated into wealth for some of the more industrious families. The New England families of the Griswolds, Lows, Howlands, and Grinnells were all key figures in shipping circles and individual members of these families possessed personal fortunes exceeding $100,000, the equivalent of nearly $2 million in today's currency. Nearly half of the wealthiest individuals in New York were not native to the city. Most of them were from New England.

In his book, *Old Merchants of New York City*, J. A. Scoville, a shipping merchant turned author during the period, wrote of the character of the New England boys and why they were successful, whether they sought their daily bread at sea or in the countinghouses of Manhattan.

Wherever this boy strikes, he fastens. He is honest, determined and intelligent. From the word "go" he begins to learn, to compare, and no matter what the commercial business he is engaged in, he will not rest until he knows all about it, its details—in fact, as much as the principals. . . . It is a singular fact that a foreign-born boy, or one from the New England states, will succeed in this city. . . . The great secret of this success is the perfect willingness to be useful and to do what they are required to do, and cheerfully.

Take for instance such a firm as Grinnell, Minturn & Co. In their counting room, they have New York boys and New England boys. Moses H. Grinnell comes down in the morning and says to John, a New York boy—"Take my overcoat up to my house on Fifth Avenue." [The boy] takes the coat, mutters something about "I'm not an errand boy. I came here to learn business," and moves reluctantly. Mr. Grinnell sees it, and at the same time, one of his New England clerks says, "I'll take it up." "That is right. Do so," says Mr. G., and to himself he says, "that boy is smart, will work," and gives him plenty to do. He gets promoted—gets the confidence of the chief clerk and employers, and eventually gets into the firm as partner.

It was quite fitting, then, that the two most important men aboard *America*, Richard Brown and Nelson Comstock, were Connecticut Yankees and that three of the crew were as well. These men not only knew their work, they loved it with an ardor few others matched. The yachting culture, its glamour and glitz, the cigar-toting fellows in the clubhouse all chattering on, it was far outside their ken. The sailors vowed to sail the schooner as fast as she might go, to do their duty without hesitation, and most of all, win the contest against their British peers. It was for them a simple match of one good boat against another, a chance to ply their skills and trade on the other side of the Atlantic.

Brown and Comstock both surveyed the water around the yacht as the breeze gradually increased. The ripples flowed toward the yacht and finally surrounded her, and moved on to darken the sea to the north. The wind tousled their hair, tickled their skin. Brown, in his usual soft-spoken way, simply said, "Let's put her in full dress, boys. We've got wind at last."

Comstock went forward to supervise and pitch in himself as the crewmen untied the lashings around the sails in preparation for hoisting. They made sure the boom and gaffs were set to run up without snags. They manned the halyards, lines used to raise the gaffs and the boom of the mainsail. The mainsail and foresail went up almost at the same time, followed by the gaff topsail. The wind filled the sails with a pleasing flutter and snap. The nimblest of the men worked their way out on the bowsprit and readied the jib for hoisting. Soon it, too, rose skyward and the schooner gathered way.

The sound of the water gurgling at the bow, running aft down the sides of the vessel, and swirling behind in a small wake replaced the creaks and groans of the wooden hull working in the swells.

"Don't trim her too tight, Nels," Brown said, as he set his course, just south of due east. He felt the yacht respond to the subtle shift of the tiller, a long, intricately carved extension of wood attached to the rudder. *America* did not have a wheel with a series of pulleys and lines affixed to the rudder, as was the case on large ships where a mechanical advantage was needed. As a consequence, Brown could better feel the schooner's every move as she picked up speed. It took a special talent to work the tiller of a schooner of *America*'s size to the best advantage. A man might spend his entire life sailing schooners and still not get the hang of it.

"We'll be on a close reach when I get her steady," Brown said, smiling broadly. He did not need to manhandle the tiller. With her sails perfectly trimmed, yacht *America* sailed in balance, her sails and hull working together in harmony. Brown steered with just the tips of the fingers of his left hand resting on the smooth finish of the tiller, his back against the mahogany coaming of the cockpit, his eyes on the sails he had borrowed from *Mary Taylor*'s inventory of spares expressly for the transatlantic voyage. At only sixty-six feet *Mary Taylor* was much smaller than *America*, and as a consequence, her sails did not reach to the tops of the yacht's towering masts. The reduced sail area was safer in heavy weather. Also, as long as *Mary Taylor*'s sails were set, the racing sails stored below decks remained safe from potential damage during the passage.

The schooner's racing sails were special, a strictly American innovation at that time. They consisted of a mainsail and a loose-footed foresail and jib. These sails were made of machine-woven duck, heavy, strong, and tight cotton fabric that kept its shape under high loads from the force of the wind—a big advantage when coaxing every bit of possible speed from a sailboat. With the pilot boat rig, the lower edge of *America*'s mainsail was lashed to the boom along its entire length. This further aided retention of the intended shape of *America*'s largest and most important sail, the powerhouse that drove the yacht.

When she arrived in England *The Illustrated London News* described *America*'s sails with admiration:

> Her sails come close down to the deck and are what may be termed body sails, whereby the mast head leverage is much decreased. She has no [topmast], merely carrying a pole at her mainmast head for the purpose of setting a flying gafftopsail, and hoisting a flag. By having only three sails, and spreading a large quantity of canvas, there is as little escape for the wind as there is with our yacht schooners that spread perhaps an equal quantity, but who have it in a large number of small sails.

The writer for *The Illustrated London News* did not mention another major advantage *America* enjoyed over her British competitors. The many smaller sails of British yachts were made from flax, a flowering plant less well suited for conversion into woven materials than cotton. Flax sails stretched and allowed air to pass through the material, slowing the vessel down. To increase speed, crews frequently poured seawater over the sails to help tighten the weave and reduce the amount of air that passed through the fabric, but the technique was not very effective. A further disadvantage was in how the sails were set. Aboard British yachts, the sails were loose-footed, or unattached, along the entire length of the lower edge to a boom. Thus, the optimal shape for aerodynamic lift was not easily achieved or kept.

The effectiveness of *America*'s racing sails was of no concern at the moment, however. Brown concentrated on the business at hand, sailing the yacht as the wind filled in. With the wind came the fog. It swept toward the yacht in a wide swath of white illuminated from the diffuse light of the sun. Brown watched it come. He felt its damp touch as the world around the yacht disappeared. Only the blue sky was visible in a patch immediately above the mastheads. Drops of water dripped from the rigging and pattered on the deck. The Steers family went below to get away from the dampness, along with the men of the port watch. Although *America* was not a merchant vessel and none of the usual formalities were required to keep discipline, the division of the crew into two watches to stand in shifts of four hours on duty and four hours off was a simple tenet of the sea that extended even to a private yacht. Comstock commanded the port watch, Brown the starboard.

Brown posted a lookout at the bow and strained to hear the first telltale sound of an approaching steamship, that rhythmic splash-splash of the paddle wheels as the floats churned the water with every revolution. An approaching sailing packet posed an even greater danger because the vessel moved silently through the water. It was almost impossible to hear one coming in time to avoid a collision. Ships of this period did not routinely sound a fog horn. Steamships were not equipped with mechanical whistles. At best, the captains posted a lookout with a trumpetlike horn at the bow, which the lookout blew every few minutes until he became winded. There were no traffic separation zones that kept ships moving together in one direction. These were not instituted until 1859, when Lieutenant Matthew Fontaine Maury of the United States Navy included separation zones on his charts for the transatlantic service.

Pilots, whose job it was to stay where the traffic converged, were particularly cognizant of the danger posed by large steam and sailing ships, and the tactics needed to avoid calamity when the weather came in thick. While waiting offshore in the shipping lanes for the fog to lift, pilots positioned their schooners to present the bow or stern to oncoming traffic. They never lay broadside to, as so many of the Gloucester schooners did, their captains unaware of the simple, yet effective method to diminish the odds of disaster.

America sailed onward with a building sea breeze pushing her eastward in the deepening twilight. Off the port beam, lost in the fog and darkness, was the low sandy shore of Long Island. Beyond the beach the water remained shallow for miles out to sea until the broad gradual slope of the continental shelf dropped abruptly away. This shelf was once dry land and the island a rocky ridge only twelve miles long. During the Ice Age, before the level of the sea rose and covered the continental shelf, the edges of the glaciers terminated along the ridge, depositing moraines that gave the present island its form and character. As *America* sailed farther east, she faced the remains of the glacial influences in the sandbars that swept southeast of Nantucket. The natural processes that created the coast left behind dangers for the un-wary mariner. Brown, with his knack for science and his understand-ing of the hydrography of the coast, was keen to avoid these hazards and the trouble they might cause for the yacht. He adjusted his course to put more southing in it, to ensure he did not run inside the Nan-tucket Lightship on station at the terminus of the shoals.

The yacht moved easily through the small waves that began to run with the rising wind. She heeled slightly to port, but otherwise remained steady. Out off the coast of Long Island in the complete cloak of darkness Brown had no way of telling exactly where he was. He was reduced to making an educated guess based on the age-old practice sailors call dead reckoning. A navigator can calculate his po-sition using the vessel's speed traveled over a specified course dur-ing a given time period. Multiplying speed and time will give an approximate distance covered for that period, which, together with the course steered, and other considerations, can allow the naviga-tor to plot the vessel's approximate position on a chart. If *America* sailed for two hours at a rate of five knots, Brown knew she made good approximately ten nautical miles along her course. It was a simple method of navigation, but effective enough for his purposes provided that he stayed well offshore.

Brown, however, did not know *America*'s speed through the wa-ter, and he was quite interested in finding out, both from a naviga-tional standpoint and from his mounting curiosity about just how fast the schooner was actually sailing. She seemed to fly through the water without any fuss or bother. No spray shot over the bow. She did not pitch or yaw. Brown asked a crewman to bring up from be-low a lantern, and a device called a log, which was used to measure a vessel's speed through the water.

A log consisted of a triangular-shaped piece of wood called a chip. It had weights at the base to allow it to turn perpendicular to the surface of the sea, to create drag when towed behind a vessel. Attached to the chip was a long line marked at intervals of forty-eight feet with the bulge of a knot. Each knot represented the equal of one nautical mile traveled in the space of an hour, hence the rea-son why a boat's speed is referred to in knots, not miles per hour.

Using a sandglass as a timer, the log was heaved and the number of knots to come off the line in the specified time indicated the vessel's rate of progress through the water.

The light of the lantern lit up the cockpit as the crewman moved aft, the log line tucked under his arm coiled on its reel. The yellow glow shone on Brown's face, and the faces of the others gathered together for the first heaving of the log. George Steers, in particular, could barely contain his curiosity. While one crewman held the reel and Comstock held the twenty-eight-second sandglass used to time the run of the line, Brown grabbed the chip and prepared to heave it over the stern.

"Ready, Nels?" Brown asked.

"Ready."

Brown tossed the chip overboard and said, "Turn!"

Comstock turned the sandglass over and replied: "Done!"

The sand began to run. The line spun off the reel. Brown concentrated on counting the knots in the dim light until Comstock shouted: "Stop!"

The crewman holding the reel stopped the line from running. Brown squinted at it. He was surprised at how many knots had run off. Thinking he miscounted the number, he had them repeat the process and the results were the same. *America* was sailing at ten knots, a very fast rate of speed given the moderate strength of the wind and her small sails from *Mary Taylor*. George Steers smiled and clapped his brother James on the back.

"She's sailing almost as fast as a Collins liner!" George said.

The men broke out some brandy and sat in the cockpit and laughed. The warmth of the liquor drove away the slight chill. Brown gazed out toward the bow into the impenetrable blackness looking for the indistinct smudges of light that revealed the presence of another vessel. Ten knots. In this breeze!

CHAPTER TEN

TO OPEN SEA

The south-southeast wind blew fair through the night and into the dawn of Sunday, June 22, carrying with it the billowing swirls of fog that had closed in the afternoon before. Fog rolled over the yacht and obscured all but the waves breaking gently as they came in on the starboard beam. As the sun rose, the gray of the mist whitened and created a sometimes beautiful overlay atop the green and black of the water. At times the fog thinned and revealed the empty horizon out to a mile or two. Just as quickly, it came in thick again and repeated the cycle once more.

The wind slowly faded as the day progressed, leaving yacht *America* to roll with the swells. When a swell larger than most forced the air from the canvas, the gaffs and the boom of the mainsail swung back and forth. The spars worked against the fittings on the masts that held them in place. Brown ordered the sails trimmed in tight to prevent the annoying slat and bang, and the creak and groan of the wood. He meticulously checked all the gear for signs of weakness. He examined the halyards, sheets, downhauls, and other running rigging for wear. These lines were used to raise, lower, trim, and shape the sails. He pulled and tugged the stays and shrouds that supported the masts to test the tension, making sure the ropes were set up tight enough to keep the masts from excessive bending or whipping in a fresh breeze. These tasks were part of his daily routine, just as they were aboard *Mary Taylor*. Gear failure at sea meant potential disaster. It was up to the captain to ensure that the vessel was in good working order at all times.

James Steers, who was keeping a journal to chronicle the events during the voyage, wrote that the "sails [were] set like boards," well trimmed and shaped to catch the breeze. He also noted that the "air was as thick as mush, the fog like rain" and that the captain set the crew to scrubbing the hatches and the decks. While the men worked, the pleasant odors of the Sunday dinner wafted up from the companionway and mingled with the tart tang of the salt air. Below in the galley the cook and his assistant prepared a noonday meal of roast turkey, green peas, boiled beef and pork, with bread pudding for dessert, which James Steers enjoyed, along with drinks later in the afternoon in keeping with true yachting style. The voyage began as a pleasure cruise for the Steers family. Although the business at hand was serious, they considered the journey an adventure. Only one or two yachts had ever crossed the Atlantic Ocean, and none of them to race. It was indeed a rare undertaking for them to sail *America* across, rare on many levels. Little George took particular joy in it as he conversed with the crew and listened to their tales of the sea.

The yacht sailed on for a while and slowed to a stop. She fell into a rhythm timed with the ebb and flow of the fog. When she lay idle, the sun burned away the fog and visibility increased. When the wind puffed, it blew in a fresh layer of mist to obscure the world around the boat. The crew worked with a will to take full advantage of the zephyrs, and they were delighted at how the vessel surged forward even in so light and fickle a breeze as she made her way past the tip of Long Island, past Martha's Vineyard and the Elizabeth Islands, well out to sea at the outer edge of Nantucket Shoals.

With no sun to use for a celestial observation with his sextant, a device needed to navigate a vessel while offshore and away from navigation aids like a lighthouse or a buoy, Brown continued to guess at the yacht's position through dead reckoning. He had done this hundreds of times aboard *Mary Taylor*, especially in June, July, and August, months known for heavy fog off the New England coast. Nevertheless, Brown was a cautious man not given to taking the sea for granted. Swift, unseen currents flowed in baffling, unpredictable directions in the waters they sailed through. These currents might easily move the schooner into danger without a steady breeze to keep a good course. He ordered Comstock to take soundings, a time-honored method of navigation along coasts where the sea was not bottomless deep.

Comstock went up to the bow with a long line twenty to thirty fathoms in length, or a maximum of 180 feet, a fathom being the equal of 6 feet. Attached to the line was a seven-pound lead sinker with a hole in the base. Appropriately enough, the line and lead was called a lead-line. Comstock inserted some fresh tallow into the hole of the lead. When the lead hit the seafloor the tallow collected a specimen of the bottom, which might provide a useful clue concerning their whereabouts. The type of bottom—sand, mud, gravel—was marked on the chart. Comparing what the tallow brought up to the bottom on the chart in their assumed position might confirm Brown's dead reckoning, at least to within acceptable margins for error. It might also alert him to a severe deviation of course or a bad mistake in his dead reckoning.

Comstock held a coil of the line in his left hand, and with his right hand he slowly swung the lead back and forth like a pendulum. As the momentum increased, he skillfully raised his right arm and swung the lead around his head. He gradually let out more line to widen the circle, increase the centrifugal force needed to carry the line well forward of the bow, and give the sinker enough time to sink before the vessel drifted past it. Comstock released the line. It flew straight ahead and splashed into the water. The weight of the lead dragged the line deep, until it finally reached the bottom and the line hung straight down at the bow. He noted the markings on the line as it ran free, each of which denoted a specific water depth. A single piece of rope dangled above the surface of the water, the mark for twenty-five fathoms.

"By the deep twenty-five," he called.

"By the deep twenty-five, aye," Brown called back to Comstock.

Based on the sounding Brown estimated they were in between

DANGERS OFF THE NORTH AMERICAN COAST

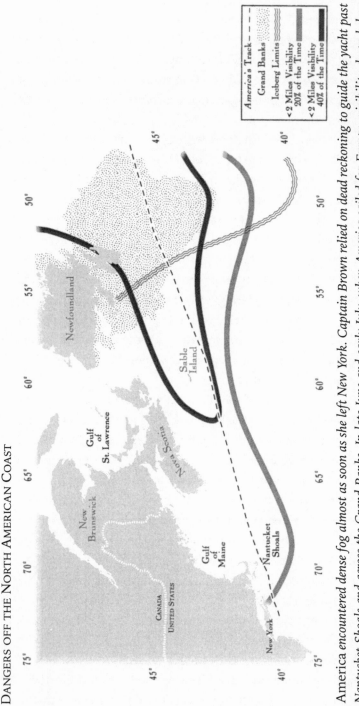

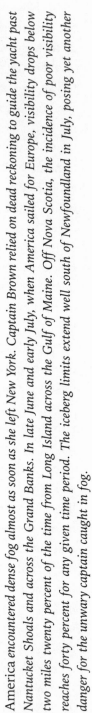

America encountered dense fog almost as soon as she left New York. Captain Brown relied on dead reckoning to guide the yacht past Nantucket Shoals and across the Grand Banks. In late June and early July, when America sailed for Europe, visibility drops below two miles twenty percent of the time from Long Island across the Gulf of Maine. Off Nova Scotia, the incidence of poor visibility reaches forty percent for any given time period. The iceberg limits extend well south of Newfoundland in July, posing yet another danger for the unwary captain caught in fog.

twenty to twenty-five fathoms of water, or just a bit less than 150 feet. He consulted his chart and noted that these depths were consistent with those off Nantucket Shoals. If he was correct in his dead reckoning, the island of Nantucket lay roughly thirty-two miles to the north of their current position. Just under three miles to the north was the seaward edge of Davis South Shoal, a dangerous patch of water less than twelve feet deep in places. Named after the sixteenth-century English explorer John Davis, who was thought by his backers to be "a man well grounded in the principles of the arte of navigation," it was a stretch of Nantucket Shoals seamen sought to avoid.

The waters off New England did not compare with those Davis sailed in his quest for the Northwest Passage in the Labrador Sea and off the east coast of Baffin Island. He encountered fierce tides, ice flows, and gales in one of the most treacherous reaches of ocean in the world. Davis South Shoal would have been tame to him, and possibly caused him to smile if he had known it bore his name. But despite the vast differences between the sea above the Arctic Circle and the waters Brown sailed through, navigation off New England's coast required caution as well as an innate sense of "the arte of navigation." Thirty miles to the east lay more dangers at Phelps Bank, an area known for tidal rips that churned and boiled as the sea rushed from deep water to collide with the sandbars. Steep, confused seas broke. Standing waves similar to those found in river rapids formed when the tide ran fast. One of the most notorious tidal disturbances was Asia Rip, about sixty miles southeast of the shoulder of Cape Cod, dead off *America*'s bow.

In 1609, when explorers had turned temporarily away from the high northern latitudes in their search for the Northwest Passage, Henry Hudson's *Half Moon* experienced the tides and dangerous shoals in *America*'s general location. Robert Juet, the chronicler of the voyage, wrote in his journal: "Very thicke and mystie all day . . . Wee sounded many times, and had difference of soundings, sometimes little stones, and sometimes grosse gray sand . . . And at ten of the clocke we heard a great Rut [roar], like the Rut of the shoare. . . . and presently came an hurling current, or tyde with over fals, which cast our ship round."

Throughout the day Brown updated his dead reckoning after the log was heaved. The crew checked the yacht's speed four times and found she sailed at one to six knots. Determining the yacht's position was made all the more difficult because of the light wind and the unsteady progress of the boat. The schooner drifted more than she sailed, at the mercy of the tidal currents. Brown ordered the topmast staysail set, hoping she might move faster. The topmast staysail was set between the main- and foremasts. It filled the gap between them to provide maximum sail area. Brown had already set the extensions of the jib and the foresail, called bonnets. Bonnets were set at the lower edge of the sails to enlarge the total amount of canvas spread to catch the wind. *America* carried every inch of canvas she could fly, but progress was slow. The wind shifted from the south-southeast to the northeast, and went calm, and clocked back to the southwest for a while before coming in from the south nearly off *America*'s starboard beam on the morning of June 23. Soundings revealed the water depth in their stretch of ocean measured only fourteen fathoms.

Brown was a patient man. Yet he found himself wishing for a good wind to come, feeling a little uneasy as he steered the boat. Few experiences at sea proved more vexing than fickle winds aboard a vessel shrouded in fog drifting about in close proximity to a dangerous coast. Another pressure exerted itself on Brown in addition to the adverse weather conditions. John Cox Stevens, his brother Edwin, and Colonel James Alexander Hamilton and his wife were soon to set sail aboard the steamship *Humboldt* of the Havre line. They expected to arrive in Le Havre, France, in advance of the yacht, where she was to be made ready for the races in England. They made it clear to Brown that he was to drive *America* as hard as safety allowed and bring her across the Atlantic in two weeks. The peak of the British sailing season had arrived and the syndicate feared time ran short for a skirmish with the Royal Yacht Squadron's fleet, hence the need for haste. However, given that the much larger and loftier sailing packet *Isaac Wright* set the record in 1848 for the fastest passage from New York to Liverpool at just over thirteen days, a record that stood until the mid-1850s, it seemed impossible that *America* might equal her time. With her much shorter waterline and much reduced sail area it was theoretically unlikely that she might even approach *Isaac Wright*'s record-setting passage.

Brown still hoped to make a fine showing in his race against time and the record set by *Isaac Wright*. Occasionally, a rare captain surfaced who managed to overcome the most unfavorable odds. Captain David G. Bailey had set the westbound record from Liverpool to New York at sixteen days aboard the packet *Yorkshire* in 1846, and he had set the eastbound record aboard *Isaac Wright* two years later. The success of a vessel rested as much on her captain as it did on her design, as Bailey had demonstrated. Brown had no reason to think himself unable to achieve similar success.

Thus, while Brown paced about on deck, wishing for his wind to come, like all good captains he realized that his control of the sea amounted to no more than his ability allowed under a given set of circumstances. He could not cause the wind to blow with a snap of his fingers, nor could he breathe deeply and blow the fog away, so he might get a visual fix on the Nantucket Lightship, which must have been somewhere nearby. He stood his watches with the belief in one of the ocean's only predictable elements—that nothing remained constant at sea. The sea was ever changing, almost alive, capable of kind and cruel ways just like a human being. And, as the morning of June 23 wore on and the crew stood the forenoon watch, the sea did change its quiet mood.

The south wind increased, gradually at first, kicking *America*'s speed up to six knots, then to ten. The yacht heeled to the freshening breeze, her port rail close to going under. She came to life as she fell into harmony with the waves as they built over the course of the day. Wedges of white foam shot out to leeward when she came down off the face of a wave and rose to meet the next. Astern, her wake stretched far back arrow-straight before it disappeared in the crests. Brown was pleased to see the schooner responded well to the helm despite the push of the seas coming in on the right side of the vessel, and the wind that blew broadside on. Many a schooner under these conditions with a full press of canvas developed what sailors call a weather helm, the tendency of a sailboat to want to come up into the wind. Even at her quick rate of travel she did not need much more than a light touch on the tiller. It was a good sign, a very good sign, Brown thought.

"She's got good balance in fresh conditions, George," he said to Steers. "She likes this better than light air." Smiling at George, Brown gave him a turn at the helm. It had been a long time since Brown had seen him so happy. The fatigue was gone. The dull, despairing look in his eyes had vanished.

As he steered, George rejoiced in the adventure, in the vessel he designed and built, and in the majesty of the sea. He shouted in delight to his brother and nephew as the schooner romped eastward. With his sou'wester hat pulled low, his rain gear buttoned tight against the showers that came and went, he even looked like a sailor. He gazed over the windward side of the yacht at the procession of waves, at the low, gray clouds scudding over the mastheads, and at the empty horizon. It was a wild scene devoid of all shoreside comforts, a waste of heaving swells broken only with the sight of a lone gull swooping above the breakers. Although he had conceived of and fashioned many a yacht, George had never been to sea on a small craft, never ventured far from New York Harbor aboard his creations. He turned the boats over to the yachtsmen, who took the sloops and schooners out racing or on cruises to Newport, or to the owners of companies for whom he built commercial craft. The experience of sailing aboard *America* felt good. He looked forward to reaching France, and he was already thinking about ways to make *America* faster.

By early evening, *America* reached speeds of twelve knots. Her swift progress took her beyond the dangers of Nantucket Shoals out along the edge of Georges Bank. The wind hauled aft of the beam as the clouds to the east grew pitch-black, and those to the west glowed a pale gray over the horizon. The waves merged with the shadows and became invisible. Only the roar of the crests bearing down on the schooner told the men aboard her that a good sea was getting up. Brown surveyed the sails, checked the wind direction by feel and by compass, and determined he might set Big Ben, the large square-sail *America* carried for the transatlantic voyage. The square-sail was set on a single spar fitted in front of the foremast. The spar, known as a yard, supported the upper edge of the sail and presented the wide spread of canvas perpendicular to the hull of the boat, like the sails of a square-rigged ship. Big Ben, as Brown called it, achieved maximum efficiency when the wind blew from astern.

Brown called to Comstock and the crew on watch, "Set Big Ben!"

Comstock grinned. "Aye, Captain," he said.

They would see what *America* had in her.

Comstock went forward and rapped on the hatch over the crew's quarters to muster the men off watch below in their berths in the forecastle. All hands spilled out onto the deck to set Big Ben and soon stood at their stations ready to work. Together with a group of the lightest and strongest sailors, Comstock made his way carefully toward the foremast, keeping well inboard of the schooner's rail. There were no lifelines attached to stanchions that could keep a man from washing overboard. The fewer lines and structures alow and aloft meant less resistance to the wind, a compromise that favored speed over safety. Comstock timed his next steps well, as he scurried nimbly across the deck to the foremast shrouds and climbed the short distance to the yard used to set Big Ben. When not in use, it was customary to lash the yard to the forward shrouds to keep it out of the way. Comstock straddled the spar, bracing himself against the motion of the schooner. Two other men did the same.

"Come on, boys!" Comstock shouted. "Look lively!"

Already taken from the sail locker, the big square-sail was ready for the crewmen to send it up to their peers perched on the yard. They got it aloft and Comstock and his helpers attached the top edge to the ends of the yard as well as at the center. The canvas was held in a loose roll with lines light enough to break away when the men raised the yard up the foremast. The sail would unfurl on its own, with the men safely on deck. Once off the yard, the crewmen clung to the shrouds and cast all the lashings off. The yard swayed violently as the schooner battled the swells. The men below hauled the control lines taut to steady it. Down the shrouds and back to the deck, Comstock checked to make sure the square-sail was finally set for hoisting.

"All ready forward!" Comstock cried.

"Send him up, Nels!" Brown answered.

Working together, the sailors lay to the control lines with a will. The yard soared skyward, flying free and away from the foremost shrouds. At the same time, crewmen yanked the sheets hard. Big Ben unfurled with an explosive whoosh and rumble as the sail spread to the wind. The sailors worked fast to trim the yard using the sheets and braces, lines attached to each end of the yard that enabled the crew to pivot it to the best angle to catch the wind. Big Ben bellied out in a balloonlike curve. *America* rushed forward under the new press of sail and began to roll a bit—quite common when sailing fast downwind in the open sea. She rolled to port, dipped her rail almost under, then to starboard. She cut through the water like a knife and parted the seas with a steady roar at the bow.

As the wind continued to increase, so did *America*'s speed. She sailed on the verge of skittering out of control. Brown concentrated on his steering. He was in tune with the slightest change in the boat's feel and even a modest shift in the wind's direction. He was playing it close. The square-sail was trimmed as far forward as possible to make the best use of the wind blowing off the right side of the stern. If *America* slid down the face of a large wave and he failed to compensate for the motion, he might find her sailing too high for the square-sail to hold its air. A momentary lapse of attention meant the wind might swing round to catch the front of the sail and slam it aback against the mast. In such a stiff breeze, his error might tear the foremast out of the boat. It was a calculated risk, flying Big Ben when the wind angle was just within the limits of the sail's capacity to use it efficiently. But that was the way of it aboard any sailer out to push the edge of her potential for speed.

Brown worked hard at the tiller. No longer was he able to steer with a light touch. His muscles strained as he guided the schooner downwind, weaving through the waves and concentrating on the wind, which began to shift slowly forward on the right side of the boat. As it did so, the danger of going aback increased. Brown compensated by turning the bow further to the left, bringing the wind back to a more manageable angle aft toward the stern. But he could not keep bearing off. The shallows of Georges Bank lay to port. He

had seen the breakers flash white and aquamarine in the bright sun-
light on a blustery day. He had heard their frightening din from a
safe distance in the years he frequented the banks aboard his fishing
schooner, and in more recent times, sailing aboard *Mary Taylor* on
the eastern chance. He had no wish to run up on the shoals at night
with heavy weather approaching. At *America*'s current speed, trouble
lay less than an hour or two off the port beam. He held his course as
long as he dared, hoping the wind might shift back closer to the
southwest. But as each exhilarating minute passed, he realized Big
Ben posed too much of a danger.

"Call all hands, Nels," he said, almost shouting above the wind.
"I'm afraid old Ben won't stand much more."

"Aye, aye," Comstock said.

The crew mustered on deck once again, ready to tangle with the
big square-sail in the pitch-black of the windy night. They moved
quickly along the windward side of the schooner, the spray flying in
sheets over the rail. When all was ready Brown turned *America* until
he brought the wind almost directly astern. The crew slacked off on
the sheets of the mainsail and foresail. The sails aft of Big Ben partially blocked the force of the wind, blanketing the square-sail. The
sailors eased the sheets to rob it of its shape and to spill the wind.
The canvas blew toward the bow and thundered and shook. Blocks
banged. Ropes whipped and vibrated. In moments, the sailors lowered the yard to the deck. The wind caught the square-sail and blew
it forward, flogging in the stiff breeze and momentarily resisting attempts to subdue its immense power. The work was exhausting,
though the men did not realize just how taxing it had been until
they finished the job at hand. Panting, wet to the skin, and cold, the
crew off watch went back below to the cramped confines of the forecastle and tried to sleep until their next shift.

America sailed on through the night, reeling off the miles, and by
the morning of June 24, she labored hard in the rising gale, the
clouds as dark as the inside of a hat. The seas broke out to the horizon, painting the ocean in splashes of white. Foam flowed on the
leaden backs of the waves. The wind lifted spindrift into the air to
mix with the intermittent rain pelting the sails. Brown and his men

tasted salt when they licked their lips, and their eyes stung when they rubbed them with their knuckles to drive the sleep away. The constant wet chaffed and chapped their hands and the backs of their necks under their oilskins. The wind hauled back to a favorable slant for Big Ben, and Brown ordered it set yet again. The crew stifled their complaints and obeyed their captain, despite their aching backs, and the bruises they sustained when thrown against the bulkheads and door frames below. Drive her hard, John Cox Stevens had told him, as hard as you can to get her across. Brown had promised he would and he was a man to carry out his word to the letter. As long as he felt it was safe, he intended to push the schooner to the limit.

Far off to leeward, Brown caught sight of a brig bound west for the approaches of New York, for she was too far along the eastern chance to find a berth in Boston. She disappeared hull down below the crests of the waves and the next moment came into full view as she mounted the summits. She sailed under reduced canvas, with just her topsails and a reefed spanker. The Steers brothers huddled in the cockpit with Little George and watched the vessel draw closer, fascinated at the splendor of the moment, despite its inherent misery in terms of the weather and the rough motion of the schooner.

Suddenly, the brig hauled up her colors as a show of respect. It was customary for ships passing on an otherwise empty sea to hail each other, or to show their country's flag as a form of gesture, a nautical greeting. The British flag billowed in the wind from the mizzen truck of the brig. Brown ordered a sailor to fetch the Stars and Stripes from below to return the salute. But as the crewman tried to set the colors, the lines snagged, and he could not raise the flag.

"A pity," Brown mumbled as he watched the brig fall away astern. "The captain will think we've slighted him. Stow the colors. We'll not need them now."

At noon the cook and the boy found it too difficult to prepare any kind of formal dinner. It was too dangerous to light the stove. The men ate cold beef and bread washed down with a bit of water. When the log was heaved Brown turned to Steers and winked. "The schooner makes thirteen and a half knots! She's keeping pace with a

Collins liner, boys!" he shouted to the crew. "A Collins liner!"

George smiled weakly. The rough going was making him feel a little seasick, though he did not admit it to anyone, not even to James. It would not do to be seen as a lubber. But as the time passed and the yacht drew ever farther from New York, Steers felt the pangs of homesickness set in along with his physical discomfort. He felt a growing desire for the boat to stop pitching about, for the sweet smell of the trees and grass and late spring flowers, the sound of songbirds, and most of all, the security he found in focusing entirely on his work and family. He needed the stability a predictable existence brought, where he was in control and not at the mercy of nature. He looked at Brown, his stocky frame bundled in a rain slicker and rain pants, with sea boots on his feet, and to top off the garb a sou'wester hat pulled snug over his head. The man's eyes sparkled. His voice boomed with confidence. He seemed to exude strength with every agile move, every soft-spoken word. Truly the man was in his element, at one with the sea, and in love with it. Steers realized how different he was from his friend. Where Steers was timid even of horses, actually scared of them, much less the power of the sea, he wondered if Brown knew the meaning of fear.

The fury of the blow continued to rise. The rigging strained under the high loads the wind imposed. Two men were needed at the tiller. At one o'clock, caution got the better of Brown. He ordered the crew to reduce canvas to bring the yacht's speed down. She slowed just a little, but it was enough. By Brown's reckoning she had made good 284 miles in a single day's run, the equal of a fine rate of travel for a grand clipper ship or a swift steamer. *America* continued her surge and roar to the eastward, leaving the shoals of Georges Bank astern, her bow to the last leg of the eastern chance before she proceeded on to the deep sea beyond the rocky coast of Newfoundland still more than 700 miles to the northeast.

CHAPTER ELEVEN

TURN OF SPEED

The layer of low, dark clouds that obscured the sun since *America* left New York remained with her as she sped east toward the Grand Banks of Newfoundland. It was as if she sailed into an endless night never to emerge from the gloom. The crew went about their shipboard duties with the change of each watch resigned to endure whatever the North Atlantic sent in the way of misery. They knew the hardships of a cold, midnight watch at the helm, and the monotonous passage of time that stretched minutes into hours, and hours into days. But regardless of the discomforts, the work at the sails, the coming and going of storms and calms, and the ebb and flow of the rotational deep ocean tide imparted a uniquely satisfying rhythm to their lives.

Judging the yacht's position based on the information he gleaned when the log was heaved, his courses, and his knowledge of the currents in that rough and dreary area of ocean, Captain Brown updated his dead reckoning on a regular basis. The schooner lost soundings northeast of Georges Bank, the water too deep for the lead line to find bottom. Brown was thus denied one of the more effective means of determining his whereabouts. However, he was not overly concerned. There were no shoals to threaten *America* until she passed over the banks. The only danger came from possible collisions with the ships traveling along the busy route between Europe, and Halifax, Boston, and New York. There was also the increasing likelihood of encountering an iceberg the closer the schooner came to Newfoundland. The lookouts kept a weather eye on the horizon at all times.

With the exception of a brief calm, the schooner sailed well and fast with a brisk northwesterly wind blowing off the left side of her stern. Every sail was set. She averaged ten to twelve knots from June 24 through the morning of June 26, putting her almost 1,200 miles from New York since her departure. Even with her slow start in the calm and fog off Long Island, she had covered roughly one third of the passage in just five sea days. Brown began to think he might well get her across in only two weeks, or perhaps less. If the schooner kept up her daily averages of 250 miles, he theoretically might equal the passage of *Isaac Wright*'s famous crossing. He knew in his heart that the odds of actually accomplishing such a victory were extreme. But he let himself hope. What a grand way to make an entrance in Europe, with a schooner that equaled or bested the finest of the New York packets on her first transatlantic crossing.

The lookouts aboard *America* spied several ships as the yacht closed with the Grand Banks. She passed two under full sail on June 25. The excitement aboard reached a new high. It was one thing to run thirteen or more knots off the log. It was another far more tangible evidence of the yacht's speed for her to bring the topgallants of a full-rigged ship over the horizon, the large vessel still hull down, and to steadily creep up on her until the people on deck became visible. Several hours later, the ship's hull was again invisible, and so, too, were her highest sails not long afterward. James Steers recorded in his journal: "Everything set. The way we passed every [ship] we saw was enough to surprise everyone on board." And later, he wrote of the schooner that she was "the best sea boat that ever went out of the Hook. The way we have passed everything we have seen must be witnessed to be believed. The captain says she sails like the wind."

On the morning of June 26, under a hazy sky that looked as though it might clear at last, the yacht bore down on an English

brig. Brown brought *America* in close enough to speak her. The officers on deck shouted to the people aboard the schooner, but the
yacht pulled ahead fast. There was no time to exchange the usual
greetings. Again, as on the day before, the square-rigger fell behind
and soon grew small on the horizon amid the rolling swells that partially obscured her black hull. The schooner's performance impressed Brown and gave him hope for a fast passage across the
Atlantic and success in the matches against the British yachting
fleet. He did not question the fact that the British had not formally
invited the schooner over for a race. He left those matters for his
employers to sort out, though it did strike a man with his practical
nature that purchasing a yacht for $20,000 and dispatching her on
the transatlantic crossing without a commitment bordered on the
foolish. It was easy to imagine that a race might not come off, and
that the entire ordeal George Steers suffered in connection with
building the yacht, and Brown's labor in bringing her over to England might amount to nothing more than a show without a song.

The clouds slowly broke apart as the morning ended, the
watches were changed, and the cook served up a dinner of roast
turkey and chicken potpie. The intermittent warmth of the sun
when it peeped out from behind the clouds prompted the men to
smile and joke with one another as they worked, pleased and accepting of the gift the sea had given them in the form of a temporary
break in the weather. Brown was delighted. For the first time since
leaving New York, he was able to use his sextant to shoot the sun,
albeit with some difficulty. He waited patiently for hours, sextant in
hand, ready for the sun to peak through the scud and the overcast
sky above. He took several observations throughout the day, starting
at noon, when he got his latitude. Down below in the main saloon
he worked out the yacht's position. She sailed 170 miles southeast
of Cape Race, the southernmost tip of the island of Newfoundland.
Le Havre, France, lay on a bearing of east by three-quarters north approximately 2,000 miles away.

The observations confirmed what Brown already suspected, that
the schooner had reached the Grand Banks. In the space of 20 miles,
the ocean depths shoaled from eight thousand feet to just 250. This

accounted for the pronounced change in the ocean's color from the bottomless blue of previous days to its present green hue, and the shorter, steeper seas so different from the long, undulating rollers of deep ocean. Gulls, gannets, fulmars, and many other birds filled the sky, darting and soaring above the schooner. Their shrill calls remained loud and strident only for a few moments. The wind quickly carried the lonely sounds away as the birds flew past on the wing to nowhere. It was a repetition of a scene played out for more than three centuries, as men and ships came to the Grand Banks on their way to explore new lands or to reap the rich catches of cod.

Like the gold rush unfolding in California, the rush to cash in on the Grand Banks fishery needed a spark, that first discovery at Sutters Mill to get it started. John Cabot's explorations of North America in 1497 brought him to the banks and provided the impetus for the events to come. The first European explorer of the western sea after the Norse, he made landfall at the northern end of Newfoundland, sailed southward down the coast past present-day St. John's, and turned back near Placentia Bay, where he observed huge numbers of cod numerous enough for his crew to catch, using weighted baskets lowered overboard. The baskets went into the sea empty and came back full of cod. The men had never seen anything like it in European waters.

Although the expedition did not bring back word of treasures, merchants in France and Portugal, and a little later in England, noted the value of the cod fishery and set up a new territory for the age-old profession of fishing. French fishing vessels began the long tradition of cod fishing in the vicinity of the Grand Banks. The first recorded foray occurred in 1504, taking the French ships on a profitable venture between Cape Bonavista and the Strait of Belle Isle, which separates Newfoundland from Labrador. They brought their valuable cargoes back home to the port of Rouen on the Seine River. Rouen soon became a key depot for the distribution of cod into the interior of France, and for exports to England. The Portuguese began sending ships at around the same time.

Robert Juet, aboard Henry Hudson's *Half Moon*, witnessed the early fishing activity on the banks. Several times, the men aboard the ship sighted the vessels of the French fleet. He also wrote in his journal about the great number of cod in the waters off Newfoundland:

> We takt [tacked] and stood backe to the Banke, and had five and twentie fathoms; and tryed for Fish, and it fell calme, and we caught one hundred and eighteene great Coddes, from eight a clocke till one, and after Dinner wee tooke twelve, and saw many great Scoales of Herrings. . . . We had sight of a sayle on head off us . . . and spake with a French-man, which lay Fishing on the Banke of Sablen [off Halifax, Nova Scotia], in thirtie fathoms, and we saw two or three more.

As *America* sailed onward over the banks, her crew observed seven schooners from the Gloucester fleet. Like the French, Portuguese, and English before them, the banks drew the hardy men from New England to carry on the fishing tradition. The thousands of tons of cod each schooner took home every year went to Boston and New York, and to a multitude of small towns and villages in the interior. The owners of the schooners measured their wealth in terms of fish, and the men working the banks were paid a share of the profits earned from the sale of the catch. The Gloucestermen were much like their whaling brethren of New Bedford and New London. They relied on the bounty of the sea for their livelihoods rather than on the business of carrying freight and passengers aboard the packets and liners, whose owners paid seamen a steady, though modest salary.

Once off the banks, the schooners anchored or drifted. The fishermen launched a seaworthy type of rowboat called a dory, and put to sea in them two men to a boat. The dorymen worked eighteen hours a day to fill the holds of the mother ship. They fished with long lines, known as trawls. These lines were more than a mile in length, armed with hundreds of sharp, barbed hooks. The work of hauling a trawl loaded with cod back into the dory taxed the strongest men. All day they floated on the waves, baiting and deploying the trawls, and hauling the long lines in again, until the boat sank low under the weight of a ton of cod. The work did not end there. The men gutted and cleaned the fish below in the stinking hold of the schooner. The meat of the cod they salted down for the dinner table. The livers were boiled for the oil they contained. The heads were sometimes made into soup, and the tongues were fried and eaten as a delicacy.

The Gloucester schooners were cousins to yacht *America* and the pilot boats that had inspired George Steers in fashioning her unique design. Like the pilots of New York and Boston, the Gloucestermen prided themselves on the speed of their vessels. They raced against each other to arrive first back in the harbor with the freshest catch. They crowded on all sail, drove the lee rails under, and sailed on through gales to get home, the crews exhausted from their labor on the banks.

James Steers watched the schooners as one by one they hove near and quickly dropped astern. The dories peppered the sea. The fishermen paused from their work and gazed at yacht *America* sailing fast through the fleet, admiring her clipper lines and lofty spread of canvas set on masts raked aft. They waved and shouted and stood up in the boats to get a better look at her. She was a grand sight, one that inspired the fishermen and made them think of their many fast passages home from the banks. James Steers waved back at the men in their dories, along with the rest of *America*'s crew. He turned to the captain, a gleam in his eye. He stroked his long, gray beard and said to Brown, "The fishing looks good here. I bet the cook could do justice to a freshly caught cod."

Brown shook his head. "We'll not waste a fair wind on any old cod, James." He laughed. At over 200 pounds, Brown enjoyed a good meal as much as James evidently did, judging on how the man cleaned his plate of every morsel at dinner. "But you're right. Fresh cod on the table would be good. If we weren't on the commodore's errand, we might have stopped to try a line or two."

Sailing at such a swift pace, *America* soon passed over the Grand Banks and left the fishermen to their work. The color of the water changed back to a dark shade of gray-blue. The waves steadied out and the schooner's motion became smoother, less jerky. The birds

flocking around the yacht, thinking she might have fish to offer, became discouraged and flew west back to the banks where the pick-
ings were better. The evening closed in and the schooner raced
ahead into the broad Atlantic. The last of the North American continent receded farther away in her wake with every passing minute.

Toward the next morning, June 27, the northwesterly wind gave
out and the boat slowed. The wind shifted to the south and came in
light, allowing her to sail on through the swells but not fast enough
to keep up her usual pace. The south wind also brought in more
foggy weather and deepened the overcast sky to blot out all vestiges
of the sun. Brown counted himself lucky to have gotten at least one
accurate fix of his position the day before. He shaped his course to
slightly north of east, bringing the south wind to come in aft of the
starboard beam at a fine slant for swift sailing even in the light
breeze. Every sail drew fair, the working sails, with bonnets on the
foresail and jib, the topmast staysail, main gaff topsail, and Big Ben.

Although the yacht sailed in the westerly wind belt above a latitude of forty degrees north, the localized winds were always less
predictable. In late June and July, the winds often blew from a
southerly quarter. With each low-pressure system blown off the
North American continent out to sea, the winds progressed in a
counterclockwise movement around the compass, usually ending in
a blustery northwester such as the one *America* had ridden for the
last couple days. The westerlies of the northern latitudes varied
greatly in their direction because of the continental influence. In the
southern latitudes down around Cape Horn and the Cape of Good
Hope, the lack of large landmasses in the southern reaches of the
Southern Hemisphere made for much steadier west winds.

Thus, the captain of any sailing vessel on a transit between
North America and Europe faced a set of challenges different from
those of his counterpart on the southern sailing routes. The Gulf
Stream's influence added to the mix of variables. Its half-knot push
to the east and the dramatic temperature differences between its
flow and the surrounding waters created stormy weather notorious
for its potential violence. Nevertheless, sailing masters preferred to
stay well within its influence on eastbound passages. Riding the cur-

rent added as many as thirty miles made good over the bottom on a single day's sail.

Brown was familiar with the southern and northern westerly wind belts from his many years at sea sailing all over the world. He knew what demands might be made on him, his crew, and the yacht. Even in the early summer the possibility of a strong gale loomed large in the North Atlantic. The break in the northwesterly wind might foretell the calm before the next low-pressure system gathered strength to the west and came roaring out to meet them, as they sailed farther into midocean. He gazed southward at the sea looking for the telltale clues of the larger swells that indicated heavy weather below the horizon. The ocean remained as it had been. There was no sign of a blow. But Brown knew it was only a matter of time before his crew was put to the test. The unstable weather meant a challenge lay ahead. The only question was when it might come.

Brown paid special attention to his usual daily check of the yacht's gear. No weak links in her rig, no line out of place, no lapse of vigilance could he tolerate. The safety of all aboard depended on him and the abilities of all the men to carry out their duties like the professionals they were. He noticed the jib sheet had chafed where it rubbed against the starboard rail on the foredeck. He set some of the men to rigging a buffer of canvas to reduce the wear on the line. It would not do to have the line part in a big wind. Brown kept the men busy working on the schooner, cleaning her decks, and the insides of the cabins, and he pitched in himself when necessary. Hard work and dirty hands were part of his life. He may have been captain, but he was no better or worse a man than the men under his command. It was his intention to work them into a cohesive team, one capable of the smart sailing he knew was needed in the competitions to come. If the men saw him working side by side with them, it helped form an important bond between him and them and among themselves. A well-found boat with a well-practiced crew might meet most anything the ocean sent to test them and any challenge the British might have in store.

The light southerly winds continued for the next two days. The schooner sailed onward at half her typical fast clip, making good an average of only five or six knots. Yet the progress eastward was steady and sure. The sun did not show itself. The fog stayed with them. It thinned occasionally and came in thick again. Brown's sextant remained below decks in its varnished, felt-lined case, useless without a view of the celestial bodies that hid behind the heavy cloud cover and without a view of the horizon obscured in the fog. A rising swell from the south and east began to make itself felt. Little George, like his uncle, complained of seasickness. Although only eight sea days had elapsed since their departure from New York, the Steers family grew unhappy with the wet, miserable conditions aboard the yacht. The jokes came less frequently. They sat in the cockpit as much as possible. Every time they went below, the motion of the vessel made them feel sicker.

Brown was well aware of the rising swell as it continued to build. When the wind shifted from the south to the southeast and kept going counterclockwise around the compass it confirmed that another storm system was on the move. As the wind shifted, he ordered the men to sheet the sails in to maintain the schooner's speed. Soon the yacht sailed close-hauled, as close to the true direction of the wind as she could make. She heeled over from the press of the canvas and drove her bow through the crests. Spray flew aft. Water ran overboard off the deck in steady streams through the openings cut through the bulwarks. A bad sea kicked up on the afternoon of June 29, their second Sunday under sail. The rain drove all but those on watch below. The crew off watch crawled into their berths cold and damp. There was not a bit of dry clothing left in their seabags. James Steers wrote in his journal: "Thick and foggy with rain. I do not think it ever rained harder since Noah floated the ark."

Brown drove the yacht hard through the night. Sailing close-hauled against a heavy sea she did not make fast progress toward their destination, but she held her own. As the night wore on, the men at the tiller found the schooner harder to control. Still more ominous was the foremast. It began to show signs of weakness. The spar worked and flexed and groaned under the force of the wind against the canvas and the violent motion of the vessel. Brown grew anxious. The risk of carrying on with everything set was too great. He might push the yacht to her limits. However, it was up to him to see that he did not exceed them. He did not know just how much she might take before her rigging parted and the masts crashed down. In the predawn darkness, he ordered the men to shorten sail. All hands tumbled to and manned their stations.

"All ready forward!" Comstock cried above the wind.

Brown answered the first mate. "Stand by."

Brown waited a moment, hoping to time the sail work when the wind let up some. He felt the vessel pitch and roll and he listened to the sounds of the wind and sea, looking for clues in the motion of the yacht and the level of the din. When the schooner rode more steadily and the noise dropped off to indicate a lull, he turned the vessel closer to the wind until her sails lost some of their power. The boat heeled much less as she got to her feet and slowed down.

"Ease the jib sheet!" he shouted.

The men slacked off on the sheet, spilling most of the air without letting the sail flog. Others eased off on the halyard that raised and lowered the sail, and the jib dropped low enough for the men to reach the bonnet. Several sailors moved slowly out onto the bowsprit—five, seven, ten, fifteen feet out in front of the boat. The water rushed past close under them with a roar that mingled with the howl of the wind. As the yacht rose on the back of a crest, the bowsprit pointed toward the sky and the men hung on tight, ready for the drop down into the trough sixteen feet below. Their situation was often compared to riding a bucking bronco, and it was just as dangerous. The up-and-down movement repeated with every crest to hit the yacht in a cycle of six waves per minute.

Anxious to get their work done and to return to the relative safety of the foredeck, the sailors reached up with their right hands while holding onto the boat with their left hands. They pulled the twelve-foot-wide bonnet down until they were able to reach the ropes used to fasten it along the forty-three-foot lower edge of the jib. Men on the foredeck worked to untie the inboard end of the bonnet. It was tough, exhausting work. The canvas tore and bloodied their hands and fingers, and bruised their bodies. Spray ran down the insides of their oilskins. The wind swept away their curses and grunts.

Brown stood at the helm and concentrated on making sure not to point the yacht too high, lest she lose all headway and find herself at the mercy of the blow. He noted how hard the sails were to handle in such a big wind and he began to think his crew was a bit shorthanded for the crossing. He put the concern out of his mind as the sailors hoisted the jib up tight and trimmed her true. They repeated the same procedure with the foresail. The bonnets removed, the men moved aft to deal with the mainsail and main gaff topsail.

Away from the bow as it plunged deep in the troughs and bucked high on the crests, the motion was less extreme. The sailors gathered at the mainmast and waited for Brown's signal. Again, the captain waited patiently. A fierce series of gusts ripped through, heeling the yacht way over on her side. She soon recovered her footing and surged on. Confident as he was, in another lull Brown ordered the men to reef the mainsail. He pinched the yacht close to the wind and trimmed the mainsail in tight to keep the massive fifty-eight-foot boom from swinging back and forth and tossing the men overboard. The sailors eased the halyards to partially lower the main gaff. This spilled the air from the mainsail and caused it to shake violently. The men acted fast. They furled up the loose canvas at the base of the sail and tied it securely with the lines sewn into it for that purpose. With less of the mainsail exposed to the wind, it was easier to control.

The men moved on to take in the main gaff topsail, a triangular sail flown above the main gaff. It was an important sail that added power to the mainsail. But in the blow it was too much canvas to have set so high up the mast. As the sailors struggled to strike it, the wind caught the canvas and flogged it back and forth. The twenty-eight-foot main gaff swung wildly in the night, out of control and in danger of tearing the mainsail. Suddenly, the gaff topsail split from end to end in an explosive report the men on deck heard above the howl of the wind and the crash of the waves. The situation got out of hand fast.

CHAPTER TWELVE

PERILOUS MISHAP

Sailing under reduced canvas at close to eight knots, *America* raced through the violent seas that became gradually visible in the gathering light of early morning. More than seventy feet above the deck, the torn gaff topsail flapped and shook. Although it might work loose from its lashings, it was too dangerous to take it down for repairs. Brown knew that task had to wait until the time was right, the ocean in less tumult, and the crew fit and in better spirits.

Shorthanded as they were, the sailors fought the fatigue that sapped their strength and clouded their minds. Slowly, but with certainty, the sea's power was winning a victory over them. The schooner demanded much effort to keep her in proper trim. When the wind blew strongly, the men had to reduce sail as they had during the previous night. When it slacked off, they had to set all the canvas she might carry. A schooner required fewer crewmen to sail than a mighty square-rigged ship. But, at times, fewer hands meant an increased danger of calamity. There was no reserve to call upon in an emergency. Every man's strength and knowledge was needed.

Brown nursed a mug of hot coffee in the cockpit, warming his thick, rough hands on the surface of the glass. He glanced up at the gaff topsail. Had the accident been an inevitable consequence, just one of those things that happened at sea? Or had the mishap been caused by human error that resulted from lack of sleep? The sea presented a wide variety of dangers for the mariner, and physical and mental exhaustion was one of the worst. It crept up on a man to strike him unawares, like an insidious disease that seemed to come from nowhere. Many a ship had driven ashore because her master's thinking became muddy and slow after months of interrupted sleep and the drain of command.

The problem with the foremast continued to nag at Brown, as he sat ruminating on the matter of the yacht, the state of her crew, and the incessant bad weather that taxed even his usual patience. Shortly after the trials against *Maria*, George L. Schuyler published on May 20 in the *Morning Courier and New York Enquirer* a letter in which he stated:

> In our first trial it became evident that the spars of the *America* were too light, and our experiments were brought to an abrupt termination yesterday morning, by the loss of our foremast and main gaff . . . the builders of *America* feel confident that with new spars of the proper dimensions and by some alteration of sails that [she will prove herself].

Steers carried out additional modifications to the yacht after the syndicate purchased her. Where he deemed it necessary, he added heavier spars and reinforced the rigging. Perhaps he had gone too far, favoring spars that were now too heavy. This might pose a danger aboard a vessel rigged with the simplicity of the pilot boat design. Only two shrouds supported each mast from the sides. Her sail plan allowed for only the minimum of stays for support fore and aft. Raked aft at such a sharp angle, much of the strength needed to keep the masts upright came from the wood itself. *The Illustrated London News* described *America*'s masts as "large for the tonnage of the vessel, but not much encumbered with rigging, and she has but few ropes." There was also the additional consideration that her masts were loftier than they would be on a pilot boat of similar size. *America* was meant for racing. She needed to spread as much canvas as possible on masts that were high, so high that they neared the limits of safety. At sea, with the waves breaking and the wind howling, she was a challenge to handle and a potential danger to the men aboard.

The same *Illustrated London News* article that described the yacht's masts reported that "seven men brought her across the Atlantic; but the men themselves say she ought to have had ten men at least." Taking the Steers family, the captain and first mate, as well as the boy serving as the cook's assistant out of the picture, *America* really did have only seven seasoned sailors to work her as she sailed across the Atlantic. That left four or five men to a watch, including the officer on deck. It was no small wonder that the men grew tired as the days passed and Brown called all hands every time the schooner needed sails set or taken in. James pitched in to help, as did his son, Little George. When brother George was able to overcome his seasickness, he helped however he could. But the brunt of the work rested with the sailors and there was no way for Brown to relieve them of the strain. He had to get the schooner across as fast as possible. He could not slack off or dally. He was glad he had selected the best sailors he knew along the waterfront, but he grew concerned about their ability to stand much more of a prolonged thrashing.

George Steers followed Brown's gaze aloft, then stared at the captain. "She'll hold up, Captain," he said. Steers thought of the sprung foremast during the trials, of his miscalculation with the ballast, and many other small things that created trouble. Was it possible his boat, so swift and fleet, was also a danger? He put the gloomy reflections and self-doubt out of his mind as best as he could manage. He bolstered his spirits by telling himself she was a stout little ship overall, built of the finest oak, pine, and other wood, copper-fastened throughout, her frames reinforced with diagonal iron braces, as was the fashion with the large steamers and the California clippers. She might display weaknesses, but he had to have faith in her and in himself.

"She's a bit tall for this kind of work, George," Brown said. "All that weight aloft is stretching the shrouds."

George looked at the captain and returned his gaze skyward.

Comstock chimed in from the helm: "But she's a damned good sea boat just the same."

"Mind your course, Nels," Brown said.

Just as quickly as it had come, the wind dropped away to a light breeze. The seas, however, pounded the boat. She rolled and pitched and lurched. No matter how tightly the sails were trimmed, they slammed and shook. Without much wind to press against the canvas, the boat lost stability. The men wedged themselves in the cockpit or in their berths. The cook and the boy found it almost too difficult to stand in the galley to prepare dinner. Tempers frayed, though everyone tried to make the best of a bad stretch of days that seemed never to end. The Steers brothers, particularly James, began to drink rather heavily and their store of liquor dwindled.

The wind came up again and fell calm and went through the same cycle one more time over the next two days. The Connecticut sailors among the crew cursed the sea and the wind. "The damned wind is up and down more than a new bride's nightgown!" the saltiest of the sailors said more than once. The rest laughed and nodded their heads in agreement.

"The girl's gown, she's up again!" they yelled, as they scrambled on deck for yet another bout with the sails.

Brown continued to eye the foremast with mounting anxiety. The "swashing" about, as James Steers called it, was more taxing on the masts and rigging than a sustained gale with the sails properly reduced and set. Each time the yacht careened off the face of a wave, her masts whipped and tugged against the shrouds and stays. The intermittent loads were slowly working everything loose and, no matter how often the sailors took in the slack, the wear continued. During a calm spell longer than the rest, the seas diminished in size enough for Brown to set the crew to work on the rig and sails. They brought the gaff topsail down, mended the tear, and reset it. To lessen the strain on the foremast, the sailors removed the large jib and replaced it with a small one. When it was hoisted and trimmed, it looked ridiculously tiny, like "a shirt on a bean pole," James Steers wrote.

Brown's caution proved well founded. The wind freshened and

the wild ride across the mid-Atlantic commenced yet again. The yacht roared past a clipper brig and left her astern, even as she sailed close-hauled and climbed the mountainous seas on a wet, tough slog to windward. The clouds tore apart, let the sun shine for a while, and came together once more.

Below in the main cabin George Steers lay prostrate on his berth, unable to move or eat. The seasickness, his worry about the yacht, and his longing for the comforts of home was just too much for him. His brother nursed him, felt sorry for him, and grew tired of the ordeal of the voyage. Even the food, which James looked forward to with characteristic zeal for a man of his voracious appetite, lost its attraction. The situation aboard *America* he described in his journal entry of July 2:

> Brother George sick. I am making him some gruel. Our cook is not a very good caterer. He can boil a piece of beef or pork, or roast a piece of beef or turkey; but the puddings are heavy and the crust of his pies is as tough as a leather apron. He made some wheat fritters and you wanted better teeth than I have to chew them fine enough to digest. But we are here on the tossing waves 1,300 miles from Havre, and if this wind will only last 6 days we will be snug in harbor,—barring any accident.

The journal entry's reference to concern about "any accident" revealed the extent to which those aboard were wondering about their safety. It was more than just a prudent sentiment. Steers's journal entries on the same day remarked: "Had to get the yard out 5 or 6 feet outside the rigging to help support the foremast. There was a heavy head wind and she [the yacht] was making the water flow some."

Brown was worried enough to take preventive action with regard to the foremast. He had changed to a small jib. With less sail set forward, the pressure on the mast and rigging was much diminished. Next, he had figured out a way to add strength to the foremast, using a series of ropes attached to the yard for Big Ben and run down to the deck to provide extra support for the mast. With any luck, the jury-rig might hold, he thought, surveying the handiwork of his men. As time passed, the wind and seas increased, and this time they did not go down. The yacht made good progress, however.

On July 2, for the first sea day since June 26, she made good more than 200 miles in one twenty-four-hour period. The sun even cooperated and showed itself long enough for Brown to accurately fix their position at one 1,160 miles due west of Le Havre, France. The Azores lay about 600 miles to the south.

The head seas rumbled toward the yacht and broke in long stretches more than a quarter-mile along the crest. The noise was frightful down below, as George Steers moaned and perspired in his berth, his brother and nephew at his side. The pitch of the wind howling through the rigging went from a low, haunting whine to an intense scream. All the crewmen remained on deck working the yacht to windward at speeds of ten to eleven knots. By midevening on the night of July 2, the danger of keeping on with all sails set forced Brown to command his men to reduce canvas. The tiny jib he left alone. It was already little more than a scrap. But he told the sailors to take the bonnet off the foresail and single reef the mainsail. They also took in the main gaff topsail. The work done, the main gaff down lower on the mast, the sail's area less expansive, the yacht roared onward. Brown was taking a calculated risk. She was still sailing too fast for complete comfort. Yet, he continued to drive her. Drive her to Le Havre, by God he would. It was a matter of pride and urgency, and a bit of a stab to his ego that his chance to best or equal *Isaac Wright*'s passage seemed lost for good, all because of the cycle of calms.

The light faded into dusk toward nine o'clock. Purple and deep gray streaks laced the clouds to the west. A dull yellow and white light illuminated the waves as twilight deepened into night. To the east the darkness was nearly complete. Brown and another man stood at the helm. He skillfully guided the yacht up and over the waves, turning this way and that to weave between them when the opportunity presented itself. At all costs he avoided slamming directly into the breaking and seething crests. When he miscalculated and took a big one hard on the bow, the schooner staggered under the impact, slowed for a few moments, and recovered to keep flying along toward France. Each time this happened, however, the hull endured a pitiful pounding and the rig whipped above the men's heads. A slight bend was barely perceptible in the boom, the wind blew with such force.

Suddenly, the men looked skyward toward the foremast at the sound of a loud snap and crack. They all stared for a few seconds in disbelief and horror at the sight. The fore shrouds on the right side of the foremast up near the top had separated, leaving the all-important rigging on the weather side of the vessel slack and limp. There was nothing to support the foremast as the wind pressed against the foresail and jib. The foremast bent to leeward. The wood creaked and groaned as the mast started to give way.

"Jesus!" Brown muttered through gritted teeth. He responded to the disaster almost instantly. He carefully, but quickly, turned the boat through the eye of the wind to bring the gale-force winds over onto the left side of the yacht. The tiny jib slammed aback, the wind now on the wrong side of it as the gale blew across the port rail hard on the bow. This was what Brown wanted. The strain was transferred to the port-side shrouds, which were still intact. The foresail also slammed aback. It pulled hard on the sheets and might soon blow to tatters.

Brown ordered Comstock to trim the mainsail in tight. He put the tiller to leeward and lashed it. The yacht's bow fell off the wind about forty-five degrees. The motion steadied out, the noise decreased. She went over the waves without taking much water on the foredeck. *America* rode the gale nearly parked in place in a position sailors call hove to. Without a minute to spare, all hands, including Dick Brown, rushed forward to secure the foremast before it toppled over the side, possibly smashing a hole through the hull or taking the mainmast down with it.

"Douse that foresail! Look lively, boys!" Brown yelled.

The men released the sheets. The sail flogged, creating a wicked thunder of canvas as it shook, filling and emptying in the wind. The sailors released the halyards and eased the fore gaff down. They fought hard to control the sail. Every man grabbed the canvas and bundled it up into a furl. Others took hold of the halyards now freed up with the foresail lowered and ran them to the starboard rail, where they rigged a block and tackle for extra purchase. They heaved on the halyards, which ran through blocks at the top of the mast down to the rail, and snugged them up tight to act as temporary shrouds. In the storm, with the wind and waves running so high, it was difficult to get enough tension on the halyards to keep the foremast from swaying back and forth. Just the sight of it flying loose and unsupported struck fear into them all. But slowly, the men set up the temporary rig. All lines were hove bar tight. The foremast stopped its terrifying dance.

Winded, wet, and utterly tired, the men slumped back to the cockpit. They looked at each other, but no one said anything. They all knew how close they had come to potential disaster. Losing the foremast in a gale might have sunk the boat. If that had happened, there was little chance any of them would have survived the night in the small boat *America* carried as a tender. It was not a lifeboat. Its purpose was to ferry the owners and crew and any supplies back and forth from shore to the boat. The big waves running that night would have made short work of it. Once in the water, the cold would take the men in ten or fifteen minutes, if they did not drown first. The sea took men on a whim.

Brown caught his breath, tried to calm down. He glared up at the foremast and fought the emotions that swept over him. It was always the same at times like this. He thought of his good boyhood friend, Captain Starke, lost aboard *John Minturn* in the blizzard of forty-six, and of the three other companions he had grown up with in Mystic, all of whom had died at sea. He was known among his friends to have been haunted by these deaths. When the warm glow of hard liquor settled over him on a dark, cold winter's night at the fireside—or aboard *Mary Taylor* at sea on a beautiful starlit evening, the air fragrant with the scent of pine blowing off the gentle sloping beaches of Long Island—Brown often said: "There is something strange about the drowning of all my associates in that freak of my boyhood, and that this will be my death, too."

It was a sentiment he could not shake or chase away even with the help of a bottle, or upon hearing the soft, tender reassurances of his wife in bed at night, the two of them snuggled under a layer of warm blankets in their home in Brooklyn, the taste of the sea strong in the air come in off the harbor. The near-miss with the foremast summoned these dark thoughts to the fore. Brown struggled to fight them off, tried not to let them sneak into his consciousness, and he failed. He turned to Comstock and said: "We best get her moving, Nels. We're doing no good hove to."

"Think she'll take the strain?" Comstock asked, aware of his friend's anxiety, and very much cognizant of his own.

"The boys have her trussed up good. We'll last the night through," Brown said, his voice just loud enough to hear above the wind.

"Aye, Captain." Comstock replied. He ordered the sailors to man the sheets of the jib and mainsail. He unlashed the helm and turned the boat's bow off the wind as the men eased the port jib sheet and hauled in on the starboard. Others trimmed the mainsail. *America* gathered way through the waves. When she had sufficient momentum, Comstock turned her bow to bring the wind and waves off the starboard side once more, and the men sheeted the jib and main home. The schooner surged through the water back on her course for France, her bow plunging into the pitch-black of the stormy night.

CHAPTER THIRTEEN

STAYING THE COURSE

The strength of the gale gradually decreased as the night passed and gave way to dawn. But the wind still moaned in the rigging and howled in the gusts. The waves crested out to the horizon. They flashed white and brilliant green near the tops when the sun caught them at just the right angle. The scene was wild and yet oddly beautiful. Streaks of bright blue sky showed through long, jagged rents in the cloud cover and exposed the summits of the whirling gray masses of vapor to shine like the peaks of snowy mountains. The crew manned their stations during the forenoon watch and prepared to heave the yacht to. Brown called out his orders, the men jumped to their duty with a will, and *America* soon rode the waves without making much speed forward through the water. She drifted lazily to leeward, ready for her men to put her right again.

One of the younger crewmen, a man nimble and strong, slowly climbed aloft on the port side of the boat up to the very top of the foremast. He had with him a marlinespike, an iron tool used to work on rigging, extra ropes to renew the seizings of the shrouds, and other tools jammed into the pockets of his oilskins. Although the schooner lay hove to, she rolled enough to make his job hazardous. He wedged himself against the mast and leaned way over to reach the section of the upper shrouds that needed attention.

Looking down made him dizzy. He tried to keep his eyes on his work, his mind off what might happen if he slipped and fell.

Shouts from the crewman aloft carried faintly down to the men on deck, as they worked with him to effect the repairs. The man needed plenty of slack, then he needed tension on the shrouds. Meanwhile, other sailors hove taut the halyards to force the mast over as far to the right as possible. The tension of the repaired shrouds had to match the tension of those on the port side, thus ensuring that the mast did not bend right or left. The spar had to run straight and true up and down its entire length. Otherwise, the sails would not set properly and might cause a potentially significant loss of efficiency in the forward part of the sail plan.

James and his brother, who was feeling somewhat better, watched the sailors at work with awe and admiration. They had never seen such antics, nor witnessed the pure danger of the sailor's job to such an extent. The lone crewman perched precariously at the top of the mast more than sixty feet off the deck, the yacht all the while trying to shake him off. It was frightening. "She [the yacht] shook him so I could hardly think he could hold on," James wrote later that day, "but he fixed [the shrouds] and came down. We made sail and were all right again."

Brown tested the tension on the shrouds and sighted up the length of the mast to see that it ran true with no bends. He smiled and told the sailor he had done well. While the man was up the mast he had inspected the rest of the upper rigging and reported no additional problems. No signs of chafe or wear, cracked fittings, or weakness in the masthead were visible. Greatly relieved, Brown patted the foremast with his right hand. He gazed at the seas as the schooner tore through the water and wondered how much more time might elapse before they made landfall at the west end of the English Channel. Let the wind hold. . . . It was a wish everyone aboard shared. Let it hold and Le Havre might heave into view in less than six days.

The crew worked on the yacht throughout the day as she sailed on with all her main working sails set. They cleaned, painted, and otherwise set everything in order. They inventoried the stores

needed for the overhaul at Le Havre, and made what advance preparations were possible at sea. They may have been tired, but they
worked hard just the same. The previous days had accomplished
much, despite the high level of frustration and some exciting moments. The crew had become a cohesive team. Each man knew his
shipmate's strengths and weaknesses, where he might best serve
the boat and in what capacity. Some showed a talent for setting the
sails to perfect shape, others a deft hand at the helm. Still others
were better aloft than on deck or were known for their brawn at the
lines. Most important of all, however, was their keen sense of the
boat and how to sail her at maximum speed in varied weather and
sea states. They were in good spirits, all circumstances considered.
When the fog rolled in again, they complained little about the cold
and damp. They were on their way to France, with the yacht sailing
well and fast, a prodigious wave at the bow, a long, straight wake
astern.

As the wind dropped and the seas subsided, the crew set the gaff
topsail. The big topmast staysail went up next. The schooner responded each time with more speed to make up for the decrease in
wind velocity. She averaged eight to ten knots into the morning of
July 4, a very special day for all the men aboard.

"There will be no hard work today!" Brown announced to the
men at the start of the forenoon watch at eight o'clock in the morning.

Brown's words brought cheers from the sailors. They found
comfortable places on the deck in the lee of the companionway
house, the skylight coamings, the capstan. They smoked and talked
about home and what great celebrations were scheduled throughout
the land for the seventy-fifth anniversary of the birth of the United
States. The fog cleared away as the sun climbed high. For the first
time in days the south breeze carried warmth enough for the men to
take off their oilskins and bring their damp, mildewed clothes out
on deck to dry. The wind continued to slack off, but given the festive
feelings of the yacht's company, the slower pace did not much mar
the mood.

At dinnertime, the crew gathered and ate their ration of the cook's usual fare—roasted beef, chicken or turkey, an apple pie or pudding. They beamed at the captain, lifted their glasses of gin poured from the bottle he had given them, and toasted him, the yacht, George Steers, the United States, and President Millard Fillmore. Their toasts roamed into the realm of the bawdy and brash, and the irreverent as well. James Steers took delight in it all. "You would laugh to hear the toasts at the dinner," he wrote, adding that the wind dropped off almost completely in the midafternoon, that the sea became as still as a "mill pond."

America drifted, at peace in her element. She was so nearly at rest she might well have been secured safely in a berth on the East River, a very rare event at sea in midocean when there was almost always a swell come in from a far distant weather system. Her sails hung limp, but they did not slap and bang. There was no "swashing" about. The celebratory drinking continued. The men enjoyed their day of rest and relaxation, content to let the schooner see to herself in the calm.

More than 2,000 miles away in New York, fireworks were prepared for the coming evening. Although it was Friday, the rich and poor of the city stopped their work and enjoyed themselves at picnics, parties, and balls. Apart from all of the celebrations, however, the press of business kept up its typical high profile. Readers of *The New York Herald* opened their morning editions to find headlines quite fitting of the boom times at hand. Word from the steamship *Prometheus,* which arrived in the harbor the previous day after a fast trip from the Chagres River in Panama via San Juan de Nicaragua, indicated that nearly $3 million of gold dust from the diggings in California were on the way to New York, the nation's economic capital.

> We learn by this arrival, that the large sum of nearly three millions of dollars worth of gold dust is en route to New York. This is, indeed, surprising intelligence, when we take into consideration the vast quantity of gold which has been received from the same quarter since the commencement of the present year. There is very little doubt now, we think, that the gold de-

posits of the celebrated region [California] are literally inex-
haustible, and that the amount that they will yield will here-
after be proportionate to the number of persons engaged in
searching for it . . . The yield this year will not fall far short of
sixty millions of dollars; and we would not be at all surprised
if, within the twelve months coming, it should amount to one
hundred millions.

In Washington, D.C., the residents of the sleepy little capital received an inrush of their neighbors from the countryside, and small
towns and hamlets, to hear the famous Senator Daniel Webster
speak. He boomed out a speech for a large crowd anxious to take
part in the glory of the United States and all of its accomplishments.
Even though it was still a young nation and much disparaged by the
countries of Europe, most particularly by the British, who regarded
it as crude, simple, and arrogant, it was to Americans a shining example to the world. The level of nationalistic pride swelled with
every new advance, every new piece of territory added to the country's holdings, and every step forward in the amassing of a huge surplus of wealth and prosperity for an increasing number of the
people.

The opening lines of Webster's speech drew great applause and
cheers from the throng gathered to hear him. He said:

Fellow citizens:—I congratulate you—I give you joy on the return of this anniversary, and felicitate you also on the more
particular purpose of which this ever memorable day has been
chosen to witness the fulfillment. Hail!—All hail! I see before
and around me a mass of faces, all glowing with cheerfulness
and patriotic pride. I see thousands of eyes turned towards
other eyes, all sparkling with gratification and delight. This is
the New World, this is America, and this is Washington, the
capital of the United States. And where else among the nations, can the seat of government be surrounded, on any day of
any year, by those who have more reasons to rejoice the bless-
ings which they enjoy? This is the anniversary of American In-

dependence. This bright and brilliant morning witnesses another return of a nation, and that nation, of however recent origin, now among the most considerable and powerful, spreading over the continent from sea to sea. . . .

By July 4, news of *America*'s possible skirmish with the British was raising interest among members of the elite in Britain and France. People took notice of the short articles that appeared in the press, noting that some New Yorkers were sending a yacht over to have a go at the best Britain had to offer. There were many jokes about it. Individuals of all classes, but especially the members of the Royal Yacht Squadron, thought the idea crazy that a Yank schooner might actually challenge the well-established and moneyed yachting gentlemen of England to test their boats in a trial of speed. Britain reigned supreme in all matters maritime. Surely these Yanks understood that. The American ambassador to France agreed with those who considered the actions of John Cox Stevens and his cohorts as overly confident and downright dangerous to national pride in the event of a defeat.

While Captain Brown sailed *America* across the Atlantic Ocean, John Cox Stevens, his brother Edwin, and Colonel James Alexander Hamilton, along with his wife, basked in their own glory in Paris. Due to illnesses and prior business commitments, none of the other syndicate members could come to see how *America* might fare in races against the British, assuming a race was actually held. The Stevens brothers and Hamilton were to act as their representatives, both of the syndicate and the New York Yacht Club, and in the larger context, the United States of America. They had arrived in France on June 28, after a routine and dull passage from New York to Le Havre aboard the steamship *Humboldt*. They saw the sights and dined well. They sampled the wines of the country and bought cases of it to take to England with them to "entertain our guests in the most sumptuous manner," Hamilton wrote many years later in his autobiography, *Reminiscences of James A. Hamilton*.

While in Paris during the interval between the syndicate's arrival in France and the arrival of yacht *America* at Le Havre, Hamilton discovered that sentiments among his fellow Americans ran strongly against engaging in any kind of race between their new schooner and the yachts of Great Britain. Among those concerned was the American ambassador to France, Mr. William C. Rives. Hamilton recalled the encounter in his book:

> Such was the want of confidence of our countrymen in our success, that I was earnestly urged by Mr. William C. Rives, the American Minister, and Mr. Sears, of Boston, not to take the vessel over, as we were sure to be defeated. My friend, Mr. H. Greeley [publisher of the *New York Tribune*], who had been at the Exhibition in London, meeting me in Paris, was most urgent against our going. He went so far as to say: "The eyes of the world are on you; you will be beaten, and the country will be abused, as it has been in connection with the Exhibition." I replied, "We are in for it, and must go." He replied, "Well, if you do go, and are beaten, you had better not return to your country." This awakened me to the deep and extended interest our enterprise had excited, and the responsibility we had assumed. It did not, however, induce us to hesitate. I remembered that our packet-ships had outrun theirs, and why should not this schooner, built upon the best model?

Hamilton's dislike and mistrust of the British was legendary. He regarded them with every bit as much civilly disguised contempt as they, in his view, regarded his beloved American nation. He, like John Cox, wanted nothing better than to send the Brits a message loud and clear that the Yanks now ruled the seas and were well on their way to becoming a dominant global power. Had the United States not already surpassed Cunard's plodding steamships with the grand and glorious liners of Edward Knight Collins? Had not the New York packets consistently sailed faster than those of Liverpool? Had not the new, revolutionary clipper ships set records from Canton to San Francisco, and proven so fast that British merchants chartered them to bring tea to the great island nation that seemed so proud of herself, so smug in her own security concerning the vast superiority she maintained that she possessed in all matters of the world? Indeed, the United States had done just that.

Yet, despite the bombast and nationalistic pride the syndicate knew well that the British were very good seamen, that their yachts were nothing to poke fun at. The simple matter was the British might well best their schooner in a match. The risk of further humiliation at the hands of the British, already extreme in connection with the Great Exhibition, was real. It took faith to proceed with the venture. This was especially the case as the Stevens brothers and Colonel Hamilton vamped about Paris. These men had only seen yacht *America* fail at the trials. True, she had put up a good fight, but *Maria* clearly was faster. The British might field a boat against the schooner that was designed expressly for racing, one that might be incapable of crossing an ocean like *Maria*, but was well able to sail circles around the heavy, full-keel yacht George Steers had built for them. None of the men knew just how fast she really sailed. They had never seen her overtake a full-rigged ship with all canvas spread to a fair wind and still leave the bigger vessel astern of the yacht in the space of hours. John Cox and company put their anxiety aside as best as they could. They had a fine yacht, a seasoned skipper in Captain Brown, and the advantage of what they did know for a fact, that there was nothing like the design of *America* in England. The Brits, they hoped, would be in for quite a surprise.

The calm that settled over *America* on July 4 continued through the weekend, and on Monday as well. It seemed never to end. A low, undulating swell came in to make life aboard the yacht miserable for the men. George Steers was once again confined to his berth as *America* rolled about. Her sails slapped "enough to tear them to pieces," James Steers wrote. July 5 was "dead calm." The schooner's only progress through the water came in fitful, feeble puffs of wind, and from the weak eastward push of the last power of the Gulf Stream, known in their stretch of the ocean as the North Atlantic Current. It was really not much of a current at all. However, it helped move the schooner thirty-three miles along her course on Saturday.

Hoping to cheer his brother up, James helped George into the cockpit. The young man had difficulty standing. His face was ashen, his eyes sunk deep into his head. But he was game for the fresh air and for what his brother had in store.

His brother James insisted he have a shower bath.

The crew kept a respectful distance, aware of the designer's terrible physical state. They did not mock or jeer him, as they might another landlubber in a similar condition. They all saw George as part of their team, the man whose keen mind and skill in the shipyard had led to the creation of the schooner. Brown, who was ten years George's senior, regarded him with paternalistic affection. Seasickness was a severe handicap when becalmed in a swell. Brown understood that and was compassionate for George.

James threw a bucket overboard to fill it with cold sea water, which he dumped over George's head, eliciting an immediate cry of shock and a weak smile from his brother. James repeated the process. The stench of vomit emanating from George disappeared.

"That'll get your blood moving!" James shouted, and laughed. George shouted and laughed, too, and really did feel a little better. He felt even more so with a change of clothes.

James Steers, along with the rest of the yacht's company, grew increasingly frustrated as the calm progressed day after day. He wrote on July 6, with the boat less than 1,000 miles due west of Le Havre:

> This calm is very much against us. We had hopes of making the passage in 14 days, and would have done it, let the wind come from any point as long as it blew a breeze; but here we are tumbling about and not making any headway and what little breeze we had right ahead. . . . If George was not so homesick we would enjoy ourselves much better. I drink to those I love and respect. Amen.

Brown, the first mate, and the carpenter joined James Steers in a drink to reduce the tension. He ordered some of the ice brought up from the icebox, crushed it small enough to fit in a tall glass, and

poured generous servings of port over it. They finished off the bottle. The drinks flowed rather freely during the calm. But Brown kept
discipline, in his loose, soft-spoken way. The men did not sit idle.
He set them to coppering the forward rails to help reduce chafe on
the jib sheets, and James, with nothing better to do, lent a hand.
Other sailors sewed a canvas cover for the capstan, spliced and
rigged ropes for the gangway, and went over the rig to search for any
weak points that showed wear. The sails of other vessels appeared
on the horizon. The ships stayed in view for many hours, as if to
drive home the fact that these windless days belonged to the
steamships, not the sailers.

At last, late in the afternoon on July 7, the first signs of a north
wind riffled across the smooth sea. The men cheered as the patches
of dark water swept toward the schooner, surrounded her, and filled
in off the port beam, spreading away toward the south at a good clip.
The sailors jumped to the sails and trimmed them to catch the
breeze. *America* suddenly came to life as she gathered way. The welcome sounds of water gurgling past, the hum of the rigging, the flutter of canvas were sweet to hear. The gentle cant of the deck as the
schooner heeled to the right, her massive mainsail, foresail, and the
diminutive jib bellied to the wind was at once familiar and alien after four days of calm. The wind freshened and came in from the
northwest to blow off the left side of the yacht's stern, a fine slant
for fast sailing. Whitecaps began to appear, just a few at first, but
more as the time passed.

"We'll set old Broad Mouth!" Brown cried, his voice full of exu-
berance.

James Steers grinned at the captain. The skipper had taken to
calling the big square-sail Broad Mouth, instead of Big Ben. It
seemed a better name for the sail, Steers thought. Up went Broad
Mouth, the staysail, and the gaff topsail. The schooner picked up
speed. He wrote in his journal after the calm:

> At 5 P.M. she [the yacht] commenced stepping along pretty
> lively, which I tell you was very gratifying to all on board, after
> four days rolling about and not wind enough to keep her

steady. . . . We have 3 vessels in sight. One is a large ship with everything set, and she can go. We passed them like leaving a dock. . . . All hands well and in good spirits. [Except] our liquor is all but gone.

The next day James Steers raided John Cox's store of liquor, liberating four bottles of rum, which he expected might last him and, to a lesser extent, his brother, for three or four days until the yacht reached Le Havre. He justified the theft easily enough. He wrote in his journal that he needed the rum to help soothe George's "belly ache" and that he would be damned if he was to "starve in a Market Place."

Brown did nothing to stop him, as he would have had one of the crew done the same thing. The Steerses were guests of the syndicate. George had built them one of the finest schooners Brown had ever sailed. The young man had endured the extreme discomfort of the voyage solely to help experiment with the sails, to gauge the yacht's performance in a wide variety of conditions, and to make suggestions for any recommended modifications to the vessel in France before meeting the British yachts off the Isle of Wight. He was not getting paid for his efforts. He offered them out of an appreciation for the importance of any potential race that might materialize, and out of a personal desire to see his creation outsail the British. He also saw the potential value a victory might mean to his career.

George's brother had a gluttonous appetite, and a bit too much fondness for drinking. But that was the man's business, not Brown's. Neither James nor George were under his command or answerable to him, except in matters of emergency aboard the schooner, where the captain always had the final say. Brown thought little of the incident, but he was to find out later that his perception of his place on the yacht, and that of George Steers and his brother, was altogether different from the view of John Cox Stevens.

Richard Brown, captain of yacht America, *is pictured here in a rare photograph made from a newspaper sketch. Captain Richard Brown was one of the most famous harbor pilots in New York in 1851. He was master of* Mary Taylor, *the fastest schooner in the pilot boat fleet.*

Brown's skill at sailing and navigation made him an ideal captain for yacht America, *the schooner that brought off the greatest sporting victory of the century.*

When a ship approached New York Harbor, the pilot took command. New York Harbor pilots stood apart from common sailors. Pilots in training spent nine years learning the location of channels, shoals, and navigation aids—until they were able to draw a detailed chart of the harbor from memory. In addition, they studied navigation and honed their seamanship. A pilot's wages exceeded $1,500 per year, about twice that of a typical middle class worker in the 1850s. This photograph shows a pilot in his usual working clothes.

In February 1846 a terrible blizzard caught many of the pilot boats at sea, including Blossom, with pilot Thomas Freeborne aboard. Despite his best efforts, the ship drove aground on the New Jersey coast. She was stranded for two days before sinking in the surf. Freeborne gave his coat to the captain's wife and his sweater to a child. He froze to death as a result. This painting shows a hero's funeral procession of pilot boats that sailed the day Freeborne was buried in Greenwood Cemetery in Brooklyn. Captain Brown was in this procession.

This engraving shows a pilot boat on the left hove to in a blizzard at sea. Her mainsail is reefed, and her jib is aback, set to help keep the boat positioned in place. The square-rigged ship is also hove to, waiting for the rowboat to reach her. The pilot schooner shown here provides a good view of what America looked like as she faced adversity on her transatlantic voyage.

This engraving shows a group of pilots signaling a ship during a snowstorm. The crew of each pilot boat pooled their earnings, which were paid to them by the owners of the ships they guided into port. The pilot boats often raced each other to be the first to reach an inbound ship. This fostered a high level of skill at racing among the pilots, and Captain Brown was the best schooner sailor of them all.

George Steers, designer of yacht America, was only thirty-one when he became one of the best-known yacht designers in the United States. Instead of designing hulls with broad, rounded bows and sharp sterns, Steers did the opposite. Many traditionalists thought he was wrong to build boats this way, but the speed of two of his vessels, Mary Taylor and America, proved he was right.

John Cox Stevens, commodore of the New York Yacht Club, was a member of New York's leisure class, and spent much of his time engaging in sporting activities ranging from horse racing to yachting. In 1844, he and a group of other yachting enthusiasts founded the New York Yacht Club, the first successful yacht club in the United States.

In the autumn of 1850, John Cox and five of his friends determined to challenge the best of the British yachting fleet to a race the following summer. With that in mind, the members approached a prominent American shipbuilder whose key designer was George Steers.

George L. Schuyler was chosen by the New York Yacht Club to negotiate with the shipbuilding company. In the contract, he stipulated that the vessel must outsail every boat brought against her in the United States and in England before the syndicate would pay the staggering sum of $30,000.

Naval architects of George Steers's day typically carved what was known as a half model. The half model showed the shape of the hull, which could then be recreated to scale in the shipyard.

Steers carved the half model in the photograph above as a gift for Queen Victoria after the famous race around the Isle of Wight. Notice the knifelike bow and that the depth of the keel becomes greater aft toward the stern.

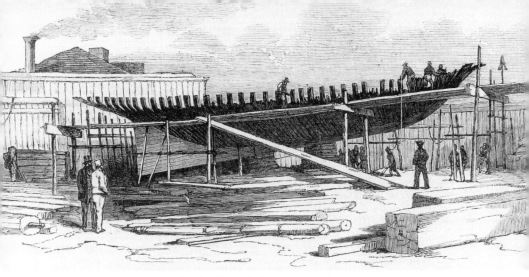

The winter of 1850–51 was harsh. Blizzards delayed the work on the schooner, causing Steers to miss the April 1 deadline. Schuyler extended the agreement, but he added conditions that put Steers at a further financial disadvantage. This woodcut shows America in the shipyard.

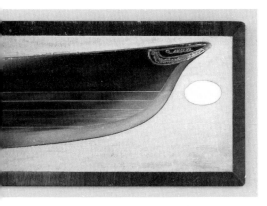

After missing his April 1 deadline for completing America, Steers redoubled his efforts to finish the work by May 1. He missed that deadline as well, but not by much. America was launched on May 3, 1851. This woodcut shows America fully rigged and ready for the trials of speed to test her sailing capabilities.

The sloop Maria *was considered the fastest racing boat in the United States. She was America's rival during the trials. Much was riding on the outcome. If* America *lost, the syndicate did not have to pay the agreed-upon price. So, when the trials went badly for* America, *Steers was forced to cut a deal. This illustration shows* Maria *in the foreground, beating* America.

America *set sail for Europe under Captain Brown's command on June 21, 1851. When she arrived in England she outsailed all the British yachts she met in informal races, causing the British to initially avoid a formal match. Outraged that their own countrymen refused to race against* America, *the British press compared their own yachtsmen to cowardly "wood pigeons."* America *is pictured here off the Isle of Wight.*

Weighing more than eight pounds and standing twenty-seven inches high, the America's Cup is an example of the decorative trophies handed out to winners of yacht races in Great Britain in the mid-nineteenth century. But this particular bauble made a lasting mark on maritime history.

(left): *The Great Exhibition was housed in an innovative glass building at Hyde Park in London. More than six million people came to see the thousands of displays from dozens of countries. The British press lampooned the American displays which included revolvers, Bowie knives, wheat threshers, and other utilitarian items.*

When New Yorkers sent a schooner across the ocean to challenge the best British yachts, it was seen as an additional threat to the national pride of the United States. America *had became the joke of the world in connection with its displays at the exhibition. Most people believed the schooner would be defeated.*

This illustration shows the opening of the Great Exhibition at the Crystal Palace in May, 1851.

This painting shows America *off the Isle of Wight in the English Channel during the great race of August 22, 1851. Notice the flying jib set on the long jibboom in the front of the boat. Captain Brown objected when the owners insisted on adding this sail to America's sail plan. Brown felt the extra canvas so far forward might put the boat out of her best sailing trim—and he was right. However, the jibboom broke during the race, eliminating the problem.*

This painting is based on a sketch drawn during the race. America *has just rounded The Needles, a headland at the west end of the Isle of Wight. A light wind blows from behind the boat. Not long after this sketch was made,* America *glided to victory off West Cowes to the cheers of thousands of spectators.*

CHAPTER FOURTEEN

WELCOME LANDFALL

After the long cycle of calms interspersed with fresh breezes and gales, fog and rain, the North Atlantic treated the men aboard yacht *America* to a spell of fine, fast sailing. The schooner raced ahead at the heels of the northwester. Her speed never fell below ten knots, and she often sailed along at twelve knots or more. In two days she made good more than 500 miles. With every possible sail set, the yacht rapidly closed with the continental shelf off Europe and the outer islands perched upon it. The sky cleared of clouds. The sun shone brightly. The crew worked in their cotton shirts and reveled in the excitement that struck deep into the heart of every mariner about to make a landfall at the end of a long, tiresome passage.

Brown's observations with his sextant on July 9 put the yacht at just 180 miles southwest of Cape Clear, off the southern extremity of Ireland. The cape marked the approaches to St. George's Channel and the point of departure for ships westbound across the North Atlantic. It was a busy sea lane that led to the Irish Sea and the British ports of Bristol and Liverpool. The waterway was a vast funnel for the shipping bound to and from the United States and other nations of the world. At the time, Liverpool was the busiest harbor on the planet, outdoing even New York in the tonnage and value of cargoes that came and went. On any given day, hundreds of sailing vessels and dozens of steamships crowded the docks built along the Mersey River.

About 220 miles dead off the schooner's bow lay the Isles of Scilly. These islands marked a crossroads. Ships inbound from the North Atlantic for the British ports of Falmouth, Southampton, Portsmouth, and others cut close to the Isles of Scilly and cruised up the English Channel. Those headed for Bristol or Liverpool turned northward toward St. George's Channel. The sheer number of ships traveling these waters created an ever-present chance of collisions. The waters around the Isles of Scilly, a group of more than one hundred islets, most of them mere protrusions of barren rock, churned with fierce tidal races and held an abundance of dangerous reefs and ledges hidden beneath the surface of the waves. Seamen the world over called the Isles of Scilly the graveyard of the North Atlantic and regarded any landfall in the area as a time for both celebration and extreme caution.

Brown consulted his chart and noted with slight uneasiness that the yacht sailed nearly straight toward Great Sole Bank, a place at the edge of the continental shelf that abruptly rose from depths more than a mile deep to just thirty-nine feet deep in certain spots. Even on a relatively calm day the breakers in that section of the sea at the outermost approaches to the English Channel inspired awe and fear in their fury. Brown adjusted his course to leave the bank a safe distance to port.

Toward late afternoon, with Great Sole Bank astern, *America* passed from the deep sea to the lip of Europe. The water changed color, taking on a greenish-blue hue that indicated that land was near. The waves grew shorter and steeper. The influence of inshore tides became apparent. On the ebb, when the tide rushed out to sea from the English Channel, the outgoing flow met the last of the incoming North Atlantic Current and kicked up a chop the men had not experienced since leaving the Grand Banks of Newfoundland. The warm flow of water from the far-off Sargasso Sea tempered the cold of these northern latitudes. The average temperature on the Isles of Scilly during the early summer was sixty degrees, allowing the islanders to grow produce for London markets many more days per year than their counterparts on the farms farther north, which had a much shorter growing season. The warm waters made the entire coast of Europe temperate, providing comfort for the people from Norway to France. As on the Grand Banks of Newfoundland, the great currents of the ocean off England mingled to create an ideal habitat for sea life. Seabirds filled the sky. Fishing boats dotted the horizon, and merchant vessels hove into view and disappeared with clocklike regularity.

The sun set astern in a brilliant display of reds, oranges, and purples cast against the thickening clouds over the ocean to the west. The wind piped up and the waves built higher. The yacht plunged onward, faster and faster, until Brown ordered Broad Mouth taken in. The men jumped to the task, their energy renewed, the excitement palpable as they worked. In just a few minutes, the sailors had the sail safely furled. *America* slowed a little and became easier to steer. The first of a series of hard squalls blew through. The sea boiled with breakers and flying spray as the crew double-reefed the mainsail, took in the gaff topsail, and removed the bonnet on the foresail. Brown drove on as hard as he dared. Although he was confident that the problems with the foremast were behind him, he did not wish to press his luck too far.

Through the morning of July 10, Brown pushed the men to their limits. He was bent on taking advantage of every decrease in wind velocity to set more sail. The crew shook out the reefs in the mainsail, exposing its full breadth to the wind. The schooner roared ahead heeled hard over on the port tack. But that was not enough for Brown.

"Lay to there!" he cried, his enthusiasm spreading to every member of the crew. "Set Broad Mouth!"

The men complied. The yacht sailed even faster. Another squall ripped across the water and howled in the rigging. "Take that square-sail in! Set the gaff topsail!"

The crew was becoming exhausted. But they worked with a will. Every maneuver and every sail change was executed well and without mishap. "Three square-rigged ships ahead of us," James Steers wrote. "They have got everything set they can carry, but we are picking them up very fast. The sight is very exciting."

As the morning progressed, the yacht closed the gap between the sea and the land. Brown shaped his course for Bishop Rock, the outpost of the Isles of Scilly and the southernmost band of reefs. The craggy rock cliffs of the larger islands loomed above the gray horizon. At first, the man at the masthead thought he was seeing yet another of the thousands of cloud banks he had observed over his life at sea. But his practiced eye soon discovered the true nature of what he saw—land, the first he had seen since leaving the purple hills of the Highlands of Navesink astern shortly before the fog rolled in after their departure from New York Harbor.

"Land ho!" he cried. "Land ho! Broad off the port bow!"

The sailors, and the Steers family, all raced to the left side of the yacht's foredeck and peered ahead over the heaving seas. There it was indeed. England! Le Havre lay only one day away as long as the wind held fair. Brown carefully guided *America* closer to the Isles of Scilly, the wind still strong, the waves still high. He was anxious to pick up a pilot to take the yacht safely through the unfamiliar waters of the English Channel to Le Havre. He knew well the importance of local knowledge, and he knew equally well that the channel was no place to fool around. Making a landfall on the French coast was a dangerous proposition in poor visibility, and thick weather was likely. The prevailing westerly winds made France a lee shore, which meant that the wind forced sailing vessels toward the coast and might drive them onto the rocks if the captains were unwary.

The heavy shipping traffic in the vicinity of the Isles of Scilly kept the British pilots quite as busy as those that served New York Harbor. The imperative of engaging a pilot was also as equally acute. According to W. S. Lindsay, writing about the pilots: "Seven separate [offshore] stations are allotted to the boats on the look-out for inward-bound vessels, which must be strictly kept, so that it is hardly possible, even in the thickest or most stormy weather, for any ship approaching the banks to miss a pilot-boat, if the captain adopts the most ordinary precautions."

Brown was intent on taking the "most ordinary precautions" as he ran the schooner in to hail one of the pilot boats he knew sailed in the area. When he was close enough to the islands, and yet still a safe distance off to account for any unpredictable currents or wind shifts that might catch him unaware, Brown called to Comstock: "Stand by to heave to!"

The crew manned their stations, ready for the maneuver. With the northwest wind blowing off the left side of the stern, Brown slowly turned the yacht to the left and gradually brought the wind forward of the beam. Little by little, with the men trimming the sails while the schooner turned, the wind and waves traveled at an angle up the left side of the vessel. The wind came abeam to blow broadside off the rail, then at a sharper angle until she sailed close-hauled.

"Ready forward?" Brown shouted to Comstock.

"All ready forward, aye!"

Brown turned *America* to bring the bow through the eye of the wind to back the jib. Right as he did so, the wind gusted strong. The jib slammed aback against the starboard side of the rig. The men working the mainsail were caught off-guard. The gaff and boom swung over before they could trim the sail in tight enough to slow the momentum of the heavy spars. Aloft there was a loud crack as the collarlike fitting that kept the main gaff attached to the mast parted. Only the halyards kept the spar aloft. It sagged and banged against the mast.

"Let go the jib sheets!" Brown called and immediately headed the yacht up into the wind, relying on the schooner's forward momentum through the water to power her. The sails flogged and shook with a thunderous roar. The schooner lost way and began to pay off. Her bow pointed out to sea. As she slid to leeward, she pitched and rolled without her canvas drawing full to keep her steady.

"Get the mainsail in! Lively, now. Look lively!"

The sailors worked fast and took in the sail before it tore to pieces. Brown frowned at the crewmen on the main sheet. But he said nothing to rebuff them. The sea was unpredictable. The gust came on fast, catching him off-guard as well. He shared the blame for the minor mishap. He set the men to repairing the parrel, the rope slide attached to the gaff. Soon *America* was again under full sail, hove to and waiting for a pilot.

A small, single-masted vessel, known as a sloop, sailed near *America*. Aboard were several men lined up along the rails, waving and hailing them.

"Ahoy, schooner! Do you need a pilot?" the captain of the pilot boat shouted across the waves, his voice amplified with the speaking trumpet he grasped in his right hand.

Brown answered that they did. The sloop hove to a short distance away from the schooner. The crew aboard *America* watched as a tiny rowboat, a punt, was put over the side of the sloop. The men in it rowed skillfully through the crests to the side of the yacht. *America*'s sailors helped the man up over the low rail of the foredeck. The pilot strode aft to meet Brown.

"Good afternoon," the pilot said, his eyes darting about the schooner, taking in her bright, clean decks, the neat set of her sails, the shining varnish finish and white paint. "You have sailed far."

"We're eighteen sea days out of New York bound for Le Havre," Brown said. He noticed the men in the punt remained close to the schooner.

The pilot looked impressed. However, he got right to business. "Well, I can get you to the harbor, but then you'll need a local pilot to guide you in."

After a quick bout of dickering, the matter of the pilot's fee was settled.

"Have you a bottle of spirits aboard for the boat?" the pilot asked, nodding to the men in the punt.

"No, sir. We don't," Brown said.

"Well, then. Have you any pork?"

Brown looked hard at the man. Such questions were never asked of captains the men of *Mary Taylor* met while sailing the eastern chance. But he told the cook's assistant to hurry below for some pork for the pilots. Were these men hungry? The pilot's appearance struck him as odd as the man's questions. His clothes were soiled and worn, his beard unkempt, his hair matted. He did not look the part of a gentleman, not at all like the Sandy Hook Pilots. James Steers described him as "dirty as a chimney sweep." The cook's assistant gave the pilot some pork. He smiled.

"Could you spare some tea or coffee?" the pilot asked.

Brown grew angry. "We'll fill away now, Nels," he said to Comstock.

Seeing the crew preparing to get the schooner under way, the pilot frantically waved the punt over. He dropped the bundle of pork into the boat as the yacht's sails filled and she rapidly gathered way. The pilot boat dropped astern and was soon out of sight. *America* cut through the waves at eleven knots, bringing Start Point on England's southern coast abeam by early evening. James Steers chatted with the pilot as he watched the course. He revealed that begging padded the small income the pilot boats brought in for their crews.

"Every boat we see we try to speak and ask for spare provisions," he said. "Why, just last Wednesday we supplied a ship with two hundred pounds of beef and pork, and some other things. The captain paid us three pounds for it. A nice haul, that."

The pilot complimented Brown on the way the schooner sailed so quickly along without "making much fuss."

"Twelve knots, I'd say," Brown said, a twinkle in his eye.

"Can't be twelve knots, Captain. Not so smooth."

Brown offered to let the man heave the log himself. The pilot accepted, and was empirically corrected.

The strong northwesterly wind held fair through the night. By noon the next day, July 11, *America* was just eighty-five miles from the entrance to Le Havre at the mouth of the Seine River. Brown drove hard with all sail set in hope of reaching the port at high tide, which would occur in the early evening. The tidal range of the Seine estuary topped out at more than twenty feet. The approach to the docks and canals of the inner harbor was made very difficult, due to the strong tidal currents that flowed in and out of the river. The pilot told Brown about the famous mascaret, a tidal bore, a natural phenomena Brown knew about from the fishermen of the Bay of Fundy, where the tidal range ran to forty feet and created incredible whirls and eddies and the well-known wave of the bore.

When the sea swept in on the flood tide to the shores of Fundy's Petitcodiac River, it seemed to come in all at once. A wave washed over the mud and stones bare at low water. It came quickly enough to drown the unwary caught out on the flats. The mascaret behaved in much the same way. Hence, the harbor of Le Havre was built with canals to keep the water in and the ships afloat out of the current. The first work on the harbor began in 1517 shortly after the fishery of the Grand Banks of Newfoundland became a major source of commerce for France. Francis I saw the merit of the location as a depot for the fishing fleet. He ordered his subjects to build a harbor of refuge. From there the cargoes brought from the New World were transported seventy-five miles up the Seine River to Rouen. Small craft moved the cargoes still further inland upriver to the city of Paris. The French were hard at work on the port in Brown's day to improve its facilities for the ships that were always increasing in size. It was one of the most important harbors in France, a clearinghouse for Paris, and a major jumping-off point for émigrés bound for the United States.

Because of the tides, Brown felt it wise, indeed, a necessity, to go in at high water before the tide turned and the outgoing ebb began. But no matter how hard he drove the schooner, she still had too many miles to sail to arrive in time for the slack at the top of the flood. At eight-thirty in the evening, with the ebb tide already beginning to flow out the English Channel, *America* tacked back and forth off the approaches to Le Havre.

"We'll stay hove to for the night, Nels." Brown said. "We'll have a fair tide in the forenoon watch to get us snug to the quay."

Comstock set the men to work and soon the yacht rode peacefully. She was at rest after a passage of close to 3,200 miles in nineteen sea days. The boat and the men who sailed her had done well even with the adverse weather and the spate of calms. *America*'s crossing was four days faster than the average sailing time of the eastbound New York packets.

Comstock gazed toward the land rising from the sea off the starboard beam. The pleasant aroma of grass and trees filled the air, scented with a faint hint of the salt and the earthy pungency of the flats that became exposed as the tide continued to ebb. The twilight faded into night and the captain ordered the running lights lit to ensure the schooner was seen in the event other vessels came near. The lights of ships traveling up and down the channel sparkled in the blackness. Ashore, the loom of Le Havre lit up the sky with a dull yellow glow that warmed the hearts of all the tired men aboard *America*. They had come from the isolation and indifference of the sea back to the bustle and vigor of civilization. Their work was just about to begin.

CHAPTER FIFTEEN

RACING TRIM

The early morning sun shone brightly down on the city of Le Havre on Wednesday, July 16, as the cool of the predawn hours gave way to the heat of the day. Captain Brown and his men sat idle on the deck of the schooner under the shade of an old sail suspended from the fore gaff, lost in their thoughts and in the sounds of the city that reached them on the breeze lazily stirring the makeshift awning. The sailors took advantage of the last of their brief time to rest before they began the hard work of putting the yacht into shape for her adventures across the English Channel. There was little to talk about. They had already laid out their plans, each man knowing his tasks for the overhaul.

The summer of 1851 in Europe was unusually hot. The London correspondent for *The New York Herald* wrote in one of his late June dispatches: "It is now just such summer weather as you have in New York; the heat is just as oppressive. The country looks charming, like a garden, the crops of all kinds are promising, the farmer looks forward to a rich harvest, the laborer is contented, for bread and beer are cheap." After the long days at sea in the cold and damp, the heat might have seemed a welcome change. But, for the sailors, the rising temperature meant the work was going to be harder. They were not yet readjusted to shoreside life, its vast differences from that of an existence measured in watches on and off duty while the schooner surged forward on the cresting waves.

When the tide was right, Brown told the crew it was time to move the boat over to the government dry dock reserved for their use at the arrangement of John Cox Stevens. The commodore came down to the schooner as soon as word of her arrival reached him and the other men of the syndicate in Paris. He congratulated Brown on a fast passage, and he made it clear that the yacht was to look as fine as any that sailed in New York. The Steers family had gone up to Paris to see the sights, but Brown expected them to return later in the day. George suggested several minor modifications to the hull, which John Cox approved. George's presence was needed in the afternoon to see that the modifications were done to his specifications.

With the assistance of a steam tug, the yacht was towed into the wide maw of the dry dock. She was made fast with lines run on both sides of the vessel to the bollards that protruded from the stone top of the bay. As the tide went out, the yacht dropped lower and lower, like a barge in a lock on the Erie Canal. Her rail, at first above the quay, sank below it. The crew slacked off on the lines just enough to keep her secure with the proper tension in the center of the rectangular enclosure. As she settled down on the aft section of her keel, the men jammed wooden blocks under the bow. She was much shallower forward than she was aft. The blocks kept her level when she sat high and dry. She was also propped up with timbers to keep her balanced from side to side, upright and stable. The tide rushed and whirled away with surprising rapidity. In a couple of hours, the water receded completely. The gates of the dry dock were swung closed to lock out the flood tide when it once again swept into the harbor.

The men swarmed over the yacht. They broke out paint cans and buckets, brushes and rags, scrapers and sanders, planes and mauls. The most junior of the sailors got the dirty work. Standing ankle-deep in muck, they scraped the thin layer of slime off the copper sheathing below the waterline and burnished it to feel as smooth as glass. A clean hull was an important ingredient for speed; the least bit of growth slowed the boat down. Other men scraped and sanded the topsides to prepare them for painting a jet-black with a gold stripe along the top as well as the gold carvings on either side of the bow.

George Steers arrived with his brother and Little George, the three of them relaxed and cheerful. Each was happy to have put an end to the passage across the North Atlantic and each vowed never to repeat it in such a small craft. They all looked forward to their planned trip to London. Once there they would collect James's other son, fifteen-year-old Henry. He had come over on a steamer to meet them and share in the wonders of the Great Exhibition, along with other members of the English side of the Steers clan, who had made Henry their guest until his father arrived in the city.

"Ahoy, Dick!" George called, as he stepped down on the ladder built into the wall of the dry dock.

"Afternoon, George!" Brown called back, looking up from the stern. He and Comstock were painting the eagle that decorated the transom. It was a large golden bird with a nine-foot wingspan perched atop a shield endowed with the Stars and Stripes, and a profusion of carved green flowers. White banners carved to look like folds created the base for the eagle.

"I see I am just in time," George said.

George and his brother changed into work clothes below and climbed down into the muck with the rest of the men polishing the copper. They brought an assortment of tools with them. George started work on the bow. He thought the schooner might sail faster if he made her even sharper forward than she already was. He removed a small portion of her forefoot, the point at which the stem joined the keel. He felt this might reduce drag and increase speed. Next, George moved aft to the rudder. He carefully planed its trailing edge to reduce its width, hoping that this might also help the water flow more easily as the yacht cut along under full sail.

The day ended with the work well in progress, but still far from finished. The gaffs, main boom, mastheads, and bulwarks needed new coats of white paint. The hull was not yet brought to a lustrous black shine. The sails used for the crossing had to be taken off and the racing sails put on. The yard for Broad Mouth had to be sent down, since it was not used for racing. The fancy furniture, pictures, bedding, china, silverware, crystal, and numerous other items required unstowing and putting into their proper place. Cases of French wine waited for loading, and there was the reprovisioning to look after, including the acquisition of a huge quantity of ice for the galley icebox to keep the food fresh. In all, Brown expected the chores to take close to a week, possibly more before *America* would be ready to receive her owners.

Having completed the modifications to the yacht, the Steerses wished Brown and the crew well and left for London by way of Southampton. They crossed the channel on July 17 aboard a steamship and got their first look at the Isle of Wight. It was a beautiful, diamond-shaped island, green in the verdance of summer. It stretched out at its greatest length from west to east, approximately twenty-three miles, and twelve miles from north to south. From afar, the high white and dun-colored cliffs topped with a carpet of low vegetation caught the eye. Some of the bluffs rose abruptly from the sea to reach heights of 500 feet. Other sections of the craggy southern coastline fronting the English Channel dipped down to create a pleasantly irregular profile. The steamer rounded the Nab Lightship five miles off the east end of the island at Bembridge Point and turned into Spithead Channel. As she passed Nomansland buoy, the mainland of southern England presented an expansive view, with the gun batteries protecting the outer reaches of Portsmouth harbor abeam and the approaches to Southampton westward off the starboard bow.

The Steerses stood at the rail of the ship and took in the panoramic vista that slowly unfolded before them. Dozens of yachts and fishing smacks rode peacefully at their moorings off the Isle of Wight. Their masts created a thicketlike appearance off Ryde and still farther west at Cowes, home to the Royal Yacht Squadron. Beyond Cowes was another narrow slot of water known as The Solent. Spithead and The Solent were protected from the big seas of the English Channel and provided an ideal habitat for pleasure craft of all sizes. The north side of the Isle of Wight was indeed a haven for yachting enthusiasts, but it was also a resort for all classes of people during the summer months, including Queen Victoria and Prince Albert, who owned Osborne House. The residence was one of their favored retreats.

But no matter how popular the Isle of Wight may have been as a vacation spot in most years, the vast majority of pleasure-seekers streamed to London for the Great Exhibition in the summer of 1851. The Steers family joined them. After taking a train from Southampton up to Waterloo Station in London, they reunited with Henry and went to see the Crystal Palace with its varied array of displays covering all manner of human creation from the whimsical and sublime, to the practical and functional. The tens of thousands of people mopped their brows and sweated under their many layers of clothing. They drank copious amounts of ginger beer for sale at the concession stands. The authorities in charge of the exhibition tried all kinds of ways to increase the ventilation in the Crystal Palace, but without much success. Nothing alleviated the heat. Gallons of perfumes were opened and strategically positioned to exude a pleasant odor that would conceal the less pleasing scent of the crowds. The Steerses merged with the other spectators and gawked at the locomotives, four-in-hand carriages, jewels of all kinds, including the Koh-i-noor diamond, sculptures, paintings, fine china, gold and silver plates, bowls, and other silver- and goldsmith works.

The London correspondent for *The New York Herald* sent numerous dispatches back to New York to re-create what it was like to visit the Great Exhibition and to see all the sights, so many in fact that visitors came back day after day to view displays that they had missed.

> The Crystal Palace is thronged by the curiosity-seeing multitude, and keeps up its receipts to between 2,000 and 3,000 [pounds] daily. I devoted the other morning to the investigation of the Russian compartment. The massive doors of malachite the vivid green of which is tastefully relieved by a line of gold here and there—the handsome clocks and elegant vases, of the same material—are magnificent; a coronet of diamonds and opals, worth 5,000 [pounds], and other jewels, are great

attractions to the female portion of the visitors. . . . I shall not enumerate the numerous banquets, concerts, fetes, and other festivities, that have taken place, or are to take place, here. London—the black smoky city—has donned a gala dress, and is making merry in honor of its foreign guests.

Each of the dozens of countries exhibiting their examples of art, science, and technology were allotted their own space in the Crystal Palace. The United States occupied a large area at the east end of the building, but compared to all of the glitter of the contributions from other nations, the Americans appeared backward, simple, and inadequate. The British magazine *Punch* remarked: "But what was our astonishment on arriving there [the United States exhibits] to find that their contribution to the world's industry consists as yet of a few wine glasses, a square or two of soap, and a pair of saltcellars."

The United States was the laughingstock of the exhibition. American displays included a long, evil-looking Bowie knife, a grain thresher, a plow, a device for mass-producing metal screws, and a safety pin, among other items. Although there were some examples of art, the number of paintings by American artists, sculptures, fine silver, and gold works was small. The Americans, true to their nature, brought to England the practical inventions and bits of technology that helped improve the lot of the people through commerce and innovation. The offerings had little to do with the luxury of the rich and privileged, and were therefore not appreciated.

The minstrel show held every hour with the performers all in blackface was popular, however. It reinforced the rather slapstick image people had of Brother Jonathan, as the United States was called. An individual American was called a Yank, which in polite British company of the day was meant as an insult. One most decidedly did not aspire to possess the characteristics of a Yank. Anything but that. It was a sad fate indeed to be an American, at least from the viewpoint of many snobs of the British elite.

The bad press stung national pride in the United States. But the editorial writers back home found humor in the situation just the same. The sardonic wit of James Gordon Bennett, publisher and editor of *The New York Herald,* was evident in his editorials, in which he conveyed his contempt for the American commissioners at the Great Exhibition:

> All accounts agree in representing the Crystal Palace as decidedly successful—as a happy discovery—a capital hit—an excellent thing—a first-rate speculation. It pays. Prince Albert has, then, proved himself something more than a mere nobody—something more than the husband of her Majesty and the father of the royal family—something more than the poor German cousin of Victoria, pensioned upon the tax-paying people of England. As the inventor, the projector, and chief director of the Crystal Palace, H. R. M. the Prince may congratulate himself and his royal consort. He has done something for himself, something for John Bull [England], and not a little for the attractive Paris and Parisians over the channel. It appears that the Crystal Palace, after having paid all expenses, yields a daily revenue of some three thousand pounds sterling, more or less, or from twelve to fifteen thousand dollars [per day].
>
> Now, as every little helps, why not keep this exhibition in active operation, to aid in the liquidation of the national debt. . . . Besides, we wish the Exhibition prolonged, in order that the "vast unoccupied area given up to the United States," may be filled up, if possible, with Yankee notions—not with baby jumpers, patent churns, straw cutters, and such like specimens of the fine arts, but with such handicraft articles as would be calculated to leave a better impression of the skill, taste, and genius of this great country. We would suggest another thing to the American commissioners of this World's Exposition: Barnum has in his museum, in this city, a collection of owls, mice, cats, rats, hawks, small birds, monkeys, foxes, hedgehogs, snapping turtles, a dog, and a bear, and what-not, all in one cage, living harmoniously together, and happily denominated "the happy family." The commissioners should apply to Barnum to make this cage his contribution to the Crystal Palace, in order to show to the wiseacres of Hyde

Park, and *Punch* and the *Times,* that "some things can be done as well as others."

As John Cox Stevens, his brother, and Colonel Hamilton had discovered in Paris, the Steers brothers discovered in London that much more than victory in a mere race rested on the outcome of a match between *America* and the British yachts. The stakes were much higher than for a chance to grab a cup or silver plate or to win a wager. The schooner took on the role of savior of United States' national pride, a last-minute entry into the fray surrounding the New World's lackluster performance at the Great Exhibition. It was not without a heightened degree of anxiety that the Steers family left London to find lodgings at Cowes, where they planned to rejoin the yacht once Brown brought her over with the owners aboard. The schooner was fast, sailed like the wind, as her captain often said. But was she fast enough to beat the incredible odds against her? She was but one. The British were many, and sailing on their home waters they enjoyed every advantage over this Yank schooner come across an entire ocean to test her mettle in a trial of speed.

Unknown to any of the Americans involved with the schooner, word was already trickling in on the waterfront in England concerning *America*. The British pilot who had guided her to Le Havre lifted his pints of ale in the pubs and told his story of how well the yacht sailed. He described her as a "wonder" and the story spread fast from pub to pub until the press got wind of it. The members of the Royal Yacht Squadron began to wonder if they had been wise to invite these New Yorkers for a visit. The press had already reported that the schooner was in England expressly to race, and the members of the yacht club were by no means sure that a match against a far superior vessel would be in their best interests. The situation, it seemed, might be getting out of hand, and this before the schooner had even dropped anchor off West Cowes.

Back in France, Dick Brown and his men put the last touches on the yacht. She was ready for sea on Monday, July 28, and was prepared to meet whatever challenges might come her way. John Cox Stevens and his brother, Edwin, came aboard and settled in. Their presence changed the prior informal atmosphere Brown allowed on the yacht to one more formal and in keeping with the protocol when an owner was within earshot. Owners were something to be tolerated; crews never liked having them around, however. Colonel Hamilton and his wife, who did not relish crossing the channel in the boat, booked passage on the steamship *Humboldt* for Wednesday afternoon. In the meantime, Brown got *America* under way in a light breeze that hardly moved her along through the water. As she sailed out of Le Havre on Tuesday with the start of an ebb tide to help her on her way, people gathered on the quay to wish her and her crew good luck and Godspeed.

Word reached England of the yacht's departure Tuesday afternoon from passengers aboard the Havre steamer, which provided regular service between France and England. As *America* sailed and drifted in calms and fog, working her way slowly toward the Isle of Wight, people interested in the schooner gathered in Cowes to be among the first to get a glimpse of her. Among the spectators was a reporter from *Bell's Life in London,* a publication dedicated to sportsmen. He was on hand when *America* came in to Spithead east of Cowes on Thursday, July 31. He wrote:

> This morning about six o'clock, a suspicious looking craft was observed working down with light winds, owing to which, and the flood tide, she shortly afterwards brought up [dropped anchor] in mid-channel, abreast Osborne. . . . Throughout the forenoon a perfect calm prevailed. At noon the ebb tide made to the westward, and a light westerly breeze also sprang up. The *Lavrock* cutter [a yacht from the Royal Yacht Squadron] got under way to meet the *America,* which shortly after followed her example.

No sooner had he arrived in England than Dick Brown faced his first challenge. The British fired the opening salvo. *Lavrock* was not out to guide him to the anchorage off the yacht club, though that may have been a secondary motivation. Her skipper was bent on an informal match. He wanted to see just how fast this Yank schooner really was, how she might do against his new cutter, which he expected to sail rings around her in the light, fickle breeze. Brown watched as the cutter, a single-masted vessel similar to *Maria*, glided toward the schooner, making good time despite the foul tide starting to run strongly against her.

"It's a poor match, this," he said to John Cox. "*America*'s not at her best in light airs, not fully loaded. We'll not have as much control with the tide running with us."

John Cox frowned, knowing his captain was right. "We'll not raise anchor then. We'll wait her out until the breeze freshens."

Lavrock closed on the yacht, her large mainsail let way out to catch the mounting westerly. Ripples darkened the water and the wavelets slapped against *America*'s bow. The crew aboard the schooner stood at their stations ready to raise the sails at Brown's command, while others waited anxiously at the windlass to heave up the anchor. Brown studied the cutter. She was a fine boat. Her bow cut through the water with little resistance. Even towing her tender astern did not seem to slow her down much. *Lavrock* drew in close and sailed gracefully by. Her crew headed her up into the wind and sailed back toward *America* to pass below her stern with the west wind abeam, every sail drawing fair.

"Ahoy, *America*! Welcome to Cowes!" *Lavrock*'s skipper called.

John Cox touched his hand to his cap. "Thank you, Captain."

"We'll show you the way up!" *Lavrock*'s skipper said.

Lavrock sailed smartly around *America*. She luffed her sails when she was off the schooner's bow and lay to with the tide pushing her away from the Americans, waiting for them to act.

"They're playing with us, sir," Brown said to John Cox.

"Do you think we have wind enough yet to try them?"

"Aye, we've a chance." Brown replied, as he continued to study his rival. *America* was larger than the cutter, but the cutter was lighter. According to the rules of the Royal Yacht Squadron's racing handicaps, allowances made for differences in rig and size of vessels, among other things, *Lavrock* was a good match for a schooner of *America*'s dimensions. *Lavrock* filled away and sailed around the schooner again. Brown let *Lavrock* sail ahead, then ordered the men

into action. He had a plan he hoped might work. If he could only get
to windward of the cutter and keep the clear air undisturbed by the
other vessel's canvas, they might stand a chance of outsailing her.

Much later, when John Cox was back in New York, he recalled
the emotions aboard *America* as they weighed anchor and set sail
with "heavy hearts," thinking their first brush with the British
might end in defeat.

> During the first five minutes [after getting under way] not a
> sound was heard, save, perhaps, the beating of our anxious
> hearts or the slight ripple of the water upon our sword-like
> stem. The captain was crouched down upon the floor of the
> cockpit, his seemingly unconscious hand upon the tiller, with
> his stern, unaltering gaze upon the vessel ahead. The men
> were motionless as statues, with their eager eyes fastened
> upon the *Lavrock* with a fixedness and intensity that seemed al-
> most unnatural.

The crew trimmed the sails to catch the wind off the port bow
and moved to the weather rail aft of the mainmast. They crouched
low to reduce the resistance caused when the breeze struck any object, be it a man or a deckhouse. George Steers emphasized the need
for clean decks free of structures. Reduced windage was one of his
key reasons for building the schooner to sail low in the water and
with few protrusions above the rails. The yacht gathered way as
Brown sailed her to windward of *Lavrock*. Slowly the schooner
gained on the cutter.

"Ready about!" Brown shouted, his voice strong, settled, and
confident.

The crew scurried to their stations at the sheets. When all was
ready, Brown shouted, "Helm's alee!"

Brown eased the yacht's bow smoothly through the eye of the
wind as his men let the jib back to push the bow through the turn,
then eased the starboard sheet and hauled in the port as the wind
came over the right side of the bow. The jib filled as the foresail and
mainsail swung over and caught the breeze. *Lavrock* tacked to block

America. The tacking duel continued as the yachts made their way steadily toward Cowes. The men aboard *America* remained silent, but their spirits soared. Their schooner glided ahead of *Lavrock*. Brown smiled broadly and glanced over at John Cox. The commodore and his brother looked relieved, and perhaps a little smug.

"Stand by the anchor! Rig for starboard side," Brown called as he gauged the speed of the current, which was with them, against the velocity of the wind. All the moored boats rode with their bows to the tide, which indicated the ebb was stronger than the wind in terms of its influence on how the yacht would act once the sails were lowered. Brown surveyed the crowded anchorage, chose his spot, and approached the position where he intended to anchor with the wind abeam off the left side of the boat, the bow pointed toward Southampton.

"Ease the main and foresail. Luff the jib!" he called. His men complied. As they let out on the sheets, bringing the sails over on the right side of the boat far enough to make them shake and lose power, the yacht slowed down and began to move sideways with the tide. Brown let the tide move her down to the place he had chosen.

"Let fly main and foresail!"

The crew eased the sails all the way out, until they no longer drew. The yacht slowed to a stop.

"Drop anchor!"

The men at the bow released the anchor. It plunged with a loud splash into the water and the chain rattled as it passed over the iron-reinforced hawshole.

"Drop sails!" Brown said, grinning as the tide slowly pushed the schooner's stern toward the westerly wind as Comstock and the sailors skillfully and quickly lowered the sails. Within minutes, *America* rode with her bow facing the current, her sails on deck, her position well clear of the many other yachts moored nearby. She eased back on her anchor, setting it deep in the mud off Cowes Castle. The towns of East and West Cowes lay before them, separated by the Medina River. They had arrived in England at last.

"Well done, Captain," John Cox said. "Well done indeed."

CHAPTER SIXTEEN

RELUCTANT RIVALS

Dick Brown strode forward to *America*'s bow to ensure that the anchor was set with enough chain out to compensate for the twelve- to fourteen-foot tides. The bight of land at West Cowes afforded modest shelter, but the anchorage was exposed to the north, east, and west. Everywhere there were plenty of rocks and sandbars that might harm the yacht if she dragged anchor and drove aground, and Brown wished to avoid such a mishap. "How much chain have you let run?" Brown asked Comstock.

"We've got out a scope of five to one," Comstock replied, meaning there was five feet of chain out for every foot of water—more than ample during the tame weather of the summer season.

"She's swinging a bit," Brown muttered. The breeze blowing from astern tried to push her round to head her bow into the wind, while the opposing current kept her facing east. There was a battle of sorts going on between the wind and tide.

Brown looked southward at the buildings on shore and took a visual bearing on some prominent landmarks. He stood off by himself away from the rest of the crew as he surveyed the boat's position relative to the structures he had chosen to watch, making sure there was no major change outside of the normal swinging to and fro of the boat on her anchor chain while the ebb tide increased its influence. He heard the water rippling and swirling against the bow, almost as if the schooner moved slowly forward. He was well aware of how different conditions were from those he was used to in New York, where the tide seldom ran fast, with the exception of the East River and a few other places near Sandy Hook. All seemed well. He gazed eastward at Queen Victoria's two yachts anchored nearby. The 1,600-ton, 225-foot steam yacht *Victoria and Albert* dwarfed most of the other vessels in the anchorage, as she did the much smaller royal yacht, *Fairy*.

Satisfied that all was secure forward, Brown passed word to the crew to furl the sails. He had kept the sails ready in case the yacht's anchor was not set properly. But they were not needed now, nor was he sure when they would be again. The men went to work putting *America* shipshape. They furled the sails and coiled the lines, hanging them neatly on the belaying pins. The sailors steered clear of the owners and spoke only when necessary, as protocol dictated. About twenty minutes after dropping anchor, several boats put off from the beach and headed in *America*'s direction.

"Ahoy, *America*!" a man called from the longboat closest to the schooner. He waved to John Cox and Edwin as the boat came alongside.

"Good day, gentlemen," John Cox replied from the cockpit. The slight breeze ruffled his wavy gray hair.

Comstock deployed the boarding ladder and the guests clambered aboard. The man who had called out introduced himself as the Earl of Wilton, commodore of the Royal Yacht Squadron. He was a dapper-looking fellow in his early fifties, athletic in build and ruddy in complexion. The earl was an avid yachtsman, the proud owner of *Xarifa*, a large and fast topsail schooner. Like many of the English noblemen, Wilton was fond of horse racing and was particularly so of steeplechases. He presented his wife, who was stunning, according to James Steers when he described her in his journal, and his four children.

One of the other guests was an elderly gentleman with a wooden leg, which had been lost to a cannon shot at the battle of Waterloo. At age eighty-three, the Marquis of Anglesey was one of the oldest members of the Royal Yacht Squadron. In fact, he helped establish it. The early roots of the club dated back to 1815, when a group of noblemen formed a loose organization of yachting enthusiasts known simply as the Yacht Club. It later became the Royal Yacht Squadron, which had been in its site at West Cowes since 1825. The Marquis of Anglesey had come down from his home in Cowes Castle just to see the American yacht and to take her measure. Like Wilton, he was one of the better sailors in the club. He peered around with keen interest. The schooner's design looked nothing like that of British boats. It seemed as if her lines were reversed, that her rounded stern should be the bow, her sharp bow the stern. "If she is right, then we are wrong," he mumbled, thinking with wry humor that if it were true that the bow should be sharp, then he had been sailing his cutter, *Pearl*, backward for almost forty years.

"I see you have met some of our members," Wilton said. He smiled and nodded toward *Lavrock* riding to her anchor, her crew looking over at them.

"Indeed, your lordship," John Cox said. "We appreciated the escort up the channel."

Wilton laughed. "An escort. Well, I suppose one might call it that. I trust you had a good passage across, Captain," Wilton said to Brown, who was standing a discreet distance away from the owners.

"Yes, your lordship. She held her own."

"Good. Jolly good. The Atlantic can be a rough place for a yacht."

Other pleasantries were exchanged, ending with an invitation for the commodore and his brother to come ashore to meet more of Wilton's friends, and to reunite with Colonel Hamilton waiting for them ashore at the hotel. The owners left and the sailors settled in with a more relaxed state of mind. Brown gave some of the men leave to go ashore. The Steers family came out to the boat. They talked with Brown about the encounter with *Lavrock*. They witnessed the skirmish from the beach after trying to signal Brown before *America* got under way, hoping to come out and sail into the anchorage with their friend and the rest of the crew.

"Do you think she's got more speed?" George asked earnestly, referring to the modifications to *America*'s hull.

"Can't be sure," Brown said. "Maybe a little."

"You did well against that cutter," James said. "From shore it was a pretty picture."

"Too early to tell how she's going to do," Brown said softly, his eyes darting uneasily to the boats in the roadstead. "They've got nice craft. Some of them are bound to give us trouble."

The men fell silent. They listened to the wind, the ripple of the water, the sound of song birds on shore. The scent of farms reached them, mixed with the smells of the sea, and combined to create an unsettling atmosphere. They were in a strange land.

John Cox and company spent little time aboard the yacht in the next couple of days. The members of the Royal Yacht Squadron wined and dined them, made them feel right at home. These New Yorkers from some of the wealthiest families in the United States were of a class of men that the British elite found easy to accept. They put out of their minds the unpleasant fact that the fathers of the Stevens brothers and James Alexander Hamilton played a part in winning the Revolutionary War, and that Hamilton himself had fought against them only three decades earlier in the War of 1812. Rather, the British noblemen identified with the New Yorkers' sense of their position, their high-minded views about the importance of the best and the brightest in any society, and the need for the "lower order" to keep the mills, mines, and farms turning out profits to boost the prosperity of the land. They shared a love of sports, sports of all kinds. The New Yorkers fit in quite well in all ways, at least on the surface. However, in spite of the shared wealth and lifestyles of luxury, the men of the syndicate differed much from the aristocracy of England.

An underlying tension quickly worked its way to the fore after the first rounds of meetings and festivities. The British danced around any mention of a yacht race with the alacrity of a ballerina. John Cox was too polite to broach the subject at the dinners and balls. But he soon grew impatient and decided to act. On August 2, he sat in his stateroom aboard *America* and composed a letter to the

Earl of Wilton that he hoped might move the matter of a challenge race ahead. His observation of the swift characteristics of *Lavrock* led him to confine his challenge to the schooners of the Royal Yacht Squadron, and any others from clubs throughout the country. He, like the British, knew full well that the cutter or sloop was the faster rig. *Maria* had proven that all too boldly off Sandy Hook when he sailed her against *America* during the trials. John Cox was not interested in a repeat performance of the failure and mishaps that had occurred in May.

Commodore Stevens presents his respects to Lord Wilton, and begs to present for his consideration the enclosed proposition. Yacht *America*, August 2, 1851.

The New York Yacht Club, in order to test the relative merits of the different models of the schooners of the old and the new world, propose through Commodore Stevens, to the Royal Yacht Squadron, to run the yacht *America* against any number of schooners belonging to any of the Yacht Squadrons of the Kingdom, to be selected by the Commodore of the Royal Yacht Squadron, the course to be over some part of the English Channel outside the Isle of Wight, with at least a six-knot breeze. This trial of speed to be made at an early day to be selected by the Commodore of the Royal Yacht Squadron. And if on that day there shall not be at least a six-knot breeze, then, on the first day thereafter that such a breeze shall blow.

On behalf of the New York Yacht Club,
John Cox Stevens, Commodore

John Cox had the challenge delivered to the Earl of Wilton. He instructed George Steers to keep watch for an answer and to send word immediately when one arrived. In the meantime, the commodore, his brother, and the Hamiltons departed for London to see the Great Exhibition. The yacht lay idle and the crew grew listless. Boats crammed with people came out to see the schooner and ask questions. Reporters showed up. The Steerses enjoyed the activity. In a sense, George, as the yacht's designer, was something of a celebrity. He told the correspondent from *Bell's Life in London* that any challenge must take place outside in the English Channel "to test the qualities of the hull, and not the skill of the pilot."

The issue of a pilot's skill in the waters around the Isle of Wight became more salient as the days passed. Brown's forays ashore provided information about the unpredictable nature of the tides, the numerous treacherous shoals, and the fickle winds that came down off the cliffs to blow in weak puffs or roar in near gale-force blasts. The news made him increasingly uneasy. The boatmen of Cowes delighted in inflaming his anxiety as they drank with Brown and his first mate in the village pubs. Hoisting their pints, Brown laughed along with his new British friends at the funnier jokes about the contributions of the United States to the Great Exhibition. They were, after all, amusing and preposterous next to those of European nations. But deep in his bones he believed his country depended on him to show that Americans were to be taken more seriously.

Brown spoke to John Cox about the need for local knowledge on these unfamiliar waters, and admitted that he needed help if he was to ensure that the schooner did well in any match that might arise. The commodore agreed and sent word to the American consul at Southampton to search for and hire a British pilot whom they might trust not to fix the odds against *America* out of loyalty to his own people. He wanted an honest, capable seaman to stand at Brown's side as he sailed the schooner. That man was Robert Underwood, a pilot of great distinction. Brown took to the man immediately. He was a large, big-boned fellow with a substantial paunch and an even more substantial taste for ale. Good-humored and talented, Underwood came aboard the yacht as one of the crew. Brown and he spent hours together in the cockpit comparing notes and hatching schemes to give the yacht every advantage against the home team.

There was also the issue of the crew. Brown made it clear to John Cox that the boat was shorthanded. More men were needed to sail her at top speed on a potentially rough racecourse. The men had handled the tacking duel with *Lavrock*. But over a long race, the exertion required to work the sails might exhaust the sailors. Again, John Cox agreed. Several men from the schooner *Surprise* volunteered to come aboard *America* and learn the ropes of the American yacht. Like Underwood, these were good sailors ready to give their best to ensure the New Yorkers were able to meet any challenges that might come. With the expanded number of crewmen now living on the boat, there was no room for George and James Steers. The Steers brothers kept their lodgings ashore in the hotel, but as Henry was keen about sleeping aboard, and Brown was able to make space for him, the boy returned to the schooner every night. Henry came off in the tender every morning to pick up his father and uncle, along with Little George, for the day's work.

John Cox returned from London after a short interval of less than a week. When he learned his challenge was not yet answered he became very displeased. His brother and Colonel Hamilton also expressed their consternation. They had spent $20,000 to build the schooner and had paid her men to sail her across the Atlantic, all based on the supposition that a race would come off. Facing the prospect that they were wrong inspired emotions bordering on quiet rage.

Hamilton wrote: "As we had been invited by them [the Royal Yacht Squadron], we believed they were bound to make us [an offer to race]." Hamilton cited the incident with *Lavrock* as a probable reason why the British were reluctant to engage in a trial of speed. "The *Lavrock* being a cutter, although of less tonnage than the *America*, was ranked by the Club as a match for a schooner not larger than the *America*. She [*Lavrock*] having been so much beaten in so short a distance, induced an estimate of the *America*'s sailing qualities, which much impaired the confidence of the Club in the superiority of their yachts."

The dark moods of the owners of *America* rubbed off on the rest of the men as they all waited for something, anything to push the events they so longed for and had worked so hard to make happen actually come true. They knew their schooner was fast, but she was as yet unproved. There was every possibility she might be beaten. All they wanted was a chance to try her against the best schooners in Great Britain and Ireland.

Some days later, after events began to unfold with rapidity, the

London Examiner published an editorial that shed some light on the reluctance of the Royal Yacht Squadron to take up the challenge of the New York Yacht Club:

The truth is, they [boats of the Royal Yacht Squadron] are built for the inside of the Isle of Wight, and for owners who take to yachting for fashion's sake, knowing nothing about the matter, having no real taste for the sea, subject to sickness, and confining their trips to Hurst Castle to the west, Ryde and Portsmouth to the east, and preferring the Southampton water if a weather-tide raises a popple on the gentle Solent. The great pleasure of these gentlemen is to swagger about in sea-toggery, and to have boats'-crews in smart equipment dangling after them. Many a yacht hardly stirs from its moorings at Cowes in a whole season, but to make up for that inaction, there is plenty of boat-work, rowing backwards and forwards, hailing and signalling. There are exceptions; there are some score of the two hundred members of the Royal Yacht Squadron who are good seamen, ay, and competent navigators to boot; but the great majority are unskilled.

The other Clubs contain a much larger proportion of sea-men among their members, because with them it is not a matter of fashion so much as it is with the aristocratic Squadron. Some years ago a member of the Thames Club undertook to man his yacht (between 60 and 70 tuns) with gentlemen, members of the Club, exclusively, not employing a single working-man, and to sail her against any vessel of the Squadron, manned in like manner. But the challenge fell to the ground. And well it might, for though there are some few members of the Royal Yacht Squadron who know whether a gaff-topsail is properly set or not, we have our doubts whether there is one who could go aloft and lace it to the topmast.

Dick Brown observed the tensions on board, and tried his best to absent himself from the friction. If there was to be a race, he meant to fulfill his duty to the best of his ability. He had given his word to

John Cox Stevens, and he did not intend to break it for any reason. That simply went against every fiber of his character. However, he found himself growing concerned for his friend, George Steers, and to a lesser extent, James. The brothers were invested in the boat, wanted her to succeed, and had done all they could to make her the fastest schooner ever built. Yet, John Cox paid them no mind. He treated them with the same indifference he showed to the rest of the crew, whom he saw as part of the boat's outfit, human equipment put in place to secure what seemed now a lost bid to outdo the British.

The Steers brothers continued to drink heavily, particularly James. Every day he stole two bottles of rum or other liquor from John Cox's ample supply, and took the bottles back to the hotel, where he and George consumed most of the contents. Both brothers felt the commodore and the rest of the "aristocracy," as they called the gentlemen who came aboard, owed them thanks, or at least the courtesy of treating them like the guests they were. They felt themselves as equals, but they were not treated as such. The Steers brothers complained about their treatment to Brown, who listened but kept his opinions to himself. His view of any man was his business and his alone, though he began to wonder what he had gotten himself into. The politics and class distinctions simmering on the boat were new to him. It was unlike the straightforward interaction he was accustomed to in working with his men aboard *Mary Taylor*. He longed for the end of his time in England, and a return to the simple and rewarding work of the Sandy Hook Pilots.

James vented about his frustration over John Cox in his journal. He wrote:

> George was looking ashore, and who should he see but Henry coming off in a boat. I was sorry when I saw him, because I am much dissatisfied myself with "Old Stevens." He is a damned old hog, bristles and all. I will tell you. On Friday night, Henry went on board to go to bed, when lo and behold the stateroom door was locked. On Saturday morning, Henry told me and George of it, and George felt bad.
>
> We have had to sleep on shore ever since we have been

here. So George went to "Johnny" and told him we were going to leave. He wanted to know the reason. Then I spoke and told him what I thought of him. He saw George at the hotel and said he did not mean anything by it, he had some things in it [the stateroom], and the door being left open he was afraid some of the men would take them. He has not even asked us to take a drink since he came on board, but we take about two bottles every day. At night, he sits down on the cabin floor in his shirt tail and counts them all over. When he finds any missing he calls the steward and says: "Where the hell does my liquor go to?" He [the steward] says: "I don't know, sir. The Messrs. Steers take some when they want any." "How do they get it when I carry the key?" The steward told him we had a key to the wine locker. He has not said anything to either of us as yet, and if he does he will get hell or something worse.

On Friday, August 8, the Earl of Wilton added to the gloom aboard *America*. He sent a note saying he intended to alert all seventeen yacht clubs in the kingdom of the commodore's wish for a trial of speed between *America* and the top schooners of the land. However, "some little time must necessarily elapse before answers can be received." In other words, John Cox would have to wait, perhaps indefinitely. The Earl of Wilton mentioned a forthcoming race that had been long on the Royal Yacht Squadron's schedule, "to be sailed for by vessels of all rigs and nations" without handicaps for size, meaning whichever boat crossed the finish line first won the event. The earl invited John Cox to enter the regatta, saying it would be a great way to test his schooner's merits. This was not what the commodore had in mind. He wanted a challenge race against boats of similar rig and size out in the English Channel, not to sail against the entire fleet of the Royal Yacht Squadron on the inshore waters around the Isle of Wight, the odds of which were unfavorable for *America*. But if that was the way the British wanted to play it, John Cox would give them all something more to chew on.

In the body of his response to the Earl of Wilton dated August 9, 1851, John Cox wrote:

I beg leave in reply to say that as the period of my visit is necessarily limited, and as much time may be consumed awaiting to receive answers from the proprietors of schooners (without intending to withdraw that proposition), and although it is my intention to enter for the cup, provided I am allowed to sail the *America* in such manner as her rig requires: yet as the issue of a regatta is not always the test of the merits of the vessels engaged in it, I now propose to run the yacht *America* against any cutter, schooner, or vessel of any other rig of the Royal Yacht Squadron, relinquishing any advantage which your rules admit is due to a schooner from a cutter, but claiming the right to sail the *America* in such manner, by such booming out, as her raking masts require; the course to be in the English Channel with not less than a six-knot breeze; the race to come off on some day before the 17th instant; the distance to be not less than twenty nor over seventy miles out and back, and in such a direction as to test the qualities of the vessels before and by the wind.

Although it would be most agreeable to me that this race should be for a cup of limited value, yet if it is preferred, I am willing to stake upon the issue any sum not to exceed ten thousand guineas.

I have the honor to be, your Lordship's obedient servant,

John Cox Stevens

John Cox raised the stakes to a new high. Not only was the commodore attempting to shame the members of the Royal Yacht Squadron into a race they did not want, but he was ready to wager 10,000 guineas, or the equivalent of more than 50,000 American dollars, on the outcome if the British obliged him in accepting the challenge. In United States currency of today, John Cox had staked his honor and reputation on a bet worth more than $900,000. When James Steers got wind of the challenge, and saw the stunned expressions of the yachtsmen along the waterfront, he wrote that the sum "was a staggerer for them all." And it was.

However bold his gesture may have been, John Cox's pushy na-

CHAPTER SEVENTEEN

INFORMAL SKIRMISH

As was his custom, Dick Brown awoke earlier than the men under his command and spent the hour just after dawn on Monday, August 11, thinking through the plans for the important tasks that lay ahead that day. He sat in the cockpit and watched the sky grow pink and orange over Spithead as the sun rose. The cry of gulls overhead mingled with the gentle ruffle and slap of the water against the schooner's hull. Beads of dew glistened on the brightwork. He ran his thick, calloused hands over the cool, moist wood, feeling a deep connection with the boat and the elements. At last it appeared that the mission he had sailed far to fulfill was to come off. The commodore had tentatively lined up a race against vessels of similar size to *America* at the annual regatta of the Royal Victoria Yacht Club at Ryde, just about eight miles east of Cowes. The officers of the club were sanguine about the prospects of including the Americans in their race, though the final decision had not been made. The race was to take place on Wednesday, and much work needed to be done in the likely event the yacht was invited to join the regatta.

Brown walked forward, gazed up at the foremast, and climbed the shrouds to better survey the masthead. From high aloft, the anchorage looked even more serene. Ashore, the shop keepers, clerks, and domestic help for the hotel began to move on the streets. Fish-

ture and his willingness to wager enough money to intimidate even the noblemen of England did not work in his favor. His moves were seen as distinctly Yank in manner and execution, and added to the determination among the British yachtsmen not to give this uppity New Yorker a chance to show them up on terms of his own making. The friendly civility continued. But there were much darker emotions and perceptions boiling just beneath the surface. It was only a matter of time before the lid toppled off the pot.

ermen busy on the smacks prepared to get under way for the work offshore. How far removed was his world now from the days past fishing off the Grand Banks of Newfoundland, and the days of his youth aboard merchantmen that traveled all the major oceans on earth. Indeed, finding himself captain of a yacht seemed an odd twist in his otherwise workmanlike life. Brown examined the masthead for any signs of weakness, any hairline cracks that indicated fatigue in the spar. He ran his hands over the seizings for the shrouds and the iron fitting for the forestay that led to the tip of the bowsprit. He sighed as he regained the deck. There was room enough for another fitting for the second stay required to fit the flying jib, and for the halyard needed to raise and lower it. But it was a mistake just the same. The schooner did not need a second jib, and he had said so to John Cox the day before when the subject came up.

"Tomorrow we fit her with a flying jib," John Cox told Brown. He did not ask for his captain's opinion. He had made up his mind already. On the advice of his English friends, those whom he trusted implicitly not to steer him wrong, John Cox felt the boat might sail better with the extra spread of canvas set on an extension of the bowsprit on a spar called a jibboom.

"Sir, she's a good boat now. Her rig is well balanced," Brown said. "Adding sail so far forward may give her a bad lee helm."

Brown feared the flying jib's extra power might well put the yacht's sail plan out of balance. She might want to turn her bow downwind as she sailed, which sailors call lee helm. To counteract lee helm meant using more rudder, not good on a sailing boat. The maximum speed of a sailboat rested on length and an ability to sail her with the rudder as close to the centerline of the craft as possible. When the rudder was pushed off to one side or the other of the keel to keep her on course it disturbed the flow of water and acted as effectively as a brake.

"More sail forward will be good for the yacht," John Cox said testily. "I'll hear nothing more about this, Captain, nothing more, do you hear?"

Brown bit back the sharp words he might have let fly, nodded, and said: "As you wish, sir. I'll have the men fit her for the new sail in the morning." He had warned the petulant commodore. He had done his duty.

"Excellent, Captain. Make it so," John Cox said.

The degradation of the schooner's performance under sail would have to be gotten around. How to best rig the flying jib required much work, work that did not merit rushing. But the race was slated for Wednesday, giving him only two days to arrange for the builders ashore to fashion the jibboom and the sailmaker to construct the massive jib to set upon it. Based on his measurements the flying jib needed a foot, or lower edge, approximately forty feet in length. The jibboom required sufficient stretch to rig the sail and yet let it pass in front of the existing stay without snagging in a tack. The jibboom itself was going to take a bit of engineering. A dolphin striker, a long slender projection of wood fitted perpendicular to the bowsprit and jibboom, was necessary to support the lines rigged to keep the jibboom secure and able to withstand the forces of wind against sail. Fittings on the bowsprit, and on the sides of the boat were also necessary. In all, the commodore was asking for a tall order. However foolish he thought adding a flying jib might be, Brown rapped on the hatch over the forecastle to rouse the crew.

"Up with you all!" he cried.

Brown heard groans and curses below, and smiled. A sailor seldom liked to leave a warm, snug berth when safely anchored in a harbor. The men tumbled to, rubbed sleep from their eyes, and gathered on deck for a quick breakfast. A boat, with Henry at one of the oars, was sent to pick up the rest of the Steers family waiting on the beach.

When all was ready, the men fed and fit and much more alert, the work began. The Steerses were sent to talk with the builder and sailmaker, both from the Ratsey clan, well-known and respected workers on the island. George, after all, had designed the yacht. Who better than he to make the arrangements for the flying jib? The friction between him and the commodore lurked beneath the surface, but it appeared to have diminished enough for him not to book passage home as they had threatened during the confrontation with John Cox. The Steerses went ashore while the rest of the men set to

the many little jobs needed to complete the refit. They worked under the watchful eye of John Cox and Edwin. To their credit they did
not interfere. They sat in the shade drinking soft beverages and eat-
ing fruit and biscuits brought to them in the cockpit. The crew ignored them, but Brown did not. He had to balance the supervision
of the men against the demands of the owners, who were not at all
timid about butting in if they felt like it. He was at their beck and
call, and could not be seen to disrespect them in any way. In this he
was successful, despite the inner conflict he fought to subdue. Years
later, George L. Schuyler, who got to know Brown during the events
associated with *America* and in connection with other vessels as
well, related the syndicate's assessment of Brown to *The New York
Herald*. He said:

> As she [*America*] was about being finished we began looking
> around for a sailing master. This, as you know, was early in the
> spring of 1851. There were no large yachts then, excepting the
> *Maria,* and she was a leviathan compared with the others of the
> New York fleet, and most of the boats were sailed by their
> owners [with the help of Sandy Hook pilots]. Mr. Steers sug-
> gested Captain Brown as being an excellent and suitable man
> and he was at once engaged. His reputation at that time as a
> boat sailer was head and shoulders above all his associates. . . .
> Brown was always a hard worker, knew his place, and, unlike
> some of the yacht sailing masters of the present day, always
> obeyed the orders of his owners and did not pretend to in-
> struct them. He was a practical boat sailer, and having the ves-
> sel, experimented [along with George Steers] until he got her
> to suit his owners and himself. He was careful, reliable, faith-
> ful, one of the best men in his position I ever saw.

Brown may have been able to pull off his role as the humble sailing master. But on this day it was something of a push because "his
owners," through their adamant desire for a flying jib, were in all
probability sabotaging their chance for victory, a victory that rested
on him to hand them. The pilots poked fun at the captains of the big

liners and sailing packets. The captains were beholden to the owners, and hosts, willing or not, to the wealthy passengers. "It's not work fit for a sailorman," the pilots said. "You might as well be a Tammany Hall backslacker." Brown was getting a look at the other side of the captaining business, and it opened his eyes and filled him with compassion for his brothers who commanded the ships on the transatlantic run. Their jobs were more difficult than he had thought, and not because of the harsh conditions of the North Atlantic, but rather because of the arrogance of the men with more money and power than was good for their humanity.

A breeze from the southeast picked up as the morning faded into the early afternoon. The flood tide began. Slowly the bare rocks covered with kelp and mussels ashore dropped below the surface of the incoming sea. The wind grew stronger and kept the vessels in the anchorage pointing eastward, despite the tide that tried to turn them around to face The Solent. Yachtsmen from the Royal Yacht Squadron, Southampton, and Ryde took to the waters. As men of leisure, there was no work for the owners of the boats to do on a Monday, when the vast majority of England's subjects were at their jobs. White sails contrasted against the green hills of Hampshire. It was a fine day for a sail. But the men aboard *America* toiled on. The commodore eyed the boats sailing to and fro, like a hungry wolf. He paced around the aft deck, stood motionless for a while, his hands on his hips.

A boat approached from the cutter *Pearl*, with the Marquis of Anglesey seated in the stern. The boat pulled alongside, and the oarsmen helped the marquis up on board *America*.

"Good afternoon, commodore," the marquis said, beaming at John Cox. "Isn't it a lovely day?"

John Cox greeted the man warmly. The marquis was a true gentleman, a man whose love of boats equaled the commodore's. The two had much in common, and a genuine liking for each other.

"Yes, indeed it is. I'm afraid we've got to miss it, though," John Cox said.

"Pshaw. Come out for a sail. Your new men need a trial before the race, no?"

Brown listened from a discreet distance. Part of him wanted the commodore to take up the invitation of the marquis. The practical side of his nature resisted. The boat was all a mess, with tools everywhere, the men tired from their work, which was by no means near done.

"We're in the middle of fitting for our new flying jib," John Cox said.

"Nonsense. The boom's not even done. Come out for a sail."

The eagerness of the marquis to get the yacht out on the water was understandable. While she was not engaged in a formal match, seeing what she could really do in a stiff breeze might tip John Cox's hand once and for all. There were many men gathered on shore watching to see what happened next. John Cox was aware of the implications, that if he sailed now, all would have a chance to take the schooner's measure. He determined that he did not much care. He trusted Brown and his men would complete the work on the flying jib in time for the race on Wednesday, and besides, the marquis was right. The crew needed a shakedown to get in racing tune. John Cox turned to Brown and told him to get the yacht under way. A gust struck the schooner. She pulled at her anchor chain. The wind whistled in the rigging, warm and pleasant as it came off the island.

"Aye, sir," Brown said. "But with the work in fitting her out we can't use the foresail."

"The mainsail and jib should suit her," John Cox said. "There's plenty of wind."

"Aye, there is that," Brown said. He suddenly felt excited about the chance to break with the work, despite the need to get it done. It was a perfect sailing day and it might do everyone some good to get out on the water. "All hands stow gear," he called. "Nels, see everything is properly secured below."

The crew looked weary. They had been working since five o'clock that morning with just a short break for a simple dinner. But as they cleared the decks and readied the sails, they moved with a bounce in their step. Looking out at the yachts sailing back and forth in the narrow gap between the Isle of Wight and the mainland, their eyes sparkled. A slight chop ran in Spithead and The Solent. There were no big ocean waves to slow the schooner, just smooth water, a fresh-ening breeze, and a crew anxious to see action after the long wait subsequent to their arrival from Le Havre, and the passage across the North Atlantic. Robert Underwood, the pilot, and Brown talked quietly together in the cockpit, and suggested to the owners a beat to windward to show the marquis, who wanted to remain aboard, how she sailed close-hauled.

"We'll take a starboard tack across to Southampton water, and swing back over to Osborne," Underwood said to Brown. "There's good water until you reach Mother Bank, just a bit past the palace. I'll give us time to tack safely off."

Brown nodded. He waited until all the men were ready at their stations, with some of the men at the bow to heave up the anchor. "Heave her short!" Brown shouted.

The men at the windlass heaved the anchor chain in.

"She's hove short, Captain," Comstock called from his position near the bow.

"Mainsail haul!" Brown called.

The men heaved on the halyards to raise the gaff. It slid up the mast and pulled the sail after it. The wind shook the sail and created a sound like thunder. Blocks and lines snapped. The boom swung from side to side, the main sheet slack.

"Jib haul, and back starboard!"

"Haul and back starboard, aye!" Comstock answered the captain.

The jib ran up the forestay and began to flap. The crew on the starboard sheet pulled the line in as the bow swung in a gust off to the left. The sail slammed aback and pushed the bow further to the left.

"Raise anchor!"

"She's aweigh," Comstock shouted.

"Let starboard sheet run! Haul port!"

The experienced hands of the crew executed the maneuver well, and the yacht gathered way as the anchor was brought up on deck. The men on the mainsail trimmed the sail to work in harmony with the jib. As the mainsail filled and added its enormous power to the jib already drawing fair, the schooner took off with a mighty surge.

She heeled hard to port, a wedge of white foam forward, and a band of whirling eddies astern.

"My, my," the marquis said. "She likes the breeze, Commodore. Likes it very much indeed. And how she points!"

John Cox grinned. "She makes little leeway, my lord. She'd take you off a lee shore in a gale, to be sure."

Brown stood at the tiller, his eyes on the sails, and the crowded waters ahead. The schooner roared across Spithead. The crew crouched low on the high side of the rail to weather on the right, adding their weight to the internal ballast below that helped keep the yacht upright and sailing in good trim.

"Ahh, there's the *Eagle*," the marquis said, pointing at a large schooner, also sailing fast. "See if you can catch her!"

John Cox nodded to Brown.

"She's in close, Robert," Brown said to the pilot. "Any hard water over there?"

"Not a rock to worry you at Stokes Bay shore, Captain. At least not where she's making the spray fly. I'll sing out when you need to steer clear."

Brown eased *America* off the wind and she gathered speed. The crew readjusted the trim of the sails. The yacht closed with *Eagle*. The rival schooner labored hard under a press of full sail, her lee rail low and sometimes under in the gusts. The two yachts sailed side by side, and tacked back across Spithead almost simultaneously. A cutter hove close abeam, then dropped astern.

"She's playing us, Commodore," Brown said, nodding toward the cutter.

"Let's give her a game, then," John Cox replied.

Brown shouted orders to the men. He jibed around and came up under the lee of the other yacht, a sleek, fast cutter of about fifteen tons. Small and nimble, the other craft tacked across *America*'s bow, forcing Brown to bear off. The two yachts reached back and forth, until *America* flew far ahead. She jibed again and brought the wind off the left side of the stern in a broad reach. *Eagle* was far down the channel near East Cowes, but the American yacht caught her and raced on. The shouts of delight from the commodore, Edwin, and the marquis brought smiles to the crew. They, too, cheered on occasion, as one after another, Brown sailed up to and raced ahead of every yacht she met. It was as if she dared the British to send out a worthy opponent.

The breeze diminished toward evening, and Brown brought the schooner back to her anchorage. The crew retired forward for supper, their voices low and indistinct all the way back in the cockpit, where the owners and the marquis enjoyed a round of drinks and some good Cuban cigars before going ashore for a late dinner. The spirits of all aboard ran high. The men slept soundly and awoke ready for work the next day. Word of *America*'s performance under sail spread along the waterfront. The members of the Royal Victoria Yacht Club heard about how fast she was, and did not like the odds. They gathered together and decided to take action. James Steers wrote on Tuesday:

> A beautiful morning, was down on the beach about 6 o'c. waiting for the boat to come off for us. Went to the yard, got the boom, towed it aboard, got breakfast, after which got the boom out, stay up, everything ready by 3 o'c. p.m. except the sail which we did not get until Wednesday morning. About 2 o'c. p.m., a messenger brought off a note to the commodore containing the decision of the Ryde Yacht Club, refusing to allow us to enter for the cup. The objections are these: According to standing rules, every yacht has to be the sole property of one individual. There being five members, owners of our boat, she was, of course, rejected. This made us all downhearted, "Old Pig" got mad, went ashore to the clubhouse, asked if our challenge of $50,000 was accepted, was answered in the negative, the sum being too much.

The rejection increased John Cox's desire to show the British up at all costs. The Royal Victoria Yacht Club might forbid *America*'s official entry in the race. However, its members could not keep him from sailing along with the fleet and racing informally. The yacht lay to at her anchor on Wednesday morning, the owners aboard, the crew ready. All they needed was breeze enough for the racers down Spithead to set sail. At about three o'clock, the regatta began and the boats headed toward Cowes. The men aboard *America* waited for them to pass, then went into action. The London correspondent for *The New York Herald* witnessed the event.

> After the [boats of the Royal Victoria Yacht Club] passed Cowes, the *America* got under weigh, with a foresail and fore staysail only [the original jib], and turned to windward against a strong southwest wind, tide going to the west. She beat a schooner of about 130 tons, with all sails set, most shamefully; but there did not happen to be any large cutter turning down at the same time [to judge how she might do against a faster rig]. Altogether I have no doubt that she would beat any of our schooners on every point; and I would be by no means surprised if she beat our cutters, as all this was in smooth water and she professes to be best at sea.

During this informal skirmish, the cutter *Alarm* of Southampton gave *America* a run for her money. The two vessels battled it out, and neither proved much faster than the other. The odds appeared stacked in favor of the Americans. But the results were not conclusive, as *Alarm* confirmed. The commodore took the boat out again the next day, and the next for a second chance to taunt the schooners and cutters of the Royal Victoria Yacht Club during their Friday regatta. The members of the Royal Yacht Squadron watched with gathering uneasiness as the schooner outsailed her rivals, and they grew concerned about the burgeoning public anger at the yachting community for refusing to accept the challenge of the New Yorkers for a race in the English Channel. The correspondent for *The Times* of London witnessed *America*'s antics of Friday, the afternoon before a grand ball was to take place at Ryde in the evening. The reporter stated:

> [*America*] passed schooners and cutters one after the other, just as a Derby winner passes the "ruck," and as the breeze

freshened slid with the speed of an arrow out toward the Nab, standing upright as a ramrod under her canvas, while the schooners were staggering under every inch they could set, and the cutters were heeling over under gaff topsails and balloon jibs. . . . The *America* . . . went about in splendid style, a little short of the Nab, spinning around like a top, and came bowling away towards Cowes as fast if not faster than ever. As if to let our best craft see she did not care about them, the *America* went up to each in succession, ran to leeward of every one of them as close as she could, and shot before them, coming to anchor off Ryde at least two miles, as it seemed to me, ahead of any of the craft she had been running against.

The same writer in the same story, datelined August 16, put the English yachtsmen to shame. He essentially pilloried them before the entire kingdom, to the glee of the lower and middle classes who shared no great fondness for the British noblemen, nor, for that matter, the Yanks with their flashy display of the Stars and Stripes and their bold, strutting manner. Part of *The Times*'s report read as follows:

Most of us have seen the agitation which the appearance of a sparrow hawk in the horizon creates among a flock of wood pigeons or skylarks, when unsuspecting all danger, and engaged in airy flights or playing about over the fallows, they all at once come down to the ground and are rendered almost motionless by fear of the disagreeable visitor. Although the gentlemen whose business is on the waters of The Solent are neither wood pigeons or skylarks, and although the *America* is not a sparrow hawk, the effect produced by her apparition off West Cowes among the yachtsmen seems to have been completely paralyzing.

I use the word "seems," because it cannot be imagined that some of those who took such pride in the position of England as not only being at the head of the whole race of aquatic sportsmen, but as furnishing almost the only men who sought pleasure and health upon the ocean, will allow the illustrious stranger to return with the proud boasts to the New World that she had flung down the gauntlet to England, Ireland and Scotland, and that no one had been found to take it up. If she were victorious, all that could be said was that the American builder had put together a lighter, swifter and better made mass of wood and iron than any the English builders had matched against her. No one could affirm there was the least disgrace attached to us from the fact.

But if she be permitted to sail back to New York with her challenge unaccepted, and can nail under it, as it is fastened up on one of her beams, that no one dared touch it, then there will be some question as to the pith and courage of our men, and yachting must sink immeasurably in public estimation, and must also be deprived of the credit which was wont to be attached to it, of being the nursery for bringing up our national naval spirit to a respectable and well-grown maturity. . . .

The correspondent for *The Times* lingered around the waterfront at Ryde on Friday evening. He noted the buzz of excitement among the working class regarding Brother Jonathan's odd-looking craft, and their mounting irritation at how she had so easily sent John Bull's yachtsmen scurrying for cover without a single one of them being willing to accept her challenge. The reporter also observed the quiet mortification of the noblemen disguised in a veneer of civility and pomp as they gathered for the ball at Ryde. The party, one of many on the social schedule for the summer, celebrated the nation's proud tradition of yachting that dated back to the founding of the Royal Cork Yacht Club in 1720, and long before that in informal gatherings of gilded craft belonging to the lords and ladies of the land. Next to these Yanks, whose only existing yacht club of any note hailed from New York and was just seven years old, the members of Great Britain's clubs were battle-hardened veterans of racing. Much of the surprise among the general public about the reticence of their yachtsmen to tangle with the American schooner stemmed from the former's obvious surplus of experience over the upstarts from across the Atlantic.

It was not generally known at the time, however, that the Marquis of Conyngham, owner of the 218-ton schooner *Constance* of the Royal Yacht Squadron, had offered John Cox "a friendly trial" to take place that eventful Friday afternoon she outsailed more than thirty British yachts. The commodore summarily rejected the overture. He held out instead for a formal race in the English Channel, where *America* was bound to perform at her best, and a wager on its outcome.

Also on Friday evening, along the docks and in the taverns, rumors of an unpleasant and ludicrous nature began to circulate in earnest about the schooner. Many people thought the Americans cheated. They clung to a misguided belief that the yacht was powered with a new type of engine, a Yank invention hidden deep in the hold to bring dishonor on all of Great Britain through cunning and trickery.

CHAPTER EIGHTEEN

FEVERISH ANTICIPATION

Dick Brown nursed his pint of ale at a table in a West Cowes pub frequented by the working men of the village. The rough, loud talk of the men at the bar reached him from across the room. He found the simple discourse of the fishermen, blacksmiths, and wagon drivers a welcoming change from the smooth sophistication he had had his fill of in recent days. Parades of noblemen and their ladies came aboard the yacht, or lounged in the cockpit to all hours of the night. The more they talked the less they seemed to say, so vapid were their conversations. It was tiresome for him and the crew, who had come to race, not to socialize. James and George Steers sat across from him at the table, pints in hand and looking glum. Brown shared their dark mood. He swirled the ale round and round in the mug, watched it foam and bubble.

Brown took another sip of the warm, brown liquid, slightly bitter to the taste and yet very satisfying. Small comforts. These were what was most important for a man. The smell of a roast turkey in the oven and the sound of his wife's gentle voice as she prepared a Sunday meal for him and the children at their home in Brooklyn, he missed that now more than at any other time since his departure from New York. How were his men doing aboard *Mary Taylor*? Brown sighed. He had been away from home and his business too long.

"Are you sure you'll not stay till Friday's race?" he asked George.

"I can't abide that man another day," George said. "The air is too rarefied around here for our tastes."

James nodded and muttered something ending with "Old Pig."

The underhanded dealing, in George's view, that he endured in connection with the building of the schooner and the financial loss he had taken as a result was the first in a series of insults. But he overlooked the syndicate's maneuvers in New York, both for the greater good of the enterprise and his own keen desire to see how his creation performed in England. The lack of gratitude shown to him even after his work on the boat in Le Havre and in Cowes with regard to the jibboom and flying jib added to the accumulating ill-will. He had long suppressed his anger and finally he could keep it back no more.

From John Cox's point of view there was no reason for him to count George and his brother as equals, nor to go beyond anything more than a simple thank-you for the Steers's continued involvement with the schooner subsequent to the purchase in May. He overlooked the theft of his liquor, and James's often belligerent attitude. There was no love lost between him and the Steers brothers, however, and their departure was not much concern to him.

"If you stay until after the race I'll leave, too," Brown said.

"You should stay, Dick," James said, taking a long pull on his pint. He wiped his lips, smoothed his bushy gray beard. "Though it would teach Johnny a thing or two if you did go."

Brown doubted very much that breaking his word to John Cox would teach the commodore anything but to have an even dimmer view of what he openly called the "lower order." There was also the issue of Brown's personal sense of duty to his men. A good captain never abandoned his ship to leave his crew to the sharks. That the sharks in this case were of the two-legged variety mattered little. It all amounted to the same thing. No, Brown thought, he would stay to see the schooner through the race against the fleet of the Royal Yacht Squadron, a race open to all rigs and yachts from all nations for a cup worth one hundred sovereigns, with no time allowances based on the size of the vessels. Thus far the race of August 22 was the only official trial of speed the British were prepared to offer. The odds were stacked against the United States. The best cutters in England were expected to enter the regatta. *America* needed him at the helm if she was to stand a chance of winning.

The men talked and drank and sometimes laughed about the way the adventure had gone, despite its gloomy end for the Steers brothers. Of particular amusement to the men was the persisting rumor that *America* was driven by a hidden propeller. Brown's eyes twinkled and a sly grin crossed his face as he thought about how James had toyed with the many boatmen who rowed round to examine the boat, and the story James told of how he carried on the joke with the Marquis of Anglesey.

Years later, James Alexander Hamilton described the general amusement on board when it came to the issue of the propeller, and the role James Steers played in perpetuating it.

There was at one time a very general impression among the lower orders of the people about the docks at Cowes, that the *America* had a propeller which was artfully concealed; and our crew amused themselves by saying to the boatmen, who came alongside with visitors (there were thousands, as people of all classes were permitted to examine the vessel): "In the stern-sheets, under the gangway, there is a grating which the Commodore does not allow any person to open." And, indeed, this opinion was entertained by persons not of the lower class alone. A sporting clergyman said to a gentleman, who repeated it to me: "I would not wager a guinea against the Yankee craft; but I will give a hundred to see her bottom."

The old Marquis of Anglesey went out with his yacht, the *Pearl* (one of the best sailers of the squadron), taking with him Mr. Steers, one of the *America*'s crew [note how Hamilton refers to James], the brother of Mr. George Steers, the builder, to sail about the harbor. The *America* went after her under a mainsail and jib only, and passed her without difficulty. The master of the *Pearl* said: "Your lordship knows that no vessel with sails alone could do that." When the *America* went slowly, he said: "Now it is stopped [referring to the engine];" and when she went on, "Now it is going." These remarks of the master were not unheeded by the Marquis, and Steers said nothing to contradict them—he enjoying the jokes. When the vessel came to anchor, the Marquis's boat was manned; he came aboard the *America*; and after a salutation he went to the stern, leaned over so far that the Commodore took hold of his leg to prevent him from going over—he was looking most eagerly for the propeller [and no doubt playing along with the fun associated with the phantom device].

The twilight deepened, the hour grew late. After a last round of drinks, Brown accompanied the Steers brothers to the hotel, where they got their baggage in preparation for their trip to Liverpool and their passage home aboard the Collins liner *Atlantic* on August 20. They made their way to the waterfront to wait for the boatmen to take them across to the mainland. They listened to the slap of the water against the quay, the voices on the street behind them, the chatter of other people waiting for the boat. Off in the harbor, *America* rode quietly to her anchor. A warm yellow glow illuminated the skylight and the forward section of the cockpit. A lantern hung from the boom. The shadowy figures of men seated aft and the red smudges at the tips of their cigars were visible. At the bow were other forms, the dim outline of the crew gathered to see George and James, and Little George off. Henry, who had wanted to stay for the race, was to remain, safe and protected under Brown's wing.

The boatmen called to board. The passengers milled about. Brown gave each of the departing Steers a warm handshake, and clapped George on the back. "I'll see she sails well in spite of the damned flying jib," he said.

"I know you will, Dick," George said.

"Good-bye, Dick," James said. He turned to Henry. "Now you mind the captain, boy, and stay out of the commodore's way." He gave Henry a quick hug and boarded the boat.

The boat pulled away from the wharf and headed out across The Solent. George took a long last look at the schooner. How beautiful she was in the near darkness, her form still defined in the remaining light. The crew aboard *America* waved as the boat passed her. George returned the gesture. He watched the schooner until she faded into the shadows and became indistinct in the deepening night.

As the week of August 18 drew to a close and the day of Friday's race approached, Dick Brown continued to train the crew whenever the yacht sailed from her anchorage off Cowes Castle. His men worked well with the British volunteers from the schooner *Surprise*. He and Robert Underwood also became a highly polished team. With the yacht sailing fast amid the other vessels, they figured out tactics that best suited the state of the wind and tide, and the boat's proximity to any dangerous shoals. Every time they sailed together each man learned more about the other, until they could almost read the other's thoughts without the need to speak. Brown respected Underwood. He saw in him many of the traits he valued in the men in the ranks of the Sandy Hook Pilots. In these unfamiliar waters Underwood's assistance was much needed, and Brown rested easier knowing he had a man of his caliber at his side, along with first mate Nelson Comstock. Between the three of them, and the skills of the crewmen, *America* had a fighting chance. He remained concerned about the flying jib, which had indeed given the yacht weather helm. But there was nothing he could do about that. It was just one more obstacle to deal with.

The evening before the race Brown went forward to address the crew. He sat on the foredeck with them and lit a cigar. He gazed off toward the Hampshire coast at the dark clouds gathering on the horizon lit with the last of the setting sun in bands of deep red and purple across the summits. Patches of clear sky revealed a splash of stars that became increasingly bright as the twilight gave way to the night. After a few moments of silence passed, he quietly encouraged the men to work with a will when the time came and he reassured them that the odds, while not in their favor, were not too extreme to overcome. With any luck at all, their schooner might carry the day. "You're all every inch a sailor, boys!" he said. "We've got a fine boat and a practiced crew. We'll show them all what *America* can do when her back's against the wall."

The men went to their berths early on Thursday evening. But few of them found sleep easy in coming. They laid in their bunks and listened to the tide gurgle past the hull inches from their ears, and to the occasional tap of the halyards on the foremast in the slight breeze coming through the hatch. Comstock thought of his brothers back in New York, racers with more experience than he had. He wondered if he was up to the task at hand, what the morning might bring for them all. Had he done everything possible to support his captain and whip the men into a cohesive team? The question nagged at him. There was no way to answer it.

No matter how hard a crew trained and no matter how good the boat was in form and design, the sea, if it was anything, remained unpredictable and crafty. It might turn good fortune to bad in seconds. The waters around the Isle of Wight were considered among England's most treacherous for the mariner not familiar with their every nuance, and even with Underwood's help, the elements might pose more of a challenge than the yachts bent on beating them across the finish line.

While the men rested aboard *America*, the Isle of Wight bustled with activity long into the night. Earlier in the day thousands of people streamed across The Solent to West Cowes, or across Spithead to Ryde to stake out a place to witness the spectacle of one American schooner pitting herself against the cream of the British yachting fleet. Every hotel, guest house, and inn was filled to capacity, and still the people came. Owners of property along the waterfront found their homes crammed with visitors.

"Wanderers were moving about the streets long after midnight, knocking at impracticable doors, and drawing nightcapped heads from windows, only to receive the unpleasing information that there was no room for them," wrote the correspondent for *The Times*, who had come down to the Isle of Wight from London on Thursday afternoon. He walked past the shops and restaurants teeming with humanity and listened to the conversations. Most focused on the upcoming contest. There were some who expressed annoyance at the Americans, and held out little hope that their schooner might lose. Others reveled in the sport of it all and rooted for the underdogs from the United States, while still more people considered the odds in favor of their own country. After all, seventeen British yachts were slated to race against the schooner. It was bound to be quite a skirmish, a sort of friendly war between two longtime rivals, John Bull and the brash, young Brother Jonathan. There was heavy wagering among all classes of people interested in the event, and more than just the crew of *America* slept fitfully that night.

Early Friday morning Brown woke the crew. They ate a good, hearty breakfast to "stick to their ribs," because the next meal might not come until late in the day, after the race was decided. The crewmen cleaned the decks and polished the brightwork with rags to remove the dew. They readied the lines, heaved in the starboard gangway, and otherwise prepared to get the schooner under way. Already the waters off Cowes were crowded with all manner of small craft from rowboats and skiffs to workboats and yachts. More than one hundred yachts from all over Great Britain rode to their anchors near the location of the starting and finish line just north of Cowes Castle. Spectators rowed near to the schooner, taking in the "strange looking craft . . . with her long, low black hull, and thick, stiff looking rakish masts . . . a big-boned skeleton . . . bent on mischief," observed the reporter for *The Times*.

The waters of The Solent and Spithead glimmered in a smooth, slick sheen. Not a ripple passed over the surface to darken it with a sign of wind. The flags at the yacht club, atop the ramparts of Cowes Castle, and on the villas along the waterfront hung limp and lifeless. The air was heavy with moisture from the mist that hovered over the land and obscured the hills to the north in Hampshire. The dark swath of weed-covered rocks revealed the low state of the tide. The last of the ebb still ran weakly, moving westward toward The Needles, a protrusion of chalk rock outcrops at the far end of the Isle of Wight.

Brown stood in the cockpit and surveyed the scene around him. It was surreal, with the mist and the thicket of masts, the gathering crowds ashore. The interest in the contest appeared to have grown exponentially since that story condemning the British yachtsmen ran in *The Times*. Now more than ever the race was about national honor, a chance to show the merits of the New World over the Old, or if things worked out badly, the other way around. As he gazed out over The Solent, Brown wondered what the schooner's chances really were. Self-doubt was not much in keeping with his nature, but, at such a time as this, it crept in to make itself known and felt.

The first puffs of a westerly wind moved across the water and brought the pungent odor of the tidal flats, the smell of mud and kelp. The ebb tide reached its lowest point and the flow slacked off for a short time. The boats in the anchorage all drifted in varying directions—east, west, north, or south, depending on the design and depth of the keel and the unseen influence of an eddy that heralded the start of the flood tide. All but one of the eighteen vessels, the schooner Fernande, entered in the race were anchored in two rows that stretched north to south across the starting line off West Cowes. The nine cutters took the first row, the eight schooners the second about three hundred yards to the west.

"Looks like we may have wind enough for a race," Brown said to Comstock, who stood nearby, also lost in his thoughts. "Are the men ready?"

"Aye, Captain," Comstock said. "We've done all we can do."

"Just let it blow today," Brown muttered. "Just give us a good breeze I can use."

The owners emerged from their staterooms and joined the two officers and Robert Underwood in the cockpit. The cook's assistant served them breakfast. As he ate, John Cox expressed concern about the calm conditions. The men talked together about the race, their expectations for what might lay ahead on the fifty-three-mile racecourse clockwise around the Isle of Wight. They were to sail down Spithead, past the Nab Lightship, along the southern shore of the island, around The Needles, and back to Cowes via The Solent. But the talk was all just going over what had already been said. The conversation helped ease the tension and keep their minds off the slow passage of time.

Soon, though, the pace changed as Lord Wilton's yacht Xarifa ran up her flags, which fluttered in the light breeze now blowing in from the North Atlantic, a good sign the men aboard America welcomed with smiles. *Xarifa* was positioned off Cowes to mark the location of the start and finish line. The race was scheduled to begin at ten o'clock, little more than an hour away. The tide began to flood and the breeze picked up. Slowly, the fleet at anchor swung bows to the west to face the current and the wind in the opposite direction they were to sail on the first leg of the course to the east.

A boat came alongside with James Alexander Hamilton. Accompanying Hamilton was a representative from the Royal Yacht Squadron, and some friends of the syndicate. The men came aboard, went aft, and talked excitedly among themselves. The United States minister, Abbott Lawrence, was to have come with them as well. Perhaps he still might make it in time before the race began, a sentiment expressed by the Stevens brothers and Colonel Hamilton more than once. They considered it an honor to have the important and influential man witness the race from *America*'s deck, part of the overall glory of the moment. In all there were twenty-one people aboard, including Henry Steers, who stayed out of the way and watched the frenetic goings on with rapt attention.

With wind at last enough to move them along with the fair tide down Spithead toward Ryde and the Nab Lightship beyond, the sailing vessels in the spectator fleet hummed with activity. The crews heaved up the sails. The sound of canvas fluttering and shaking in the wind mingled with the shouts of the sailors, the chatter of the guests on board. The boats got under way one after the other and darted between the steam-powered excursion vessels cruising back and forth close to the racing yachts. The shore of Cowes was thick with people, a colorful swath of well-dressed men and women, already fanning themselves in the gathering heat of the day.

John Cox glanced at his watch. It was 9:45, just ten minutes before the first signal gun was set to fire at the battery in front of the Royal Yacht Squadron clubhouse. He felt his heart race at the prospect, and he turned to Edwin and grinned. Edwin smiled back and pointed at the armada of boats parading past on their way east to get a favored position to witness the start of the race.

"Incredible sight, just incredible," Edwin said.

"Merry England is showing her full glory," Hamilton laughed.

Brown looked upon the scene with a much different view. With all of the traffic, he expected to face a challenge in his effort to out-maneuver his rivals. The west southwesterly wind meant he had to get his sails up and the boat headed from west to east in short order, all the while dodging the spectators. He was pleased, however, that the schooner occupied a position at the far north end of the line, with only the enormous 392-ton *Brilliant* to her right. When the fleet set sail and slipped their anchors they would all have to turn to head east. At the far end of the line he was in a good spot to make his turn without much interference from the other contenders. As big and fast as the three-masted schooner may have been, *Brilliant* was not likely to get away faster than *America*. "Nels, tell the crew we're about to make sail, and to look lively when we do. It'll be a trick to get clear without fouling one of these damned onlookers," Brown said so that only Comstock heard him.

Comstock nodded, his face serious. He, too, was caught up in the immediate demands of handling the boat. There was no time to think about the larger implications of the race, of national honor, of the personal glory the syndicate stood to earn if the schooner won. There was just the boat, the wind, and the tide to consider, and the rivals intent on vanquishing her.

CHAPTER NINETEEN

CHALLENGE BEGUN

Standing near one of the cannons in the battery in front of the Royal Yacht Squadron clubhouse, the gunner lit the punk he would use to fire the guns. The tip of the punk smoldered and burned, giving off a dense acrid smoke that drifted lazily off to the east. As he waited for his assistant holding a timepiece to give him the command, the gunner imagined the tense silence of all the crews aboard the yachts anchored a short distance away in Cowes Roads, the anxiety and excitement of the captains, and the high expectations of the owners. Of all the regattas in the history of the Royal Yacht Squadron, none had attracted such large crowds. The eyes of the nation were all trained on this stretch of water, and most particularly on the yachtsmen engaged in a duel against the Yankee stranger.

"Ready?" the timekeeper asked the gunner.

"All ready."

At the stroke of nine-fifty-five the timekeeper shouted, "Fire!"

The gunner touched the punk to the small pile of powder in an indentation atop the cannon to ignite the charge. There was a flash and sizzle and the cannon roared, recoiling backward against its tackle with a thud. A cloud of gray smoke surrounded the men as the report echoed off the buildings and rolled out over the water. Almost immediately the men saw the crews aboard the yachts go into action, hauling short the anchor cables while others loosed the sails and prepared for the start. Unlike in a modern yacht race, where boats sail back and forth behind the starting line, it was customary for the fleets to set sail from predetermined positions at anchor. The five minutes between the first and the final guns would elapse quickly.

Aboard yacht *America*, Dick Brown glanced ashore at the sound of the gun. Cheers from the spectators mixed with the resounding blast. He looked forward at his crew poised and prepared for action, their eyes fixed on him. He rested his hand on the tiller and shouted to Comstock. "Heave short the anchor."

The men at the windlass put their backs into their labor, every muscle strained. The yacht moved slowly to the west as the chain rattled through the hawshole.

"She's hove short, Captain!" Comstock cried.

"Haul away, boys! Set all sail!"

Comstock shouted a series of orders and the crew jumped to their work. The sails were soon up and shaking in the breeze. The yacht swung back and forth on her shortened anchor chain. A slight gust of wind filled the big flying jib just as *America*'s bow veered. The bow paid off and she gathered way, despite the best efforts of the men to stop her.

"Ease jib sheets! Ease off," Brown cried. He felt the yacht moving forward, the gentle tug on the tiller as she came alive in her element. Before he had time to react, the schooner rode up over her anchor chain and slewed a bit off the wind to bring her side against the flow of the tide. "Strike! Strike all sail!"

The crew hauled down the sails and the yacht slowly swung back to face the wind and tide. Loose canvas and a snaky confusion of lines littered the deck. She drifted off the anchor chain and came to rest just as the starting gun fired. The crowd greeted the second gun with even more cheers than they had the first. One after another, the British yachts weighed anchor and sailed fast downwind toward Ryde. The expanse of white canvas was beautiful to see. It obliterated much of the view forward. There was a wall of vessels ahead and crowds of spectator boats on either side of the course all heading pell-mell down the waterway toward the open waters of the English Channel. To the schooner's left, *Brilliant* raised her anchor and got majestically under way, leaving the water clear for Brown to make his turn once he got *America* moving. Brown ordered the men at the bow to bring the anchor up just as the sails were raised. Again the sailors hoisted up the sails. The schooner quickly gathered way and started to overrun her anchor chain before it came aboard. But the crew was ready this time and got the anchor aboard without smashing it against the hull. All in all, it was a dreadful start. *America* was last.

Brown patiently waited for the schooner to gather momentum as the men trimmed the sails for the port tack. They sped toward the Hampshire coast. Brown gently eased her bow more to the north. The sailors trimmed the sails as he turned, bringing the wind aft along the left side of the boat. She increased her speed.

"Prepare to jibe!" he shouted, his voice booming over the otherwise silent boat. The noise of the crowd and the wash of the other vessels seemed to disappear. There was only the sound of the wind, the water, the flutter of canvas, and the calm, firm voices of the captain and the first mate.

"All ready, Captain!" Comstock said.

Now the wind blew off the schooner's port quarter, and her bow pointed northeastward toward Portsmouth.

"Jibe ho!" Brown yelled, and nudged the tiller a little more to the left as the bow continued turning toward the right. The yacht's stern turned directly into the wind and the men at the main sheet hauled the massive boom inboard. The stern passed through the wind. The boom swung hard over to the left side of the boat, followed by the foresail, the original jib, and the flying jib. The sailors let out the sails just enough to catch the full force of the slight breeze. The schooner churned up a modest wake. She caught the maximum power of the tidal current in the deep part of the midchannel, and gradually crept up on the fleet of British yachts sailing ahead of her. Her wind was clear and no other vessels sailed near enough to block her. *America* sped closer to her rivals.

Of the eighteen vessels entered in the race, only fifteen started, seven schooners and eight cutters. Off *America*'s bow, fourteen British yachts fought to keep their position. They kept sailing on, everyone aboard silent and intent on the drama unfolding before them. Within five minutes of the starting gun, *America* passed her first competitor, close aboard on the windward side. As the schooner's sails blocked the wind, the rival boat lost power and dropped astern. Brown maneuvered the yacht through the fleet, knocking off the stragglers at the rear with little difficulty. The wind was unsteady, and always weak, but every once in a while a stronger puff darkened the water astern of the schooner. Brown told Underwood to sing out when he saw the puffs coming.

"Here's another, Captain!" Underwood said enthusiastically. "A good one!"

Brown glanced over his shoulder to see the dark water behind him. He looked ahead to gauge the distance between the bow and the next boat, and headed up a bit to get better boat speed. The crew trimmed the sails to match his every move. *America* raced ahead. Yet there were still many yachts far in front sailing in a line spread across the channel. Leading the fleet was a big schooner, *Gipsy Queen*, which was nearly as large as *America*. A similar good match for the Americans was second, *Beatrice*. The boats were so close together it became difficult for observers ashore to tell which one had the lead. There were many spectators betting on *Beatrice* to show the Yanks up. She was one of the fastest sailers in England. Others put their money on the cutter *Alarm*. A pack of fast yachts nipped at the heels of the two leaders, including the cutters *Volante* and *Arrow*, both of which were light in tonnage and well suited to the soft, gentle breeze.

John Cox grinned broadly every time Brown passed another yacht. "She's sailing well, Captain!"

"Well done!" Hamilton chimed in.

"Excellent sailing!" one of the guests said.

Brown ignored the occasional shouts of delight among the passengers. He needed every bit of his concentration to weave the schooner safely through the fleet without letting another skipper get the best of him. All it took was one mistake and he might lose the advantage he fought hard to gain. Within fifteen minutes *America* surged past every contending yacht except the leaders of the pack, the schooners *Constance, Beatrice,* and *Gipsy Queen.* The rest of the fleet sailed all around *America,* off to each side of her, and bunched close together astern. The captains of the yachts close behind *America* tried to get upwind of her to block her air. Brown took evasive action to avoid the possibility of losing the power in his sails, as East Cowes dropped astern. Other yachts in front tried to block *America's* path. Again Brown acted with nerve and courage. Once he had to bear off to avoid collision, even though as "starboard tack" boat he had the right of way according to the rules of racing.

Ashore the crowd roared and shouted and rooted for the leaders of the fleet, and some booed and hissed as *America* advanced. The passengers boarding the excursion steamers had to be prodded and pushed. They hesitated on the dock, not willing to take their eyes off the action.

"Get moving there, move on!" the boatmen yelled. "There's plenty of race left to see outside in the channel."

Riding the freshening breeze, *America* continued to press on, passing the last of the contending vessels until all that remained open to challenge was *Gipsy Queen.* Brown worked to windward of her, hoping to sweep by if the wind held. Just behind him, however, was the cutter *Volante.* At only forty-eight tons, she was one of the lightest boats in the race and well suited to light air and flat water. She spread a huge amount of canvas on her single mast. Taking advantage of a favorable gust, *Volante* glided up on *America's* windward side off to the right and just astern. Brown set his jaw, looked aloft, and confirmed his fear. The little cutter had stolen his wind. He watched her helplessly as she darted past and captured the lead.

With clear air, *Volante* opened the gap with the fleet. But the rest of the yachts skimmed along only seconds behind her. The front runners exchanged the lead at intervals of just a few seconds. Osborne House hove into view. The roar of the crowd was loud enough to hear out on the racecourse over the shouts of the officers and sailors, the snap of lines, the clatter of blocks, and the flutter of canvas.

Observing the action from a good vantage point ashore was the correspondent for *The Times,* and other members of the press. The London correspondent for *The New York Herald* was to follow with the rest of the reporters aboard a steamer to cover the race from offshore. He wrote furiously to record what he saw before he had to leave.

> Before the steamers that were going round to Ventnor had got their passengers on board, she [*America*] had taken the fourth place, the *Volante* being first, *Arrow* second and *Beatrice* third; and all that could be said for them was, that they were delaying her from taking the lead a little longer than the others. The only question now is what can the cutters do with her in beating around the island. It is said that she can go to windward with any cutter of them all; indeed, I heard yesterday, that she beat the *Pearl* to windward. . . . But I must now close this despatch, and go look after her; and as I go, an old sea-dog observes for my comfort, to his mess-mate, "D'ye see that ere steamer? I'm blessed if the Yankee don't beat her out of sight around the island," and the Signal-master, at the Clubhouse, says to a gentleman who asks for information, "Psha, sir, catch her! You might as well set a bull dog to catch a hare!" But, notwithstanding the speed it is scarcely probable that the race will be over in time to send up particulars to town.

The fleet raced past Osborne House and Ryde, and drew quickly up to Nomansland Buoy, which they were to leave to starboard. The best boats in the fleet sailed so close that there was danger of collision. Aboard *America*, Dick Brown quipped as he gave way at one time and forced his rival to bear off at another: "Shall I put our bowsprit through that fellow's mainsail, Commodore?"

John Cox offered a wry smile. "They'll protest that, Captain. Best to keep clear."

Brown smiled and shook his head. "It's a close match, this."

A cutter, a wedge of foam at the bow, nearly rammed *America*. The captain of the other vessel acted just fast enough to avoid a collision. Close calls happened faster than anyone could count. As the fleet rounded Nomansland Buoy, *Volante* held the lead by one minute twenty seconds over the cutter *Freak*. *Aurora*, the lightest cutter in the regatta at only forty-seven tons, sailed just ten seconds behind *Freak*, with *Gipsy Queen* fifteen seconds astern. *America* was two minutes behind the leader as Brown took her round the mark, with four other boats on either side hotly contesting every foot of ground.

Off to the west, the clouds thickened and lowered. The wind increased. A slight sea began to build. *America* was at last in her best element, with breeze enough to move her sleek hull to its maximum potential for speed. She roared past all of her rivals, save for *Volante*. Little by little *America* closed the gap between her and her rival's stern. The little cutter heeled in the gusts. Spray flew over her bow in sheets that wet the bottom of her massive jib. Her captain tried to cover *America*, keeping the favored air to windward. But Brown countered her every move.

Brown had noted from the first sail with the flying jib set that the yacht suffered from too much weather helm—far more than the slight bit of weather helm George Steers intended. Sailing downwind, the amount of rudder needed to counteract the tendency of the boat to want to face her bow to the wind was small and accounted for little loss in speed. But as the wind built and came in to blow off the right side of the vessel as he turned her south toward Bembridge Point, a lee helm developed and became a hindrance. In addition, with so much canvas set, the yacht heeled more than she should have. George Steers had designed her to sail well when heeled, but there was a point where too much heel slowed the boat. These thoughts went through Brown's mind as he gained on and finally passed *Volante* in a strong gust of wind that laid both boats over.

"We'll take in the flying jib, Nels," he called. He turned to John Cox. "It's necessary, sir. We're overcanvased."

John Cox did not disagree with Brown.

The crew eased the sheets to spill the wind. The sail flogged and shook. The noise drowned out the slap of the waves and the murmur of the wind in the rigging, until the sailors got the sail down. Five or six of them perched precariously on the footropes strung beneath the bowsprit, their bellies to the spar, and gathered in the flying jib as the yacht sailed on under jib alone, with her foresail, main-sail, and main gaff topsail still drawing fair. The men did not think of the danger. Their every attention focused on the boat. *America* straightened up on an even keel and picked up speed.

"We've still got too much sail up, Commodore," Brown said, turning to John Cox, who sat low in the cockpit with the others, the crew aft as well spread out along the high side of the deck to help balance her. The commodore's eyes sparkled. His gray hair blew in the wind under his cap. He shot Brown a look of approval and agreement.

"Strike the gaff topsail!" Brown called.

The men jumped to it and executed the captain's orders. Brown felt the helm ease, the schooner settle down. She was now in better balance. He glanced astern at the hundreds of boats blanketing the waters behind the leaders. Most of the spectator fleet could not keep up. The fastest yachts in the regatta sailed not far distant, but even with them the gap grew by the minute, with the race less than two hours old. Off to seaward, several steamers belched black smoke from their stacks. White water churned at the bows and aft of the paddle wheels.

The reporters on board one of the steamers accompanying the fleet were astonished at *America*'s performance. The reporter for *The Times* wrote:

> No foam, but rather a water jet, rose from her bows; and the greatest point of resistance—for resistance there must be somewhere—seemed about the beam, or just forward of her mainmast, for the seas flashed off from her sides at that point every time she met them. While the cutters were thrashing through the water, sending spray over their bows, and the schooners were wet up to the foot of the foremast, the *America* was as dry as a bone. . . . It required the utmost the steamer could do to keep alongside of her.

America led the fleet as she reached the east end of the Isle of Wight. The wind blew fair over the right side of the boat, putting her nearly on a beam reach, one of the fastest points of sail. Brown knew he could not stand directly south for long, however, because dangerous shoals lay right off the schooner's bow. The buoys marking the hazards bobbed in the distance.

"How close in can I take her, Robert?" Brown asked the pilot. "I've a mind to head inside the Nab. But I see some of the fleet is rounding her."

Underwood considered the state of the tide. The flood had begun, meaning with every passing minute there was more water over the shoals as the tide came in. But it was a close call. The east end of the island inside the lightship was well known for its hazards. One had to time the tide right to sail inside the Nab. "Hold your course, Captain," he said. "There's water enough as long as you don't head her up farther to the west."

Four of the yachts, including those closest to *America,* stood off to pass the Nab Lightship to the east. The captains watched with anger as the Americans sailed nearly due south, making way quickly through the water on a course that cut miles off the route. The usual rules always stipulated that vessels must round the lightship, leaving it to starboard, though the directions given to *America* did not specify that requirement. Nevertheless, there were some who thought the Americans cheated. Tempers flared.

George H. Ackers, owner of *Brilliant,* vowed to file a formal protest. The four yachts did not alter course, but the rest of the fleet turned to follow *America* across the shoals.

Tension mounted aboard *America* as she drew in close to the land. Bands of white water swirled and boiled over the shallows. Patches of standing waves became visible. Brown fought the urge to sheer off toward deeper water. Although the shoals posed a real danger, in the shallower water the force of the tide running around the island diminished. He decided to take her in even closer to make better way against the foul current.

"Stand by to come about!" Brown called.

The men scurried to their stations. Comstock signaled that he was ready.

"Helm's alee!" Brown eased the yacht over onto the new tack. Sailing close-hauled, the wind now blew over the left side of the boat.

Her bow pointed straight at the towering white cliffs on the shore. Surf breaking on the rocks painted the dull green water white. The roar of the larger swells reached the people aboard the yacht.

"Sing out when we run out of room, Robert!" Brown muttered. He bit back his fear and kept driving her toward the land. Minutes passed. The surf line grew more distinct. Brown prayed the wind held. If it died off now, the schooner would be left at the mercy of the tide in a bad stretch of water. There was risk in his tactics. He hoped he did not lose the gamble.

"Now!" Underwood said emphatically. "Come about now!"

Shouts rang out aboard *America*. The sound of feet pounding the decks, the clap and bang of blocks, the snap of lines, and the booming flutter of canvas mingled with the sound of the surf. The yacht's bow passed through the eye of the wind and she settled down on the starboard tack. Sailing clear of the shoals on a southwesterly course, they left Bembridge Point astern. The occasional whitecaps that flashed on the water disappeared. The yacht slowed. The force of the tide almost stopped her dead. Brown tacked back toward the land. The town of Sandown lay off the bow dead ahead. He sailed in close and tacked out again to make his way down the southeastern coast of the island. Astern, the light cutters of the fleet closed the gap. The fickle air favored them. The elements seemed to conspire against the Americans, threatening the lead she fought hard to maintain.

"We'll have the flying jib and gaff topsail up, Nels," Brown said calmly. "Look lively, boys! Not a minute to waste."

The crew set the two sails. But the wind dropped off still more, making the extra canvas account for little in the way of improved speed. The men aboard *America* watched as the fleet closed in on them. The nearest contender was just over two miles away. But the tide flowed hard in *America*'s position relative to the island. Brown looked over the side, as did the others. The wake was gone. There was not wind enough for her to stem the tide. She began moving backward toward the approaching British fleet.

CHAPTER TWENTY

WINDS
OF VICTORY

The tide continued to strengthen as the flood reached its maximum velocity. The wind came and went in puffs and cat's-paws. *America* gathered way in the stronger bursts and kept her lead. Two miles astern the light cutters *Aurora, Freak,* and *Volante* sailed close together, matching each other tack for tack as they came on in formation after the Americans. Farther astern were the cutters *Bacchante* and *Eclipse*. Not a single British schooner was close enough to give *America* trouble. The hulls of some of the contending yachts dropped below the horizon. Several dispirited captains gave up the fight and sailed home.

America closed with the southeastern tip of the Isle of Wight, just east of Ventnor. The tide ran strong as it channeled between the land and an off-lying bank. The west-southwesterly wind blew directly against the yacht. It combined with the tide to slow her progress. Brown began a series of short tacks, and the crew worked hard beating to weather in the tideway. Again and again, they manned their stations and the captain brought the yacht to her new course. As the schooner was coming about off Dunnose, there was a loud bang and the jibboom snapped off. The massive sail blew to leeward. The broken spar hung down in the water. Brown headed up into the wind and shouted to the men to clear the wreckage. In his excitement, he said: "I'm glad that damned boom is gone!"

John Cox gave him a disapproving look.

"I've told you, sir," Brown said in the heat of the moment, "I don't believe in carrying a flying jib to windward."

"That may be, Captain," John Cox said coolly. "But we'll miss it in this light air."

"Maybe so. Maybe not."

Brown returned his attention to the matter at hand. A group of sailors climbed out onto the bowsprit to cut away the sail and run in the jibboom still attached to the boat. It was tough work with the yacht rolling to the swells, her other sails flogging in the light breeze. She drifted eastward with the tide for fifteen minutes before her men put her right. Under her pilot boat's dress—mainsail, main gaff topsail, foresail, and jib—she got under way again. Her rivals had closed the distance with her. But *America* was still far ahead of the pack. The only boats to threaten her remained two miles astern, *Aurora, Freak,* and *Volante.*

Aboard the steamer carrying the press, *America*'s broken jibboom accounted for a break in an otherwise depressing spectacle. The mishap gave temporary hope for those rooting for the home fleet, only to see it fade as the Americans got the schooner sailing again. Around midafternoon, another event gave the British press something further to lament. The reporter for *The Times* wrote:

> Looking away to the east, they [most of the fleet] were visible at a great distance, standing in-shore or running in and out most hopelessly astern. . . . Soon after three o'clock the *Arrow* managed to run on the rocks to the East of Mill Bay, and the sailing committee's steamer the *Queen, Her Majesty,* an excursion boat, and the *Alarm,* yacht, at once made in to her assistance. They ran down to the ledge of rocks with a hawser, steamed away as hard as possible, and, after some 20 to 30 minutes, towed off the poor little *Arrow,* which won but the other day at the Ryde Regatta, in such a condition that she never more was fit for sea. She put about and went off towards

the Nab, with the intention of returning to Cowes; and the *Alarm*, which might have had a chance with Brother Jonathan in a heavy seaway, kept her company in the same direction, having generously run down to aid her.

America sailed in close to the southern edge of the island trying to keep out of the worst of the current. Brown and Underwood worked together, with Brown at the helm, and Underwood at his side, his glass to his eye, his every attention focused on the sea. The wind increased and shifted more to the southwest as the yacht neared St. Catherine's Point. The crew sweated as they tacked the yacht. Their clothes were wet. The salt from their bodies stung their eyes. Large black clouds gathered over the English Channel and sometimes blocked the sun, providing momentary respites of cool for the men.

"Easy!" Brown called to encourage them. "Once we're clear of the headland, we'll be off the wind."

The men looked relieved. Even with a large, well-trained crew, a long series of tacks to windward taxed the strongest of the sailors.

Aboard the cutters to the east, the hopes of besting the Americans diminished by the minute. The captains tacked close in under the tall, rugged-looking cliffs, hoping to find better wind and relief from the current. They tacked close, very close. In coming about, *Freak* collided with *Volante*. The impact sheered off *Volante*'s jibboom with a sickening crunch. The jib collapsed and dragged the broken end of the spar through the water. Curses filled the air. The boats got clear. *Volante* drifted away, disabled in the tide, while her men struggled to clear the wreckage and get her under way with the mainsail alone. The waters of the Isle of Wight had done in two of *America*'s rivals and caused at least four others to retire, including *Alarm*, which had been a cause of concern among the men aboard the boat from New York.

The cutter *Aurora*, however, kept sailing on. Her captain watched the American schooner dash ahead through the sea, growing smaller in his glass as the time passed. But, as he observed her fine sailing capabilities, he realized he stood a fighting chance to challenge her. If he could just round St. Catherine's Point with the shifting wind, he would find himself on a beam reach, one of the most favorable points of sail for a cutter. If the wind stayed light, he might overtake her. The captain drove his men hard. He yelled at them to work with a will to catch the upstart. He mopped sweat from his brow and squinted at the gathering clouds on the horizon. What did the weather hold in store now? he wondered, and would the change favor the Americans? A short time later, the schooner disappeared from view behind St. Catherine's Point.

"Blast!" the captain of *Aurora* grumbled to himself. He redoubled his efforts, brought the cutter closer to shore. The cliffs channeled back eddies and puffs as the air flowed against the obstruction. A gust caught *Aurora*. She heeled over and bit into the waves. Spray pattered on the deck. Her crew cheered. Perhaps, the captain thought, there was still hope.

St. Catherine's Point dropped astern off *America*'s starboard quarter. Surf flashed against the base of the tall cliffs. Brown steered a northwesterly course toward The Needles at the far end of the island. The only vessels in sight were the accompanying steamers. Time passed. The sun sank lower through breaks in the clouds to the west. The sails of a cutter hove into view off *America*'s bow, causing quite a stir aboard.

"What yacht is that?" John Cox asked. He focused on her through his spyglass, but he could not see the name on the transom.

"Not to worry," Brown laughed. "I think we've found a playmate. She's not in the race."

"Well, let's give her some sport!" Hamilton said.

The appearance of the cutter ahead gave the men aboard *America* something to keep their minds keen on the competition. The more than five hours under sail, with no close-quarter matches since shortly after the start of the race, were beginning to slow the responses of the crew. Brown called for the men to trim the sails at every subtle shift in the wind. He sailed the yacht with a gentle hand, feeling her balance and how it changed with each adjustment of the sails. *America* did not seem to overtake the cutter. But that soon changed as a patch of wind spread out over the sea and surrounded the schooner. She picked up her heels and flew toward her unofficial rival.

The reporter for *The Times*, along with his peers, witnessed the sudden appearance of the cutter with much surprise. Again hope surfaced that one of their yachts might have in fact gotten ahead of the Yanks, unnoticed in all the excitement with the grounding of *Arrow*, and the mishap with *Volante*. He wrote of the event:

> The persons on board the steamers were greatly astonished at seeing ahead of the *America,* after she had rounded the Rockenend, a fine cutter . . . bowling away with all speed, as if racing away for her life, and it was some time before they could be persuaded she was not the *Aurora*; but she was, in reality, the *Wildfire,* 42 tons, Mr. F. Thynne, of the Royal Cork Club, which was taking a little share in the match to herself, and had passed the end at 3:40. The *America,* however, bore straight down for the cutter, which was thoroughly well sailed, and passed her, after a stern chase of more than an hour, though the *Wildfire* when first sighted, must have been two and a half miles ahead of the schooner. At 5:40 the *Aurora,* the nearest yacht, was fully seven and a half miles astern, the *Freak* being about a mile more distant, and the rest being "nowhere."

Off *America*'s bow rose the great upthrusts of chalk and limestone rock known as The Needles, rising like pillars from the sea. The wind and tide had eased off. But the schooner still made progress toward the headland, which marked the outer approaches to The Solent. Two-thirds of the race was over, and it looked to all those aboard the yacht that victory was theirs. Brown gazed astern and caught sight of the sails of three or four yachts. They sailed well with the wind blowing abeam. He worried a little about that, knowing that when he turned *America* to sail on a northeasterly course through the waters of The Solent back to Cowes the wind would blow almost dead astern, the slowest point of sail. In such light conditions, his rivals to the east might make up the miles he had put ahead of them. No race was ever decided until a boat crossed the finish line. Brown kept his concentration, and he insisted that the crew do the same.

As *America* rounded The Needles, a soft rain began to fall. The wind fell off to a mere whisper. The schooner now sailed in the lee of the land, while her rivals out in the English Channel no doubt had more breeze to work with. Brown looked at the foresail and jib hanging limp and lifeless, despite efforts to boom the sails out. The best canvas for speed for the run toward Cowes was the big mainsail, with its boom to help keep the shape of the sail. Brown ordered the crew to take in the jib and foresail. The boat drifted and ghosted in the intermittent wind. The steamers accompanying the yacht cruised near. The royal yachts, *Fairy* and *Victoria and Albert*, also steamed in the area. Cheers from the boats carried across the calm water to the people aboard *America*. It was a welcoming sound, for although the British seemed to have lost the race, they had not lost their sense of sportsmanship. They cheered for the Americans as if they were their own. *Victoria and Albert* waited for the schooner to come up to her, then proceeded on with her in company at half steam.

"We'll give the queen what she deserves, Captain," John Cox said. The pride in his voice was laced with emotion.

"Aye, sir," Brown said. He directed the men to drop the ensign.

All the men stood on *America's* deck with their hats off in a gesture of honor for Queen Victoria. It was "a mark of respect to the queen not the less becoming because it was bestowed by republicans," wrote the reporter for *The Times*.

The royal yachts headed back to Osborne, the queen and Prince Albert convinced that the race was over. The crowd in the spectator boats and aboard the steamers cheered, and also headed away from The Needles, back to Cowes, where more than 6,000 spectators waited at the finish line. A gun battery ashore fired in salute, the blasts obliterating the noise of all the people shouting. The gray smoke hung heavy around the guns and finally cleared.

Outside in the English Channel, *Aurora* found a good breeze. Her men could not see the events taking place on the other side of the island. They did not know their queen had left the course for home, that along the waterfront in Cowes and aboard the yachts gathered there to see the finish, the news of the race's probable outcome spread fast.

"Is the *America* first?" was the question on everyone's lips.

"Yes," came the replies from the passengers aboard the steamers.

"What's second?"

"Nothing."

The band prepared to play "Yankee Doodle Dandy." There were some members of the crowd who fumed about the loss. But the overwhelming majority of the people saw the wonder of the lone stranger's victory. They did not know the race was anything but finished.

Brown coaxed every bit of speed from *America* as she moved very slowly toward the finish line still more than five miles away. Astern, the white sails of a yacht appeared at The Needles. No one noticed right away. There were so many boats around. But it soon became clear that the sails belonged to the cutter *Aurora*. She seemed to have more wind than *America*. She slowly gained on the schooner. The minutes ticked by. The cutter closed the gap.

"Is there nothing more you can do, Captain?" John Cox asked. He looked aft toward the cutter. "She's closing on us."

"She's bringing the wind with her, I'm afraid, sir," Brown said.

Slowly, *America* sailed on. The cutter grew bigger the closer she got. The details of her deck, her rigging, the faces of her men became clear and distinct. The crowds around them roared and cheered. A puff of wind caught the schooner and she came to life. Brown sensed more than felt her accelerate. The finish line lay just a short distance off. The cutter closed the gap still more, riding the same brief increase in the breeze. The sound of "Yankee Doodle Dandy" drifted over the water as the schooner glided across the finish line at 8:37 P.M., just eight minutes ahead of *Aurora*, the game little cutter that almost won the day. Cannons at the clubhouse battery boomed. The flash of the muzzles dazzled the onlookers.

The crew aboard *America* got to their feet and shouted. They waved their hats in the air. The scene was one of complete chaos.

RACECOURSE FOR THE 100 SOVEREIGN CUP ON AUGUST 22, 1851

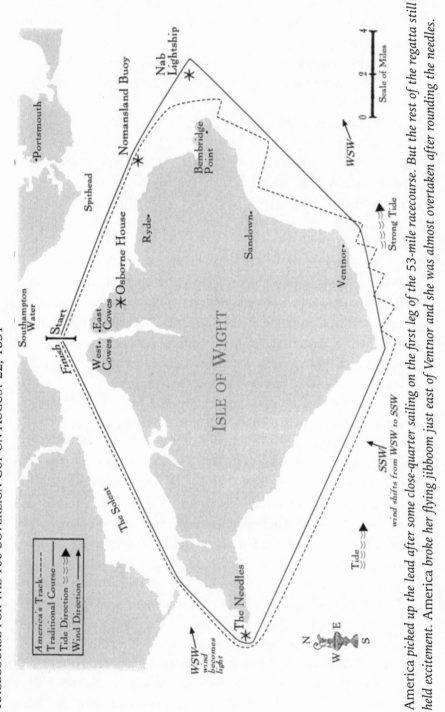

America picked up the lead after some close-quarter sailing on the first leg of the 53-mile racecourse. But the rest of the regatta still held excitement. America broke her flying jibboom just east of Ventnor and she was almost overtaken after rounding the needles.

Yachts surrounded the Americans as their boat sailed and drifted on. John Cox turned to Brown and shook his hand. "You did well, Captain. Very well indeed."

"Thank you, sir!"

The rest of the passengers shook Brown's hand and congratulated him, and they shook Comstock's and Underwood's hands as well.

"Nels, see the men are ready to drop anchor." Brown said. The sun was down and the twilight was deepening. He wanted to get the yacht safely secured right away. It would not do to collide with one of the many boats milling about.

"Aye, Captain," Comstock beamed. He went forward, calmed the crew down, and signaled to Brown that he was ready.

Brown brought the schooner slowly up into the wind. The men at the main sheet trimmed the sail to keep way on. She rounded up. The sail flapped lazily.

"Drop anchor!" Brown shouted above the din all around the boat.

"Anchor's away!" Comstock cried.

The yacht eased back on the anchor, setting it gently in the mud at the bottom of Cowes Roads.

Boats put out from the Royal Yacht Squadron and surrounded the schooner. The Earl of Wilton, the Marquis of Anglesey, and many other noblemen clambered aboard. The crew celebrated at the bow with Brown, Comstock, and Underwood. The commodore approached the crew, congratulated them for their work, and told Brown he was leaving with the rest of the dignitaries for a party ashore.

"Stay aboard her, Captain," John Cox said. "She'll need watching tonight, I think."

"Aye, sir. That I can do," Brown said. "But the men can surely go ashore."

"Indeed," John Cox said.

The commodore departed with his entourage. Most of the crew took the schooner's boat ashore and headed directly for the pubs.

Brown sat in the cockpit, a glass of John Cox's fine French wine in his hand, which the commodore generously offered as a reward for a job well done. Brown cradled a thick, sweet Cuban cigar in the other. He turned to Nels and laughed. It was not his usual hearty chuckle, but one with a bittersweet ring to it.

"You know, Nels," Brown said. "The commodore's going to be the talk of the town."

"Aye, that he is," Comstock said. He sipped from his glass of wine and looked out at the water. "But it's the boat that won the day."

The first explosions of the fireworks display rang out and split the air with a massive boom. The sky flashed bright blue, orange, and red. More fireworks went off. Rockets screamed. The crowd gathered to watch roared and shouted in delight.

Brown drew heavily on a cigar thinking of George Steers. He set his wineglass down and ran his hand along the smooth wood of the cockpit coaming. "She's a fine boat and she sails like the wind, Nels."

The two men craned their necks skyward. The pace of the explosions increased. The reports thundered and echoed off the buildings and hills ashore. The water reflected the light and illuminated the outlines of the boats in the anchorage. Dense clouds of smoke wafted toward the schooner, mingled with the cigar smoke, and drifted on. The last of the rockets detonated above The Solent and their shrieks faded. *America* rode quietly at anchor, her captain and first mate at peace and at one with her.

AFTERWORD

America's victory in the race around the Isle of Wight on August 22, 1851, stunned and amazed the British people. The schooner from New York had previously shown she was a strong match against any of the yachts in the British fleet. But the fact that she beat eight cutters, two of which were deemed the fastest sailers in England, in conditions better suited to the single-masted rig caused great surprise and embarrassment. The reporter for *The Times* described the reaction of his countrymen in his follow-up article covering the regatta.

> The result of yesterday's race appears to have come upon them [the yachting community] like a thunder clap . . . the details of the race, the peculiarities of the build of the American schooner, and the humiliating result, form the sole subject of conversation here, from the Royal Yacht Commodore, in his handsomely appointed club-house, to the ragged and barefooted urchin who offers to carry your carpet bag to the hotel, if you are lucky enough to have one.

John Cox, Edwin, and Colonel Hamilton all said later that they were surprised as well, not so much because the schooner had won but because there was no outward show of ill will among most of the people they encountered after the race. The British were anything but sore losers. Indeed, Queen Victoria and Prince Albert visited the yacht and congratulated John Cox on his victory. In his *Reminiscences*, Hamilton wrote about the response of the British after *America*'s victory over the Royal Yacht Squadron:

> I have great pleasure in referring to the courtesy with which we were treated by all persons with whom we met, and the spirit with which they accepted their defeat. Nothing could be more manly or in a better spirit; so much was this so, that I remarked to a lady, "Your friends do not seem to feel any mortification or even dissatisfaction at their defeat." "Oh!" said she, "if you could hear what I do, you would know that they feel it most deeply."

It is to the credit of the British, and particularly members of the Royal Yacht Squadron, that they retained their sense of sportsmanship in spite of their irritation at having been defeated. It is also to the Royal Yacht Squadron's credit that the sailing committee amended their rules on two counts prior to the race to accommodate the visitors. They dispensed with the regulation stating that a yacht entered in a contest must have only one owner. They allowed Captain Brown to boom out *America*'s sails, if he chose to. This gave her an advantage over the cutters, though as it turned out it was not of significant enough importance to make much difference in the outcome of the event. After the race, the sailing committee put aside the protest filed by George H. Ackers of the schooner *Brilliant* against *America* for failing to round the Nab Lightship. The committee concluded that *America* won fair and square, and that she should not be denied the One Hundred Sovereign Cup.

The Royal Yacht Squadron's loss created a lasting stir in the British press that extended well into the autumn of 1851. Essays on how to improve yacht designs, analysis of what went wrong, and arguments in favor of a renewed vigor to pursue innovation in all things lest Britannia fall far behind Brother Jonathan appeared in newspapers throughout the land. (See Appendix B.) In contrast to the magnanimous response of the British press to their defeat at the hands of the New Yorkers, the United States newspapers crowed about the victory, savoring it as a vindication of American superiority. Word of *America*'s triumph off the Isle of Wight reached New York via steamer in early September. On September 4, *The New York Herald* published the following notice:

> It appears that the yacht *America*, belonging to this port, has had a trial with eighteen [fourteen] of the best English yachts, and that she outsailed them all, with ease. Mr. Stevens' wager of ten thousand guineas had not been accepted at the last dates [the last time news came from Europe], nor do we think it will be. Truly, John Bull must, by this time, certainly think that the United States is not such a despicable nation as the London *Times* would fain make us out. We have beaten them on the sea and on land. Our packet ships never were approached by the English; our steamships have outstripped their best; our plows and reaping machines are acknowledged, by even themselves, to be superior to anything of the kind they ever saw; and now they are dared, to the tune of ten thousand guineas, or fifty thousand dollars, to put the best of their yachts, without respect to rig, in the mats with the *America*. At this rate, John Bull will have the liberty, ere long, of boasting more of what he has been, than of what he is.

What the editorial writer at *The New York Herald* did not know at the time he wrote his story was that the British did, in fact, put up a show of accepting the challenge for a match race in the English Channel. Shamed at the scathing articles that appeared in *The Times* and other British newspapers condemning the British yachtsmen as cowards and comparing them to wood pigeons, Robert Stephenson, a member of the Royal Yacht Squadron and an influential leader in Parliament, accepted John Cox's challenge. Everyone involved knew Stephenson's one-hundred-ton, iron schooner *Titania* stood no chance of winning. Stephenson's acceptance of John Cox's proposal was a face-saving measure and nothing else. If he gave the New Yorkers their race, they could not go back to the United States boasting that not a single yachtsman in England dared race alone against *America*. Hamilton wrote:

> After these efforts on our part to get up a match without success, the famous engineer, Mr. Stevenson [properly spelled Stephenson], owner of the *Titania*, to afford the American Yacht an opportunity to sail, as Commodore Stevens had proposed, agreed to enter the *Titania*, without, however, any hope of success.

The race took place on August 28, 1851, over a course from the Nab Lightship to a steamer situated twenty miles offshore, then back to the Nab. Based on the impossible odds against *Titania*, Stephenson wisely offered John Cox a wager of only one hundred guineas, the equivalent of five hundred United States dollars. It was far short of the $50,000 the commodore was willing to put up, but John Cox accepted the bet. Hamilton described how *America* thrashed *Titania*:

> Going out before the wind, the *America* took the lead a short distance and held it all the way out, although she broke the gaff of her fore-sail, which was taken in and spliced, by which she of course lost some time. She passed round the steamer ahead of her competitor, and took the lead beating back. The wind freshened to a wholesale breeze, and the *Titania* was left behind a distance which our pilot estimated at seven miles. [*America* arrived back at the Nab fifty-two minutes ahead of *Titania*.]

The one-sided skirmish with *Titania* rounded out the adventure in Great Britain. The Americans had had enough, and so, evidently, had the British. There was talk of additional challenges, but nothing came of them. The sailing season drew to a close in September, and it was time for John Cox and company to head for home. The schooner had served her purpose. Instead of paying Captain Brown and his crew to sail her back to New York, John Cox paid off the men and secured passage for them on a westbound steamship.

Dick Brown was relieved. He was anxious to get back to his wife and family, and to his friends aboard *Mary Taylor*. He was also more than ready to leave astern the constant socializing and pretense of the aristocracy, both the English and the American versions of it. His time in England had opened his eyes, shown him in stark terms just how wide the gulf was between the classes. He relished his return to the simple, straightforward ways of the workingmen and the uncomplicated lives they led at sea.

John Cox and his cohorts scouted around Great Britain looking for a buyer interested in the schooner. It did not take long to strike a deal. They sold *America* for five thousand guineas to John de Blaquiere, a captain in the British army from a titled family with extensive land holdings in Ireland. The transaction was worth twenty-five thousand American dollars, five thousand dollars over the price paid for the schooner. Subtracting expenses the syndicate cleared a net gain of $1,750 on the enterprise. (For more information about *America*'s later years, see Appendix A.)

John Cox and company were heralded as heroes upon their return to New York. They basked in the glory of it all with unabashed enthusiasm. The public adulation culminated on October 2 at a sumptuous dinner held in John Cox's honor at the Astor House, which many New Yorkers considered the best hotel in the city. Many of the most famous and wealthy men in the highest social circles attended the banquet to pay homage to John Cox.

At the center of the room, amid the plates of roast duck, quail, partridges, beef, and mutton, French cream cakes, claret jelly pastry, and ornamental confections shaped to recreate yacht *America* and *Titania*, the Crystal Palace, and the steamship *Baltic* stood the silver cup brought home from the well-appointed confines of the Royal Yacht Squadron. The cup remained hidden under a veil for most of the night while the men ate and drank, offering toasts to the commodore, Queen Victoria, the Earl of Wilton, President Millard Fillmore, and many others, including Dick Brown and his men. The one conspicuous person not mentioned by name was George Steers, who was not invited to the dinner, and nor, of course, was Captain Brown.

After midnight the speeches came to an end and the cup was unveiled. The men, many of them warmed with a surplus of excellent wine and other libations, crowded around the silver cup. It stood twenty-seven inches high from its circular base to the top of the curved handle facing a spout. Six bulbous shields girded its midsection. Intricate curls and scrolls decorated the cup, which in fact was hollow and not a cup at all, but a ewer resembling a water pitcher. The cup was the creation of R. & S. Garrard, a silversmith company engaged as Queen Victoria's Crown Jeweller. Robert Garrard, the head of the firm, designed and constructed the cup for his showroom in London in 1848. It caught the eye of the Marquis of Anglesey, who purchased it for one hundred sovereigns and gave it to the Royal Yacht Squadron as a racing trophy, according to Royal Yacht Squadron records. The first race featuring the cup was the one *America* had won.

Etched into the silver was an inscription naming the race, the defeated vessels, save *Aurora*, which was left off for some inexplicable reason, *America*, and Commodore Stevens. While George Steers was not mentioned or honored at the banquet, John Cox included Steers's name in the inscription, crediting him as the builder.

No reporters were admitted to the dinner. But the press was provided with written statements and copies of the speeches. The next day, *The New York Herald* and other newspapers in the city printed long columns recounting every detail of the event that was the talk of the town. Accompanying the story in the October 3 edition of *The New York Herald* was a letter indicative of others that had appeared in September. It seemed to many that the key to *America*'s success was not solely rooted in the moneyed soil of the city's elite, but in the hearts of the workingmen who designed the yacht and sailed her to victory. Steers and Brown received enthusiastic recognition for their achievements from the men and women working in the factories and shops, on the docks and in the shipyards. For them, Steers and Brown were the real heroes. John Cox and his ilk were viewed as an opportunistic group of hangers-on who claimed credit that did not belong to them exclusively. The letter was written by one of the many citizens who thought the commodore had crossed the line of common decency. The author of it went by the initials F. P. The complete text follows and illustrates the backlash against the New York Yacht Club that arose in circles of the "lower order."

To the Editor of *The New York Herald*.

Sir—I have noticed there has been a remarkable silence in regard to the person who built the yacht *America*. You are always willing to give honor and credit to those who deserve it, no matter whether they are working mechanics or millionaires; and when I see a man who works hard for his livelihood, that has a head to plan and a hand to form such a model as the *America*'s—a model whose equal, in my estimation, has never been seen either in England or America—passed over, and the praise given to others, I think everyone should know who that man is.

Perhaps if it had not been for the liberal offer of the New York Yacht Club the *America* would never have been built, but the club well knew who could build them a vessel that could beat all England. Why, only think, sir—she has beaten the world! Can any man, much less a poor man, afford to dispense with any of the credit to which he is justly entitled?

The previous performances of Mr. George Steers in building fast vessels convinced certain gentlemen who had the means and the spirit—for which I honor them—that if anyone could build them such a vessel as they wanted, he was the person. He is the builder of the *Una*, a small sloop-rigged yacht which bore away the prize from the *Maria* on two different occasions. He built the *Cygnet, Siren, Cornelia, Sybil, Gimcrack*, pilot boats *Mary Taylor, Hagstaff, M. H. Grinnell*, and the *Manhattan*, for years the pride and boast of every island boy. The writer of this has never exchanged fifty words with Mr. Steers in his life, but he cannot forget with what delight he looked on the beautiful proportions of his productions in their boyish days. And now when the magnitude of their performances has increased with his years, he cannot be silent when he sees his well-earned laurels taken by another.

F. P.

Upon reading this blast of criticism, John Cox replied with his own letter. It was published the next day, October 4, in *The New York Herald*.

To the Editor of *The New York Herald*.

Sir:—In your paper of this morning there is a communication headed "The Builder of *America*." The writer complains that there has been a remarkable silence in regard to who built the yacht *America*, and that he cannot remain silent when he sees his well-earned laurels taken by another. Your correspondent is, I think, mistaken. Colonel Hamilton, I know, intended, and I am positive did state, that the contractor was Mr. W. H. Brown, and that the builder was Mr. George Steers, lauding the one for his spirited offer and the other for his unrivalled skill in modeling and constructing her. In the hurried statement of such of the toasts and proceedings as were furnished to the gentlemen who reported them, or he could remember or procure, some were, no doubt, omitted or mislaid, and among which must have been the statement made by Colonel Hamilton. I regret as sincerely as "F. P." can do that the omission was made, and as I have no wish to appropriate to myself the property of another I will take this occasion to repeat—what I have over and over again stated, both in England and in this country—that the model and construction of the yacht *America* was due, and due alone, to Mr. George Steers.

Yours respectfully,
John Cox Stevens

To make up for the slight of the New York Yacht Club, some members of the city's elite threw Steers a party in his honor in December of 1851. Among these men was the shipping magnate, Edward Knight Collins, for whom Steers had designed his fast steamships. George Law, a prominent merchant, William H. Webb, a shipbuilder, John Dimon, a builder of engines and other machinery, and William H. Brown.

Interestingly enough, despite the public backlash at the time, all contemporary accounts written about the race of August 22, 1851, slant the details in favor of John Cox and the New York Yacht Club. The commodore and his cohorts are lionized. George Steers is mentioned in connection with his innovations regarding the yacht's construction, but he is relegated to a role subservient to that of the syndicate. Dick Brown is hardly mentioned at all, which probably would have suited him. His right-hand man, Nelson Comstock, appears in name only.

When asked about his role as captain in terms of assuring *America*'s success, Brown demurred and gave credit to the boat, and thereby indirectly to George Steers. He was fond of saying, "Ahh, but you see, we had a very fine boat. She sailed like the wind." He repeated this hundreds of times. He never did say much about the commodore, good or bad. He simply accepted that the ways of the rich were not his, and he left it at that. His humility and forbearing nature won him respect from the upper classes and members of the "lower order." It was part of his success as a person and a mariner, and why he was able to get along in both worlds.

Dick Brown went back to work aboard *Mary Taylor*, where he earned a good living. He also spent time as the captain of the coastal steamship *Falcon* plying the waters between Boston, New York, Charleston, and Savannah. He was unhappy with steamers, however, saying that they reminded him of overgrown tea kettles. He returned to his work as a Sandy Hook Pilot. When the fancy struck him, he took time off from piloting to serve as master aboard the growing number of yachts in New York Harbor. He was always fond of a race, whether it was at sea aboard a pilot boat or at the helm of a yacht. The thrill of fast sailing was deep in his bones and he never tired of it. Over his long life, he is credited with having sailed as master in fifty to sixty yacht races.

George Steers was less forgiving of John Cox than Dick Brown.

In a sense, this is not surprising. Captain Brown did not feel wronged at the hands of the syndicate. However much he disapproved of the pomp and pretense, it did not affect him. On the other hand, George Steers did feel slighted and financially abused. He was the only one to lose a significant sum of money on the yacht. The feud continued between George Steers and John Cox, as did the controversy of how many of the working class felt both Steers and Dick Brown were robbed of the credit for their achievement, that they were in fact the men who made the victory possible in the first place, but were nevertheless ignored because they lacked money and power. News reports to this effect surfaced again in 1854 and angered John Cox, who by then was getting pretty tired of the insults. He insisted that James Gordon Bennett, editor and publisher of *The New York Herald,* republish his letter in response to F. P.'s allegations made three years earlier. He added a few additional lines which are brief, but no less telling of the ongoing conflict.

> I can but regret it [the letter to F. P.] seems not to have answered the purpose intended. If Mr. Steers or his friends will write for me a disclaimer of all the honor of modeling or building the *America* more satisfactory to him or to them, I will sign it with great pleasure.
>
> Your obdt. servant,
> *John Cox Stevens*

By the mid-1850s, George Steers had added to his reputation as a designer and shipbuilder, after opening his own shipyard with James. Steers continued to build yachts, but he branched out to take on larger, more lucrative projects. He was noted for the design and supervision of the construction of the United States frigate, *Niagara,* the largest steam warship built in the mid-1850s in the Brooklyn Navy Yard. She was massive at 345 feet. In his own shipyard while work continued on *Niagara,* Steers built the fifth steamship for Edward Knight Collins, *Adriatic,* the largest and most luxurious steam liner the world had yet seen.

Work on both ships progressed according to schedule, and *Nia-*

gara and *Adriatic* were launched by the spring of 1856. Steers was busy overseeing the finishing touches on the ships in preparation for their first trials at sea. Life appeared full of promise for him and his family. He had at last realized his goal of owning a shipyard and he had earned the recognition he felt he deserved for his innovative yacht and ship designs.

On September 25, while on his way home to his summer residence on Long Island, he was severely injured in a carriage accident. It seemed his lifelong fear of horses was in fact justified. James found him lying in the dirt at the side of the road, bleeding and unconscious. George died that night without regaining his faculties. He never saw his family, nor his brother, lingering over him distraught with worry and grief. He never saw *Niagara* and *Adriatic* sail the seas, nor had he seen his most cherished creation, *America*, since he had looked back at her on his way across The Solent that warm August night in 1851, as he departed from the Isle of Wight. James Steers, who was very close to his brother, was never the same again. He carried on for a while in the business he and George had begun, but he ultimately closed the shipyard and retired from all matters related to the sea.

The following year, in an article about George Steers published in the *United States Nautical Magazine and Naval Journal*, the writer of the story closed with the following sentiments:

[George Steers was] a self-made mechanic, of more solid worth to the nation and mankind than legions of titled heroes and monied nabobs. . . . he had but entered the vestibule of his usefulness and fame; his sudden and violent death was a calamity to the country and a loss to the world. What he would have done in the course of the long life that seemed promised to him is now sealed up in the mysteries of the grave.

Less than a year later, George Steers's old nemesis, John Cox, died of heart and kidney disease at the age of seventy-two, leaving a personal estate estimated at approximately $1.5 million. Grief stricken after the death of his wife, Maria, from a long illness in

1855, and already feeble from his own health problems, John Cox retired from yachting. He sold his estate in New York City, and in the country, and moved to South Amboy, New Jersey. He donated a significant sum of money to local charities, including the church. The newspapers carried long obituaries after his death on June 10, 1857, and, of course, credited him with the victory off the Isle of Wight. The John Cox legend was already growing with full vigor. It continued so for the next one hundred fifty years while Dick Brown and Nelson Comstock, and, to a lesser extent, George Steers, faded into obscurity.

Before John Cox died, the matter of what to do with the One Hundred Sovereign Cup was at last settled. The members of the syndicate, with the exception of Hamilton Wilkes, who had died in 1852, had talked about melting the cup down to make silver medals for each of the five remaining parties involved in the great victory. But that idea did not win much support among them, and it was shelved in favor of another option that ended up changing the face of yacht racing forever. The syndicate gave the cup to the New York Yacht Club with the provision that it be set aside as a perpetual challenge trophy. The document outlining the terms of the gift specified, among other things, that any recognized yacht club from another country could challenge the New York Yacht Club in a race for the cup. The idea was to foster yacht racing on an international front, and in that the syndicate succeeded well beyond their own expectations.

Yachting continued to grow in popularity through the 1850s and 1860s. New designs were tried, the size of the boats increased, and even the "lower order" began to enjoy the sport, though in little sloops, not in the immense racing machines of the rich. But still no challenge came from a foreign yacht club regarding what was now called the America's Cup. In the meantime, however, Dick Brown served as a yacht captain during races, as did Nelson Comstock, and his brothers Peter, George Washington, and Andrew Jackson. One of Dick Brown's sons, Charles, who had emulated his father's career as both pilot and yacht captain, was also part of the racing scene every summer as the fleets took to the water in trials of speed that drew hundreds of spectators on land and afloat.

In the late 1860s, James Ashbury, a member of the Royal Thames Yacht Club, challenged the New York Yacht Club for the America's Cup. Numerous letters were exchanged. The contest did not come off until the summer of 1870. In fact, the skirmish began before the race, which occurred on August 8 in New York Harbor. According to *The New York Daily Times,* James Gordon Bennett, Jr., a good friend of Dick Brown's, hired him as captain of the yacht *Dauntless* to skipper the boat in a transatlantic race against the challenger, *Cambria.* Both boats drove hard in the crossing, during which a man was washed overboard on *Dauntless. Cambria* won the race, making port ninety minutes ahead of *Dauntless* after a crossing of more than 3,000 miles.

Cambria's performance inspired concern among many people that the British yacht might snatch away the America's Cup and take it triumphantly back to England, where the gloating might carry against the west winds all the way to the shores of a much-humiliated United States. To make this unfortunate outcome less likely, the New York Yacht Club fielded a fleet of boats, each with differing rigs and sailing characteristics, to defend the cup against the challenger. This underhanded tactic defied the spirit of what the syndicate had wanted. John Cox and his friends meant to encourage match racing, a boat for boat defense and challenge for the cup. The New York Yacht Club, however, thought the odds needed a little stacking on this occasion. Ashbury, of course, considered the entire proceeding unfair, but he entered *Cambria* anyway. On the day of the race, Ashbury sailed against seventeen yachts of the New York Yacht Club, including *America,* which was then owned by the United States Navy but released for duty temporarily to allow her to participate in the historic first running of the America's Cup, so named in her honor.

Excitement swept over New York City as the race date drew near. Yachting, it seemed, had taken hold of the city's residents and captured their imagination just as it had nineteen years earlier when Dick Brown sailed *America* to victory. Brown, incidentally, sailed aboard *Dauntless* during the race. His son, Charles, was captain of *America,* and Nelson Comstock's brother, Andrew Jackson, was master of *Magic*. The men who worked the yachts were a small group. Everyone knew each other, and it was part of the fun to pit friend against friend in pursuit of victory. In this case, however, the focus was on *Cambria* and the threat she represented.

The *New York Daily Times* reporter described the high level of interest in the race among the general public.

> Large crowds of people were seen hurrying to the docks for the purpose of embarking on vessels which were to convey them to the scene of the race. Women and children were especially numerous, and appeared to be as eager to see the yachts as their male relatives and friends. The majority of them presented a very respectable and genteel appearance, and it seemed as if the greater part of the middle and wealthy classes had, moved by a simultaneous impulse, turned out on the occasion, and had suddenly become warm patrons of the noble pastime, yachting. . . . The excitement even invaded the most aristocratic portions of the City, and private carriages, filled with fair and gaily dressed inmates, were seen in large numbers on Fifth and Madison avenues, carrying their owners toward the river side.

The race did not disappoint the onlookers. Bands played "Yankee Doodle" as the fleet swept away from the anchorage off Staten Island and sailed down to Sandy Hook, then out to the Sandy Hook Lightship. The breeze blew fair and freshened. The yachts made for a grand sight, their canvas spread to the wind, spray flying at the bows. The first yacht to cross the finish line was *Magic*. *Dauntless* finished second, *America* fourth, and *Cambria* eighth. The America's Cup was safe. It remained in the hands of the New York Yacht Club for 132 years, until Australia finally succeeded as the first challenger to win it in 1983.

Dick Brown was sixty years old at the first running of the America's Cup. He was, by then, known throughout the maritime trades as "Old Dick Brown." *Mary Taylor* had been run down and sunk off Sandy Hook during the American Civil War; all hands were saved.

Brown had recently left her to supervise the construction of a new pilot boat, *Mary E. Fish*. He and his men served aboard her through most of the 1880s. The deaths of Brown's son Charles and Brown's wife in the late 1870s left a void in his life. He found solace at sea with his compatriots aboard *Mary E. Fish*. He was the oldest Sandy Hook Pilot still on duty. Most of his friends from his early days were dead or retired.

Late one February night in 1885, while working to bring a steamship safely into port, Brown suffered an accident. He was seventy-four years old. His brother, Joseph Brown, described what happened for a reporter from *The New York Herald*:

> It was the coldest night of the winter, and as there wasn't steam enough to bring the vessel into port my brother caused her to be anchored. For twelve hours—in fact, all the night— he remained on the bridge unprotected, and at times his feet were so cold that they [the crew] brought hot ashes from the fire room, which they placed about them. When he reached home and took off his boots he found his left foot frozen. He had been confined to his home since that time.

Brown developed gangrene and died a long death. He had spent almost sixty years on the sea, and all that time he was haunted with the thought that it might one day take him, as it had his four friends from Mystic. Unlike the others, who all drowned at sea, Brown died in bed surrounded by his remaining two sons and four daughters at his home in Brooklyn on June 18. It was not the ocean that had taken him after all, but his sense of honor and duty, an unwillingness to let down the long tradition of his calling.

APPENDIX A

REQUIEM

Among the old salts along the waterfronts of the world, there remains a singular belief that a sailing vessel possesses her own unique personality. No two boats are alike, even if the designs are the same. It is almost as if the marriage of wood, rope, and sails with the wind and waves creates a living thing that takes on an individual character over time. In the case of *America*, her character was much like that of a thoroughbred racehorse, with a long line of noble descendants behind her pedigree, and the strength of heart to push to the limits for a chance at victory. It is dangerous to impose on an inanimate object the features of a living creature capable of feeling the pleasure that comes from the warmth of the sun or the discomfort of a wet, cold rain, the glow and well-being when one is appreciated, the pain and loneliness that stems from long neglect. Yet, for anyone who knows the sea and sailing vessels, both yacht and ship, that move in harmony with the elements across the oceans, it is a danger most are willing to abide.

America, like the handful of other famous sailing craft etched into the collective memory of people around the world, was a special boat in all respects. Her sharp, beautiful lines, her raking masts, her ability to sail fast and yet withstand the worst of storms strikes deep into the spirit of those with an appreciation for a creation as big as life itself, perhaps bigger when the lasting memory of her exploits is considered. For one hundred fifty years, *America* has occupied a stage in American maritime history shared by the likes of the warship USS *Constitution*, the clipper ship *Flying Cloud*, and the whaler *Charles W. Morgan*.

While two of these sailing vessels lasted long enough to find homes in maritime museums, *Flying Cloud* and *America* are gone forever. The passage of time wore them down. *America* plied the waters of the world for ninety years. She gave good service to her many owners. She saw the heat of battle in the American Civil War as a blockade runner for the Confederate Navy, and as a blockade gunboat for the Union. She won and lost races on both sides of the Atlantic. Hers was a full life. But like a rocket searing across a black sky, her true glory was a mere burst in the long chain of years that marked her beginning and end of her service. The few short months she was under the command of Captain Richard Brown, sailing for the syndicate of six New Yorkers in a challenge against all of Great Britain's best yachts, her race around the Isle of Wight on August 22, 1851, stands as her most important and dramatic time upon the sea. She reached her zenith in the first year she sailed.

After *America*'s purchase from the syndicate in September 1851, she went through a series of owners and spent much time idle at her moorings in England. Dry rot set in and weakened her, but she was rebuilt in 1858 and continued to sail primarily in English waters under a new name, *Camilla*, until she wound up in the hands of the Confederate Navy in 1861. The Confederates evidently paid $60,000 for her, knowing that she was the former yacht of great fame ten years earlier and that she could, in Captain Brown's words, "sail like the wind."

The Confederates sent her to England under the British flag, with her previous owner serving as captain, a British sympathizer for the southern cause. The sale of the yacht was kept secret. Aboard were agents on a spy mission to buy steamships for the South's small navy, and other arms. Her swift sailing ability enabled her to outsail the gunboats of the Union blockade, making her a valuable prize. While *Camilla* was in English waters, she engaged in some yacht races and for all appearances seemed innocent of any subterfuge. However, word reached the Union Navy that the former yacht *America* was sailing with Confederate agents aboard and was possibly in the service of the Confederate Navy. Blockade ships stationed off southern ports were advised to look for and capture her. They never did under sail or steam.

At the fall of Jacksonville, Florida, in March 1862, the Confederates scuttled *Camilla* in a creek off St. Johns River to keep her out of Union hands. She was discovered, salvaged, and put into service for the Union as the USS *America*. She served as a dispatch carrier and blockade boat for much of the war. She was credited with assisting in the capture or destruction of four enemy ships. Toward the end of the war, she was used as a training vessel for naval officers at the Naval Academy, temporarily located in Newport, Rhode Island. *America* remained in Navy service until 1873, three years after she participated in the first running of the America's Cup off New York Harbor. She was sold to a private owner, General Benjamin F. Butler, who kept her in his family for more than two decades.

Butler modified *America* extensively on four separate occasions. Donald McKay, builder of the world-famous *Flying Cloud*, carried out the first refit in 1875. Between 1875 and 1886, Butler lengthened *America*'s bow and added six feet to her stern. He lengthened her main topmast and bowsprit, and added a fore topmast. Other changes increased her sail area from the original 5,263 square feet to 13,545 square feet. He replaced the tiller with a wheel for easier steering and to provide more room in the cockpit.

Butler died in early 1893. In many respects, *America* perished with him. Without the attention and large sums of money needed to keep her in shape she began a slow decline. She was laid up for four years, then briefly brought back into service. She ran and lost her last race in 1901, and was by that time greatly weakened as a result of hard sailing and long neglect. It seemed the yachting community had forgotten her as she lay for years at her berth near the Chelsea Street Bridge in Boston. Near the close of World War I, a group of traders purchased her to go into the packet service, but a member of the Eastern and New York Yacht Clubs interceded, hoping to keep what he believed was a national treasure on American soil. In 1921, a group of men started a fund to pay for her restoration and return to the Naval Academy in Annapolis, again hoping that she might be preserved for posterity. Their efforts succeeded to a point.

America was sold back to the United States Navy for one dollar and towed to Annapolis. The Navy, however, did not allow the private funds raised for *America*'s restoration to be used; nor did the Navy foot the bill for the work she needed to keep her seaworthy. By 1930, it was estimated that more than $80,000 was needed to make *America* shipshape again. The sum was deemed too much in view of the Great Depression. The schooner slowly fell apart at the wharf. Over the next decade the yachting community lobbied the Navy for action, and finally, in 1941, the Navy agreed to start the restoration process—twenty years after acquiring her with a promise to preserve her for the American public. The Navy hired the Annapolis Yacht Yard to undertake the repairs. The yard crew hauled her out of the water and built a shed over her to protect her from the elements. Little by little, the crew began the long process of ripping out her rotten planks and frames, and replacing them with new ones.

Despite the best intentions of the men who tried to save her, the outbreak of World War II put an end to any further work on *America*. Annapolis Yacht Yard put all of its labors into the construction of torpedo boats. The yacht remained in her shed. On March 29, 1942, an unusually vicious spring snowstorm swept down on the state of Maryland and the Northeast. Several feet of heavy, wet snow fell through Saturday into Sunday, the week before Easter. Trees snapped and toppled under the weight of the snow. Blackouts cut off electricity to thousands of homes. Unknown to the few workers in the yard on that Palm Sunday, the frames and beams of *America*'s shed had nearly reached their breaking point. Suddenly, the workers heard a frightening rumble. They raced outside and discovered the shed had collapsed. Beneath the splintered planks lay the crushed remains of *America*, smashed beyond any hope of salvage.

America's wreckage lay amid the broken shed for the duration of the war. Then, one day in 1945, a crew approached the site. They carried picks and axes. One man drove a huge crane. The sound of chopping and banging mingled with the mutter of the crane's engine, the squeal of its machinery as one large section of the yacht after another was lifted away and placed in a pile of debris that grew over the afternoon.

When the men finished they wiped their brows and surveyed the pile. Some of the crew poured kerosene over the timbers. The foreman lit a match and tossed it. With a *whoosh*, flames erupted and leapt high in the soft breeze blowing in off Chesapeake Bay. Gray and black smoke rose skyward against the fading light of the sun to the west. The men stood silent for the most part, though some expressed sadness. It was a bad end for a lady like *America*, who had given so much and received so little in return. That she might have been saved was on the lips of many. But the world had seen much that might have been and was not over the last ninety-four years. Almost a century had passed since *America* sailed, proud and beautiful on the sea, with her crew of strong sailors ready to spring to action. Nothing was the same. As the fire burned out to leave a glow of embers, the last remnants of *America* crackled and hissed. She was gone forever, save for the few pieces of her that remained safe: her skylight, the cockpit seat, the eagle that once adorned her stern, her companionway hatch, a few blocks and deadeyes. Twilight settled over the yacht yard, and an age beyond reclaiming drifted off into the darkness as wisps of acrid smoke.

APPENDIX B

LESSONS

After *America*'s two victories in August 1851, the British reevaluated their traditional approach to yacht design. The form of hull, the placement of the masts on a schooner-rigged vessel, and the cut and method of setting sails all received detailed analysis. Many of *America*'s design concepts were subsequently incorporated into British yachts. However, the British did not turn their backs on all of their past practices. Indeed, the issues were hotly debated, as the following letter makes clear. It first appeared in *The Times* of London and was republished in the *New York Daily Times* on September 18, 1851.

The American and English Yachts
To the Editor of *The Times*:
Sir—It is always regarded in history as peculiar to the most distinguished generals, that they have best known how to turn disasters to profitable use, and have frequently converted the ruins of defeat into foundations of victory. We are now in circumstances which give full scope to the display of such qualities, if we possess them. We have been beaten—defeated—on our own elements. Our yacht squadron, so long masters of the Solent, hitherto victorious in all sea fights, are completely routed—I had almost said, put to flight. For a long time, not one of the Solent Sea Kings could be found to face the enemy or accept his challenge, and the American would have returned without his gage being taken up, had not the little *Titania*, of only half the tonnage, and therefore no adequate match, been courageous enough to hazard a defeat. Even the *Alarm*, which had been so long the champion of the English waters, declined battle. The victory of the *America* is complete.

[The writer then goes on at considerable length to specify the peculiarities of the *America* and concludes thus:]

I have entered thus minutely into all these points, because I conceive it to be of great importance that we should wisely and in time prepare ourselves for the probable contest of next year. We are more likely to fail next year by a blundering imitation of the unessentials of our victor than by any other course. It is most undesirable that we should be driven by a sudden defeat to abandon any of the excellent points which our own long experience may have taught us to be unquestionably excellent. The roominess, the comfort, the excellent sea-going qualities, the ease of motion in bad weather, are points in our own yacht-building which we must on no account abandon. It is our duty, therefore, to see what we must do to win next year.

1. We must build yachts of the newest construction, of as large a size as may be likely to come against us—i.e., somewhat larger than the *America*; and not allow ourselves to be caught, as this year, with a vessel of half the tonnage only fit even to accept the challenge.

2. We must adopt the best scientific principles of construction for the build of our new yachts, instead of allowing old routine to govern us. The Americans have boldly adopted the wave system, and applied it to the *America* in an unmitigated form; we must as boldly adopt it, and give speed to our vessels by offering to the water that form which shall produce the least disturbance to it, and receive from it the least resistance.

3. We must not abandon such forms of midship sections as have been found to give easy motion and good sea qualities to our own yachts.

4. We must thoroughly revise our system of rigging and cutting sails. The true theory of sails is that they are flat boards. All mechanical means must be adopted to give them that form, and make them keep it. The superior cut of American sails has long been matter of notoriety to seamen. Sail-cutters have long resisted the abandonment of cherished prejudices on this head. They must now at once adopt the true sail-theory of plane surfaces, and carry it out—whether with the use of booms or a new cut, or both, they must well consider.

5. As to rigging, the simpler the rigging, the fewer the ropes, the better. The Americans have long been distinguished in this respect for simplicity and efficiency. Multiplicity of ropes and blocks is

an old-fashioned error, out of which we are rapidly escaping, and the *America* merely gives us a fresh impulse in this direction.

In conclusion, I have only to express a hope—one which has prompted this letter—that we shall not degenerate into vulgar imitation of our victor, a course in which we shall always be behind him, but rouse ourselves to apply more independently than hitherto the resources of our science and skill to the attainment of that superiority in yacht building, which we have hitherto fancied we possessed.

> I have the honor to be your obedient servant,
> *A MEMBER OF SEVERAL YACHT CLUBS*

AUTHOR'S NOTE

This book resulted from my long affection for *America*. But it also derived from a discovery I made while researching a previous book, *Flying Cloud*. In fleshing out my knowledge of New York Harbor in the 1850s, I studied the history of the Sandy Hook Pilots. The pilots fascinated me. They sailed swift schooners far out to sea to find ships to bring safely across the shoals off Sandy Hook. They rescued mariners in distress and braved storms. These were smart, tough sailors. I admired them. When I found out that the captain of *America* was a Sandy Hook Pilot, a fellow by the name of Richard Brown, my admiration grew, and I became increasingly curious about him. I had never heard of Brown before and I wanted to know more.

After finishing *Flying Cloud*, I went looking for additional information about Captain Brown. At first I found very little. Most accounts of *America* and the America's Cup included only his name and the fact that he was a Sandy Hook Pilot. The men who worked aboard the big racing boats in the mid-nineteenth century seldom showed up in histories of early American yachting. They were names without faces and pasts. Thanks to the Sandy Hook Pilots, however, I turned up a few rare volumes that included details on Captain Brown and his life at sea. I read records and old newspapers to find still more valuable material.

A mystery surfaced during the preliminary research on Captain Brown's life, and solving it indirectly added much to the story I wanted to tell. It was one of those serendipitous moments that happen only once in a long while. In nosing about for information on Brown, specifically, his place of birth, I discovered a relative of Brown's right-hand man aboard *America*: first mate Nelson Comstock. In her eighties and living in Connecticut, near New London, Margaret Comstock Thoms is the last living relative of Henry Nelson Comstock. Stashed away in her attic were documents that helped shed light on the Comstock boys, as she calls them.

Nelson was one of seven brothers. Of the seven, five were expert sailors. For more than forty years Peter Harris, Henry Nelson, Horace Tinker, Andrew Jackson, and George Washington were mates and captains on the big yachts sailing the waters of New York Harbor. Andrew Jackson Comstock was the most well known, with twenty-seven consecutive years of service as a yacht master. He was captain of *Magic*, which won the first America's Cup race in 1870, and of *Columbia*, which won the second defense of the America's Cup. Henry Nelson, who preferred using his middle name, also did his share of skippering for the elite yachtsmen of New York.

But was this man really Brown's first mate? It seemed too good to be true, and perhaps it was. I reviewed customs house papers recorded just prior to the departure of *America* on her transatlantic voyage on June 21, 1851, and found no Henry Nelson listed as crew. The papers included a Horatio Nelson Comstock and gave his age as twenty-five, not twenty-nine, as Henry Nelson was in 1851.

Juxtaposed against the customs house papers, however, was Margaret's indisputable link to a family of yachting captains from the mid-nineteenth century. Proof positive of the Comstock connection to the America's Cup came from the fact that Margaret owned the dress flags of *Columbia*, china from the yacht, a spyglass, and other artifacts. These were handed down to her from her mother, Andrew Jackson Comstock's daughter. Margaret has since donated these priceless bits of American maritime history to a museum in New London. She has other artifacts that she intends to leave to the New York Yacht Club after her death.

A thorough check of John Adams Comstock's *A History and Genealogy of the Comstock Family in America,* privately printed in Los Angeles in 1949, provided me with the assurances I needed to conclude that Margaret's great-uncle was indeed first mate aboard *America*. According to the best genealogical records available, no Comstock by the name of Horatio Nelson, or just plain Nelson Comstock, was alive and at the right age to have served aboard the schooner. The only Comstock that matched was Margaret's great-uncle. Given the preponderance of the evidence, I felt it was safe to proceed with the facts I had at hand.

My work with the Sandy Hook Pilots and Margaret Comstock Thoms represented a good start to researching the book. Yet, there was still much work to do. I wanted to bring to life the voyage across the North Atlantic, one of the most exciting parts of the adventure, and one that is skimmed over in most accounts of *America*. I learned that a man aboard the yacht during the crossing had kept a journal. His name was James R. Steers, brother of George Steers, the designer of the yacht. In his journal, Steers included the yacht's position when Brown was lucky enough to obtain a fix in the very foggy weather they encountered. He recorded wind directions, the speed and course of the schooner, and many remarks that helped me re-create the adventure.

Using Steers's data, I plotted the yacht's track on a nautical chart. I noted the wind directions to figure out how her sails were set and to see how she progressed through the storms and calms she met at sea. Once the yacht arrived in England, Steers's journal added invaluable insights into the conflicts that arose between the men who sailed the yacht and the men who owned her.

Among other firsthand accounts that proved useful was James Alexander Hamilton's *Reminiscences of James A. Hamilton; Or, Men and Events, at Home and Abroad, During Three Quarters of a Century,* which he published in 1869. Hamilton was one of the members of the New York Yacht Club present during the events that unfolded in England in connection with the yacht. John Cox Stevens, commodore of the New York Yacht Club, was helpful as well. His views and recollections of events are related in the New York newspapers of the time.

Contemporary sources such as newspapers and autobiographies written years after events always contain errors, contradictory information, and discrepancies. Several instances deserve mentioning. Some fairly recent accounts of *America* report that Henry Steers, son of James Steers, sailed across the Atlantic aboard the yacht. Yet the custom house records do not list him, nor does his father mention him at all during the voyage; he does later, when the family arrived in England. I was left wondering how Henry got to England and under what circumstances. It appeared logical to conclude that he came over on a steamship and stayed with members of the family in London until his father, brother, and uncle met him there after they came over to England from France, where *America* fitted out for the race. No one will know for certain, however.

Another bit of contention arose in various accounts over just which parties came up with the idea to build *America*. Some authors say it was George Steers, the designer, and William H. Brown, the builder. I found this highly unlikely given the terms of the agreement between Steers and Brown and the six members of the syndicate from the New York Yacht Club. Given that the letters of agreement were all in the hand of George Schuyler, and the rather favorable slant of the terms for the New York Yacht Club, it seemed once again logical to convey events based upon the assumption that it was the syndicate's proposal that inspired George Steers to create his revolutionary schooner. The passages related to the meeting of the syndicate were all based on the knowledge I had at hand, and the dialogue contained in them, while impossible to know for certain, does indeed impart the important considerations under discussion.

There were discrepancies about even so basic a fact as *America*'s true dimensions. The ones I included in the book were taken from *The New York*

Herald, though I took care to correct the ones that appeared in error based on consultations with numerous sources thought to be more accurate. No one can know her exact dimensions. No records were kept of them at the shipyard of William H. Brown, where the yacht was built.

In addition, there was a question about when *Aurora, America*'s closest rival during the race of August 22, actually crossed the finish line. Some contemporary newspaper accounts say she finished eight minutes behind; others put her at either twenty-one or twenty-four minutes behind. I took my facts from *The Times* of London, which historians credit as the most accurate account of the race. *The Times* reported that *Aurora* finished eight minutes after *America*.

Another discrepancy worth noting concerns the name of the trophy *America* won from the Royal Yacht Squadron. In almost every article and book by American writers I consulted dating back to 1851, the prize was called the One Hundred Guinea Cup (or equally as wrong, the Queen's Cup), the equivalent of one hundred five British pounds. Diana Harding, archivist for the Royal Yacht Squadron, reported that the trophy was valued at one hundred sovereigns, the equal of one hundred British pounds, not guineas. One hundred pounds was the typical worth of cups given to the winners of yacht races at the time, and the one *America* took home was no exception. Thus, I have called the trophy the One Hundred Sovereign Cup in the book, as the British have always called it. No one knows why it was so often called the One Hundred Guinea Cup on this side of the Atlantic Ocean. It is just one more mystery that will remain unsolved.

The newspapers of the day, both in the United States and in Great Britain, were among the most valuable sources of information for the book. When accounts from differing newspapers were compared it was possible to confirm facts, provided more than one source reported the same information. Newspapers I consulted included *The Times* of London, *The Illustrated London News, London Examiner, Morning Courier and New York Enquirer, The New York Herald,* and *The New York Daily Times.* Other mysteries surfaced and I sorted through them to the best of my ability in my effort to write a factual and historically accurate narrative of how the yacht came to be built and how she earned her long-lasting place in maritime history.

The scenes drawn in the book are all based upon primary and contemporary sources. Whenever possible I relied on the journals of James R. Steers and James Alexander Hamilton, and letters published by members of the New York Yacht Club in the press. Dialogue was derived from these sources as well or reflects a logical re-creation of what was happening at any given time. In the few places where creative license was taken, my research underpinned all my narrative decisions. I avoided the use of secondary sources for key scenes and events, using them instead for background purposes.

GLOSSARY
OF NAUTICAL TERMS

Aback: A sail is aback when the wind pushes it back against the mast or rigging in a direction opposite to that which was intended. Sails can be put aback deliberately, as in heaving to.

Abaft: Toward the stern; behind some specific point or object on a vessel.

Abaft the beam: Behind the middle of the vessel.

Abeam: 90 degrees from the centerline of a vessel. Also, broad on the beam or off the beam.

Aft: Behind the midpoint of a vessel.

Aloft: Overhead; above.

Alow: On deck, or below an object that is higher.

Amidships: The center of a vessel either relative to length or breadth.

Awash: Just covered by the sea. When a deck is awash, the sea runs freely over it as if it were a beach.

Back: When the wind shifts counterclockwise, it is said to back. When a ship is backed, it is positioned so that the wind pushes against its front and slows the vessel.

Ballast: Weight placed in the bottom of a vessel to add stability.

Beam: The greatest width of a vessel.

Beam ends: A ship is on its beam ends when it is pushed over on its side, with the masts parallel to the surface of the sea.

Beam reach: A sailing direction relative to the wind when the wind blows toward the side of a vessel in a direction perpendicular to the hull.

Beam sea: Waves that strike a vessel broadside.

Bearing: The direction from a ship to an object—such as another ship or a land feature—or to a compass point.

Berth: A bed aboard ship. Also, a term used to describe a vessel at a dock. She is said to be safe in her berth.

Bilge: The bottom of a vessel's hold nearest the keel.

Binnacle: A structure near the wheel of a ship which houses the compass.

Blanket: One sail blankets another when it blocks the wind from the other.

Bluff-bowed: Having broad, wide bows. Bluff-bowed vessels are typically slow.

Bonnet: Canvas attached to the lower edge of a fore-and-aft sail to increase its size, adding to its power to drive the vessel.

Bow: The front end of a vessel.

Bowsprit: A long spar jutting from the bow. A jibboom is attached to a bowsprit, adding to the overall length of the spar.

Brace: Lines used to pivot the yards supporting square-rigged sails.

Broach: To come broadside, or sideways, to wind and seas. This is very dangerous in a heavy sea.

Bulkhead: A vertical partition inside a cabin, similar to an interior wall in a house.

Bulwarks: The part of the sides of the ship that rises above the deck to create a wall-like structure.

Buntlines: Lines run under the lower edge of a square-sail used to pull it up to the yard.

Capstan: A winch with a drum around which a line is wrapped. It turns on a vertical axis. It is the opposite of a windlass, which turns on a horizontal axis.

Chronometer: A clock used in calculating a ship's longitude. It provides Greenwich Mean Time—that is, the time at the prime meridian, or zero degrees longitude, which runs through Greenwich, England.

Claw off: To work a ship away from a lee shore.

Clew: The lower corner of a square-sail.

Clewlines: Lines used to raise the lower ends of a square-sail to the yard in preparation for furling.

Close-hauled: With sails set to drive the vessel as close as possible to the direction the wind is coming from. A vessel sailing close-hauled is also said to be sailing to windward, or beating.

Coaming: A low barrier built up from the deck at doorways and around hatches, skylights, and other openings to prevent water on deck from flowing below.

Course: A determined direction of travel from one point to another.

Cutter: A single-masted, fore-and-aft rigged sailing vessel similar to a sloop. The mast on a cutter is situated farther aft than that on a sloop. Cutters can set two headsails.

Cutwater: The forward edge of the stem, or front piece of the bow, especially at the waterline.

Davits: Arms suspended over the side used to raise and lower a ship's boat, such as a lifeboat.

Deadeye: A circular block of wood with three holes in it. It is part of the system used to tighten standing rigging.

Dead reckoning: Deduction of a ship's position based on course, speed, and time, without recourse to celestial observations.

Deckhouse: A houselike structure built on deck, usually to house the crew and galley.

Draft: The depth of the keel below the surface of the water.

Ebb tide: When the tide flows away from shore out to sea.

Fall off: To change course away from the direction from which the wind blows.

Fathom: A depth of six feet.

Fiddles: Wooden barriers around the edge of a table or counter to help prevent objects from sliding off in heavy weather.

Flood tide: A tide flowing toward shore.

Flying Jib: A triangular sail set on the jibboom. It is typically used in light winds.

Footropes: Ropes suspended under the yards. Sailors stand on these as they work the sails.

Fore-and-aft rig: A vessel rigged with its principal sails set fore-and-aft, as opposed to a square-rigged ship with its sails set perpendicular to the hull.

Forecastle: The cabin in the bow of a vessel, typically used for crew's quarters. Pronounced fo'c's'l.

Foremast: The mast closest to the bow.

Forward: The direction from the midpoint of a vessel toward the bow.

Furl: To gather in a sail.

Gaff: A spar supporting the top edge of a quadrilateral fore-and-aft sail, such as a schooner's mainsail and foresail.

Gaff-rigged: A vessel with its principal fore-and-aft sails set on gaffs and booms is said to be gaff-rigged.

Galley: The kitchen aboard a vessel.

Greenhorn: An inexperienced sailor.

Green water: Solid water that washes over a deck, as opposed to spray.

Halyard: A rope used to raise or lower a sail or a spar.

Hatch: An opening in the deck which can be closed or opened.

Hawsehole: An opening in the hull at the bow through which the anchor chain or line passes.

Head: The wind is said to head when it shifts too far forward for a sailing vessel to sail into the wind's direction without adjusting course. Also, a latrine aboard a vessel is called a head.

Headsails: Sails set forward of the fore or mainmast.

Headway: A vessel's motion forward through the water.

Heave to: To adjust a sailing vessel's sails so as to greatly reduce forward motion. A ship might heave to in rough weather, or to speak another ship.

Heel: To tilt to one side under a press of sail.

Jib: A triangular fore-and-aft sail set from the foremast and attached to the bowsprit and jibboom at the bow.

Jibboom: A spar fixed to the bowsprit to extend its length.

Jibe: To turn a vessel's stern through the wind, as opposed to tacking, which brings the bow through the wind.

Keel: The major longitudinal part of the hull, the backbone of a ship.

Knot: A term used to describe a vessel's speed through the water. It is equal to one nautical mile, or 6,080 feet.

Latitude: Lines drawn on a globe to measure distance north or south of the equator. The equator is marked as zero, and latitude measurements are designated in degrees north or south to the poles.

Lead line: A device used to measure the depth of the water and to take samples of the bottom.

Lee: The side sheltered from the wind. A vessel can be in the lee of something, such as a landmass, that blocks the wind and waves.

Leechlines: Lines attached to the leeches, or vertical edges, of a square-sail and used to pull it up to its yard.

Lee rail: The rail that is away from the direction from which the wind blows. When a ship heels, the lower side is the lee rail. The high side is the windward rail.

Lee shore: A shore to leeward of a vessel; very dangerous for a sailing vessel.

Leeward: Away from the direction the wind blows.

Leeway: The sideways motion a vessel makes when the wind, waves, or current push it off course.

Log: A device used to measure a vessel's speed.

Logbook: A document used to record daily course, wind direction, weather, and other details.

Longitude: Lines of measurement on the globe from pole to pole used to denote position east or west of the prime meridian at zero degrees, drawn through Greenwich, England.

Lubber: A landsman, or a sailor who is sloppy in his work.

Main gaff topsail: A triangular sail set above the mainsail.

Mainmast: The principal mast on a fore-and-aft rigged sailing vessel. It is set aft of the foremast on schooners.

Main topmast: A spar fixed to the mainmast. It extends the total length of the rig and allows a main gaff topsail to be set.

Marlinespike: A sharp iron tool used in working on the rigging.

Masthead: The top portion of a mast.

On the beach: A sailor ashore between voyages is said to be on the beach.

Parrell: A rope loop that holds a yard or spar, such as a gaff, to the mast.

Pilot: A mariner specializing in guiding ships in and out of ports.

Pilot boat: (1850s) Schooners used to sail pilots offshore to meet inbound ships.

Plot: A mark on a chart to denote position. To plot is to mark the chart.

Poop deck: The aft deck on a merchant vessel.

Port: The left side of a vessel when facing the bow.

Quarter: The sides of a vessel closest to the stern. There is a port quarter and a starboard quarter.

Ratline: A rope tied between shrouds. It is a form of ladder the sailors climb to get aloft.

Reef: A shoal. Also a reduction of sail area; sails are reefed to reduce strain on a vessel in heavy weather.

Rhumbline: The desired course between two points.

Roadstead or road: An anchorage offshore, usually not very sheltered.

Roll: Sideways rotational movement of a vessel in rough seas.

Run: To sail before the wind—that is, with the wind coming from the stern.

Running rigging: Lines used to work the sails. Halyards and sheets are part of the running rigging.

Schooner: A two-masted, fore-and-aft rigged sailing vessel with the mainmast situated aft.

Scud: To run before the wind in heavy weather.

Scuppers: Holes on deck through which water drains overboard.

Sextant: An optical device used to measure a celestial body's angle of elevation above the horizon, known as an altitude. It was one of the tools used to find a ship's latitude and longitude.

Shroud: A part of a sailing vessel's standing rigging. It is a rope run from the mast down to the side of a ship to help support the mast.

Slack water: The time between tides when tidal currents are at their weakest.

Sloop: A single-masted, fore-and-aft rigged sailing vessel with a mainsail and a jib.

Spars: A catch-all term used to describe masts, booms, gaffs, and the like.

Speak: One ship speaks another when the two vessels stop so that the captains can converse.

Standing rigging: Ropes used to support the masts.

Starboard: The right side of a vessel when facing the bow.

Stay: A part of a sailing vessel's standing rigging. It is a rope run from the masthead behind and in front of the mast.

Staysail: A triangular fore-and-aft sail set between masts.

Stern: The aft end of a vessel.

Sternway: A vessel's motion backward through the water.

Tack: To turn a sailing vessel's bow through the wind to bring the wind from one side to the other.

Taffrail: The rail at the stern of a vessel.

Topsides: The hull between the waterline and the deck.

Transom: Planking across the stern.

Treenails: Long, wooden pins used to nail planks to structural members. Pronounced trunnels.

Veer: When the wind shifts in a clockwise direction it is said to veer.

Warp: To move a vessel from one point to another using lines instead of sail power.

Watches: A period of time during which sailors are on duty, usually four hours on and four hours off. Also, the part of the crew that is on duty during a particular watch.

Waterline: The meeting point of the hull and the surface of the water.

Ways: The structure supporting a vessel while it is built and launched.

Windlass: A winch with a drum around which a line is wrapped. It turns on a horizontal axis. It is the opposite of a capstan, which turns on a drum with a vertical axis.

Windward: Toward the direction from which the wind blows. The wind blows over the windward, or weather, rail of a ship. If a ship sails to windward, it must be close-hauled.

Yard: The spar perpendicular to the mast upon which a square-sail is set.

BIBLIOGRAPHY

BOOKS

Albion, Robert. *Square-Riggers on Schedule: The New York Sailing Packets to England, France, and the Cotton Ports.* Princeton: Princeton University Press, 1938.

────── *The Rise of New York Port, 1815–1860.* New York: Scribner's, 1970 (1939).

Blunt, Edmund M. *The American Coast Pilot.* New York: Edmund and George W. Blunt, 1863.

Bolitho, Hector. *The Reign of Queen Victoria.* New York: MacMillan Co., 1948.

Boswell, Charles. *The America: The Story of the World's Most Famous Yacht.* New York: David McKay Company, 1967.

Bunker, John G. *Harbor & Haven: An Illustrated History of the Port of New York.* Woodland Hills, N.Y.: Windsor Publications, Inc., 1979.

Burgess, George H., and Miles C. Kennedy. *Centennial History of the Pennsylvania Railroad Company 1846–1946.* Philadelphia: Pennsylvania Railroad Company, 1949.

Burrows, Edwin G., and Mike Wallace. *Gotham: A History of New York City to 1898.* New York: Oxford University Press, 1999.

Burton, Elizabeth. *The Pageant of Early Victorian England.* New York: Charles Scribner's Sons, 1972.

Chapelle, Howard I. *American Small Sailing Craft.* New York: W. W. Norton & Company, 1951.

────── *Boatbuilding: A Complete Handbook of Wooden Boat Construction.* New York: W. W. Norton, 1941.

Chevalier, François, and Jacques Taglang. *1851 America's Cup Yacht Design 1986.* Paris, France: limited edition published by the authors.

Clark, Mark. *Red Dog & Great White.* New York: Byren House Publishing, Inc., 1986.

Comstock, John Adams. *A History and Genealogy of the Comstock Family in America*. Los Angeles: privately printed, 1949.

Constable, George, ed. *Racing*. New York: Time-Life Books, 1976.

Cutler, Carl C. *Greyhounds of the Sea*. New York: Halcyon House, 1930.

Dana, Richard Henry, Jr. *The Seaman's Friend*. Boston, Thomas Groom & Co., 1851. Reprint, Delmar, N.Y.: Scholars' Facsimiles & Reprints.

Downey, Leland Woolley. *Broken Spars: New Jersey Coast Shipwrecks 1640–1935*. Brick, N.J.: Brick Township Historical Society, 1983.

Folsom, Burton W., Jr., ed. *The Industrial Revolution and Free Trade*. Irvington-on-Hudson, New York: The Foundation for Economic Education, 1996.

Hamilton, James A. *Reminiscences of James A. Hamilton; Or, Men and Events, at Home and Abroad, During Three Quarters of a Century*. New York: Charles Scribner & Company, 1869.

Jensen, Oliver. *The American Heritage History of Railroads in America*. New York: American Heritage Publishing Co., Inc., 1975.

Juet, Robert. *Juet's Journal: The Voyage of the Half Moon from 4 April to 7 November 1609*. 1625. Reprint, Newark, N.J.: New Jersey Historical Society.

Knox-Johnston, Robin. *Yachting: The History of a Passion*. New York: Hearst Marine Books, 1990.

Lindsay, W. S. *History of Merchant Shipping and Ancient Commerce*. London: Sampson Low, Marston, Low, and Searle, 1874, 1876. (4 vols.)

MacGregor, David R. *The Schooner: Its Design and Development From 1600 to the Present*. Annapolis, Md.: Naval Institute Press, 1997.

Malone, Dumas, ed. *Dictionary of American Biography*. Vols. 4, 8, 9. New York: Charles Scribner's Sons, 1929, 1963, 1964.

Morison, Samuel Eliot. *The European Discovery of America: The Northern Voyages A. D. 500–1600*. New York: Oxford University Press, 1971.

Ogburn, Charlton. *Railroads: The Great American Adventure*. Washington, D.C.: National Geographic Society, 1977.

Pilot Lore. Washington, D.C.: National Service Bureau, 1922.

Rattray, Jeannette Edwards. *Perils of the Port of New York: Maritime Disasters From Sandy Hook to Execution Rocks*. New York: Dodd, Mead & Company, 1973.

Riggs, Doug. *Keelhauled: Unsportsmanlike Conduct and the America's Cup*. Newport, R.I.: Seven Seas Press, 1986.

Rousmaniere, John. *The Low Black Schooner: Yacht America 1851–1945*. Mystic, Conn.: Mystic Seaport Museum Stores, 1986.

Russell, Charles Edward. *From Sandy Hook to 62*. New York: Sandy Hook Pilots Association, 1929.

Shaw, David W. *Inland Passage: On Boats and Boating in the Northeast*. New Brunswick, N.J.: Rutgers University Press, 1998.

Srebnick, Amy Gilman. *The Mysterious Death of Mary Rogers: Sex and Culture in Nineteenth-Century New York.* New York: Oxford University Press, 1995.

Thompson, Winfield M., William P. Stephens, and William U. Swan. *The Yacht "America."* Boston: Charles E. Lauriat, Co., 1925.

Thompson, Winfield M. *The Lawson History of the America's Cup: A Record of Fifty Years.* Boston: Published by the author, 1902. Limited edition of 3,000 copies.

Weintraub, Stanley. *Uncrowned King: The Life of Prince Albert.* New York: The Free Press, 1997.

Willson, David Harris. *A History of England.* New York: Holt, Rinehart, and Winston, Inc., 1967.

PERIODICALS

Robert Albion, "Planning the Black Ball." *Log of Mystic Seaport,* spring 1980.

Joseph C. Bruzek, "The USS Schooner Yacht America," *United States Naval Institute Proceedings,* Annapolis, Md., September 1967.

Harold Codey, "The Schooner Yacht America: Her Life, Death, and Recreation," *Skipper* January 1967.

[Editors], "Men Who Have Made Yachting: George Steers," *The Rudder* (New York) February 1906.

[Editors], "The Shipbuilders of America: George Steers," *United States Nautical Magazine and Naval Journal* July 1857.

John Rousmaniere, "The Yacht America at 150," *Woodenboat* November 2001.

Winfield M. Thompson, "The Yacht America and Her Cup," *The Rudder* (New York) February 1914.

Also contemporary accounts from *The New York Herald, New York Daily Times, Punch, The Illustrated London News, London Examiner, The Times,* and other newspapers.

OTHER SOURCES

Data on Captain Richard Brown, Sandy Hook Pilots Association.

Data on Nelson Comstock, *America's* first mate, supplied by Margaret Comstock Thoms, great-niece of Nelson Comstock, New London, Connecticut. See also the genealogical history, *Comstocks in America.*

Data on the Stevens family and their biographical and historic accomplishments. See the Web site of Stevens Institute of Technology, Hoboken, New Jersey.

"Log of Yacht America," journal by James R. Steers, 1851.

From Mystic Seaport, Log 368, Manuscripts Collection, G. W. Blunt White Library. Additional information from a copy published in *Yachting Magazine*, December 1946, January 1947.

Contemporary newspaper accounts, letters, and other documents cited from the private library of the New York Yacht Club.

Tourism guides from the Isle of Wight, Tourism Center.

America's Cup Jubilee: Cowes 1851–2001, brochure.

DeWolf, Katherine Herreshoff. "The Story of the America's Cup." Booklet. North Plymouth, Mass.: Plymouth Cordage Company, 1930.

ACKNOWLEDGMENTS

A famous novelist once said that creating a work of fiction was like driving down a dark road without headlights. Quite a few individuals offered guiding lights along the way to keep me from falling into ditches or colliding with walls as the book came together over the space of almost three years.

As always, my wife, Elizabeth, stood by me from the start of the book when it was just the inkling of an idea that lacked shape and substance. She acted as a sounding board, listening for the most part, but offering insights and encouragement upon occasion. My good friend and agent, Jill Grinberg, got behind the book from the very beginning and shepherded it through the publication process with her usual expertise. Stephen Morrow, my much esteemed editor and sailing pal at The Free Press, Simon and Schuster, provided invaluable help in polishing the final drafts of the manuscript. I owe Jill and Stephen my gratitude and thanks for their unbridled support.

At the outset of my research, I went straight to The Mariners' Museum in Newport News, Virginia. Gregory L. Cina, archives technician, was patient and thorough, and turned up obscure information. Lisa Flick, associate coordinator, photographic services and licensing, was superb regarding her assistance in locating and furnishing the photography used in the photo insert. I must also thank Mystic Seaport in Mystic, Connecticut, for granting me permission to publish quotes from the journal of James R. Steers.

I deeply appreciated the help of Janet Hellmann of the United New York and New Jersey Sandy Hook Pilots' Benevolent Associations. She played a key part in providing information about Captain Richard Brown, the protagonist of the book. Hellmann also directed me to the few books published long ago about the history of the Sandy Hook Pilots, which revealed what Brown's daily routine must have been like. My thanks to the president of the Sandy Hook Pilots, Captain William W. Sherwood, for granting me permission to reproduce images contained in *From Sandy Hook to 62*, a rare book the pilots association published in 1929.

I am grateful to Margaret Comstock Thoms for her assistance. The great-niece of Nelson Comstock, the first mate of yacht *America*, Margaret provided access to family papers and documents, and old newspaper clippings that helped me learn more about the men who sailed aboard *America*.

The best resources for much of the information I needed to write the book came from the two organizations most directly involved in the story: the New York Yacht Club and the Royal Yacht Squadron. Joseph Jackson, librarian for the New York Yacht Club, and Diana Harding, archivist for the Royal Yacht Squadron, both spent time with me on the project. They pointed me to valuable resources and set me straight on certain facts when the need arose. I thank them both.

Many librarians at my hometown library, and at Rutgers University and Drew University, were patient and helpful in my quest for newspapers from 1851. I appreciated their efforts on my behalf. In addition, I am grateful to Margaret Westergaard for her hard work on the illustrations.

INDEX